W9-BUP-169

BUZZ SAW

The Improbable Story of How the Washington Nationals Won the World Series

JESSE DOUGHERTY

SIMON & SCHUSTER
New York London Toronto Sydney New Delhi

Simon & Schuster
1230 Avenue of the Americas
New York, NY 10020

First Simon & Schuster hardcover edition March 2020

SIMON & SCHUSTER and colophon are registered trademarks of Simon & Schuster, Inc.

For information about special discounts for bulk purchases, please contact Simon & Schuster Special Sales at 1-866-506-1949 or business@simonandschuster.com.

The Simon & Schuster Speakers Bureau can bring authors to your live event. For more information or to book an event, contact the Simon & Schuster Speakers Bureau at 1-866-248-3049 or visit our website at www.simonspeakers.com.

Interior design by Kyle Kabel

Manufactured in the United States of America

1 3 5 7 9 10 8 6 4 2

Library of Congress Cataloging-in-Publication Data has been applied for.

ISBN 978-1-9821-5226-0
ISBN 978-1-9821-5228-4 (ebook)

For Lisa and Paul

Contents

Prologue

The Top

December 10, 2019

From here, from thirty floors above San Diego, from a room that overlooks the bay, then the ocean, then the edge of the freaking world, Mike Rizzo can see everything. It is what he'd been seeking for decades. This view. A moment of closure. Perspective that only comes at the top.

And fuck, he says, over and over, about ten times in forty minutes, it feels fucking good. Look at this. Look at the bright, manicured grass. Look at the boats cutting through the water, forming waves in their wake, forgetting their way for a second, maybe two, for just long enough to enjoy the ride. Look at the sun, but not too hard, because it's busting through the window, bouncing off Rizzo's bald head, bathing everything in this suite, from the white sheets to his black sneakers, in yellow light.

Look at the top, and now look who made it there.

"The emotions are still there," Rizzo says, fiddling with his new wedding band, fighting the urge to break down and cry. "They always will be."

Rizzo can't look around without looking back. The past happened. The past is why sitting on this couch, inside the Manchester Grand Hyatt, is so sweet. He's on the West Coast for important business.

Baseball's annual winter meetings are happening downstairs. Rizzo, the general manager of the Washington Nationals, is constructing a roster for 2020. He has agents to meet. He has phone calls to make. But, these days, the fifty-eight-year-old often sinks into long bouts of reflection. You'll have to forgive him for that. You'll also have to let him explain.

He has never had a December like this. He has never walked through these meetings, a skip in his step, and had each conversation start with the same word. *Congratulations.* Everyone is saying it. It's not getting old. Because they were all watching in October, when the Nationals took their tortured history, the years of playoff heartbreak, and changed, well, everything.

The early years rush back and Rizzo leans forward. He was named GM in 2009, a little more than a decade ago, and the first real disappointment came two years later. Rizzo wanted to finish 81-81. He wanted it more than anything. But the Nationals had one game canceled, it was not rescheduled, and their final record, when six months added up, was 80-81. A win short.

Yet Rizzo soon learned that was nothing. He and Washington learned the hard way. His shoulders slump as he tells those stories, of four seasons that finished in the National League Division Series. They were one strike away from advancing in 2012, before Pete Kozma, the Cardinals' light-hitting shortstop, ripped a two-run single to rip them apart. Their next playoff run, in the fall of 2014, crumbled in San Francisco.

The run after that, in 2016, slipped in Game 5 against the Cubs, when Max Scherzer came in from the bullpen and the stadium went sideways. Then came 2017, another great club, another chance, and, by the end of it, another mark against faith. That time it was the Dodgers. The common thread was that the Nationals never won.

"It's terrible. Terrible." Rizzo remembers every time he woke in the first morning of the offseason, dazed by defeat, and had to start all over again. Sometimes he didn't even wait that long. In October of 2014, after the Nationals fell to the Giants, Rizzo worked through the flight back to Washington. He opened his laptop, the screen glowing in the dark charter plane, and stared at a list of returning players, of free agent targets, of prospects and other bits of the future. There had to be an answer, he thought, in this web of losses and loose ends. The impossible part was finding it.

"It's a terrible feeling."

Then all of a sudden, as if a reminder were whispered in his ear, Rizzo is living in 2019. His short, stocky frame, cut like a man who once played baseball, inches to the couch's edge. He acts out the highlights as they burst into his head. Soto's single off Hader in the wild-card game. Rendon and Soto hitting back-to-back homers off Kershaw in the NLDS. A sweep of the Cardinals, two wins against the Astros, three crushing losses at home, and finally, there he was in Houston, his son to his right, his wife to his left, their eyes watching a pop fly drop to earth. It wasn't over then. Not yet. But Rizzo turned to his son, to his wife, to himself, even, and let a thought escape his mouth.

"We're going to win the fucking World Series," Rizzo told them, in the last hours of October 31, 2019, two outs before the Nationals beat the Astros for their first championship. The Nationals bucked a list of modern trends to do so, blended old- and new-school tactics, didn't stay away from older players, but built a winner on their backs. They made chemistry a key ingredient. They survived a 19-31 start, when their title odds sunk to 1.5 percent, when it seemed reasonable, if not necessary, to give up and plan for next year. Then they survived five elimination games in the postseason, despite trailing in each one, and became the first to win a title with four road victories.

So after a lifetime of waiting, of wondering if the luck would flip, Rizzo could admit to saying those words out loud. They rattled around the empty hotel room in San Diego. He's still wondering how they make any sense at all.

1

"They were ready for you."

November 28, 2018

They rode down an alley off reality, beneath the dim yellow street lights, by bare bushes, bristling trees, and into a dark cul de sac, the gravel slicked and messy, the Potomac River swishing up to shore. This was where rich people went to impress other rich people, right inside, past one set of doors, then another, a pair of lit fireplaces, and a wooden, wraparound bar. So here were Mike Rizzo and Mark Lerner, at Fiola Mare in Georgetown, with millions to spend and business at hand.

This, Rizzo believed, was how they'd turn the Washington Nationals from an 82-win team, their final identity of last year, into a real contender. Rizzo was not focused on the free agent everyone was talking about. He instead wanted the top starting pitcher on the market, and wanted him bad. That pitcher had visited two teams before arriving in Washington on November 28, 2018. Rizzo knew others were in the mix. And how to show his interest, yet not come off too desperate, was what the GM had stewed over for days now. He had to nail this dinner.

"See, Pat, they were ready for you," Rizzo told Patrick Corbin while they walked through metal detectors in the entryway. Security was wall-to-wall in the Italian restaurant, and Rizzo joked that it was to protect Corbin from adoring fans. Their white-clothed table was set for six. Corbin sat down next to Jen, his wife, and straight across from Rizzo. Lerner, the Nationals' managing principal owner, and John Courtright, Corbin's agent, filled the last two seats. It just so happened that Vice President Mike Pence was dining there, too.

The dinner crowd is politicians, lobbyists, or anyone who, in a given night, can spend $125 on the cheapest caviar, or $500 on the average bottle of wine. Corbin and Jen liked fine dining, and had splurged in the past, but this was another level. They were still high school sweethearts from Syracuse, New York, modest, and smiled at each other while leafing through the leatherbound, sixty-four-page wine list.

The most expensive was a 1997 Sangiovese. It cost $10,500.

Rizzo told the group that Mr. Lerner was paying. Everyone laughed. Then food and drinks began pouring out of the kitchen, carried by waiters wearing black vests and a rainbow of ties. A seafood tower was topped by a whole lobster. There were plates and plates of caviar. There was wine, endless amounts of it, and the five of them chatted about the menu, the city, and, when small talk faded, what the Nationals were all about.

It was already shaping into a quiet off-season around baseball. A stalled market revolved around Bryce Harper, Manny Machado, and a list of free agent stars who had yet to sign new deals. The Nationals were linked to Harper because of history. For nine years, since he was drafted in 2010, Harper was Washington, Washington was Harper, and they both squinted into that mirror image for answers that never came. Harper met the world as the Chosen One, posed on the cover of *Sports Illustrated* at sixteen years old, billed as "The Most Exciting Prodigy Since LeBron." The Nationals landed him with their second straight No. 1 pick, their reward for losing 103 games the season before, when they were still trying to grip a new fan base.

They had been in DC for just seven years when Harper debuted at nineteen in 2012. They had never seen anything like him, his bat blurring through the zone, his long hair flowing, and flipping, and feeding images onto the internet. Expectations were shoveled onto his teenage back. Then they were only met in hollow bursts.

The Nationals made their first postseason in Harper's rookie year, but each playoff failure inched them closer to his free agency. He was long set to hit the market in 2018. Scott Boras, his agent, promised that Harper would sign a record deal. And if the Nationals' title window was dependent on Harper, as many believed it was, it would smack shut unless a deal was struck.

They offered ten years and $300 million in late September of 2018, and Harper declined. The contract's payment deferrals were too steep. He felt he had come too far to not even test free agency. Boras expected half the league to bid on his services. But while the press kept connecting the Nationals to Harper, and his return remained a faint possibility, Rizzo shifted his focus elsewhere.

He saw the slow drip of free agency as a market inefficiency. While most teams waded into the off-season, and many planned to not buy at all, he attacked it with urgency. He had Scherzer and Strasburg returning in the rotation, Rendon and Turner on the left side of the infield, and Soto, Robles, and Eaton in the outfield. Zimmerman was his first baseman. Doolittle was his closer.

There was life after Harper, as Rizzo saw it, and he wasn't waiting for that saga to play out. Instead, to shake the taste of an 82-80 year, he went to work. And fast.

He traded for reliever Kyle Barraclough in the middle of the playoffs. He made reliever Trevor Rosenthal the first free agent to sign once the market opened. He inked veteran catcher Kurt Suzuki to a two-year deal in mid-November and, ten days later, traded for All-Star catcher Yan Gomes. But Rizzo was set on adding another star to his rotation. That's how they wound up at Fiola Mare, their table covered in food, their waiter checking in every few minutes, pen in hand, to make sure no order was missing. Now Rizzo just needed to close the deal.

Rizzo researched Corbin before the lefty made it to Washington. Corbin's first stop on a three-city trip was to visit the New York Yankees. That's who scared Rizzo the most. Corbin grew up in Syracuse, Yankees posters all over his bedroom walls, and his family and friends pushed for the hometown choice. His younger brother even brought up the Yankees in a best-man speech when Corbin and Jen got married in the fall.

But Corbin had an open mind once he left the Arizona Diamondbacks after six seasons. He wanted to win, more than anything, and zeroed in on the Yankees, Phillies, and Nationals because they all planned to contend. He wanted to be the last piece of a blueprint, not the start of one, and Rizzo tapped into that.

He knew the lefty came from a blue-collar background, his dad a truck driver for a sausage company, his mom a nurse. Corbin landed a big signing bonus in 2009 and still spent two winters on their basement couch. He kept the same beat-up Audi he drove in high school. He officiated youth basketball, his first love, and played pickup games in the freezing cold. He wasn't big-time. He wouldn't even know how to pretend.

He'll always have tried out as a junior, unannounced, and wowed varsity coaches with a slider grip his father taught him. He didn't wear baseball pants into the Cicero–North Syracuse High School gym that day. He didn't own a pair. The legend that he wore jeans, the denim pooling at his ankles, was later debunked by coaches and teammates who witnessed the tryout. But he did walk into the end of a stretching line, scratch his name onto a sign-up sheet, then go

14-0 across two seasons. That was enough for a nearby junior college to recruit him. It wasn't enough for his head to grow.

So Rizzo didn't go heavy with compliments. He figured the Yankees and the Phillies already had. He figured most teams would. What Rizzo did do, while the rest sat and listened, was challenge Corbin to come thrive in Washington. Rizzo told him it was hard to shine next to Scherzer and Strasburg. But Corbin could, Rizzo urged, and the Nationals needed him to form a dominant rotation.

Rizzo was the Diamondbacks' scouting director when they won the World Series behind Randy Johnson and Curt Schilling. Rizzo vowed that if he was ever a general manager, his formula would center on his starting staff. He tried that with Strasburg, Gio Gonzalez, and Jordan Zimmermann in. He tried it again with Scherzer, Strasburg, Gonzalez, and Zimmermann in. He kept trying, year after year, but the mix was never quite right.

But Scherzer, Strasburg, and Corbin sounded like a winner. Rizzo kept saying it over dinner—*Scherzer, Strasburg, Corbin*—to drill the idea into Corbin's head. The wine kept flowing. Lerner promised to keep putting money into the team. Rizzo told Corbin that pitching was the timeless key to success. Corbin could tell he was at the top of their priority list. Then the check came, they went their separate ways, and he had a decision to make.

"I don't know what he's going to choose," Rizzo told Lerner as they left the restaurant. "But we couldn't have done any better than we did tonight."

Corbin, Jen, and Courtright were staying at the Four Seasons in Georgetown. It had been a long day, filled with food and information, and they were excited to sleep. But first they chatted over one last drink at Bourbon Steak off the hotel lobby. Corbin was recapping the dinner when, out of the corner of his eye, he saw a familiar face.

It was Ryan Zimmerman, the Nationals' franchise player, walking with his wife, Heather, toward the bar. Corbin shouted across the room to get Zimmerman's attention. He wasn't sure if Zimmerman would recognize him in plain clothes. But Zimmerman did, and soon enough he and Heather pulled two more chairs up to the table.

Zimmerman and Heather were coming from a gala for their multiple sclerosis foundation. Bourbon Steak was one of their go-to spots. They sat for thirty minutes and gave Corbin the player's pitch. Zimmerman loved Washington. He moved here when he was twenty-one years old, as the Nationals' first-ever draft pick, and made his home in northern Virginia. The schools were great for his two young girls. He and Heather felt the Nationals were family, and the team was strong, and Zimmerman wanted Corbin to sign there, just as Rizzo and Lerner did, if Corbin and Jen felt the same.

By the time Zimmerman left, and it was time for bed, Corbin, Jen, and Courtright were all leaning in the same direction: they were in if the price was right.

A deal came through less than a week later. Corbin signed for six years and $140 million, well above what any other club offered. The Yankees and Phillies were hesitant about a sixth season. The Los Angeles Angels, another interested team, never topped four years and $100 million. But the Nationals overpaid, and willingly, to stack their rotation to Rizzo's liking.

They only did so after carefully assessing the risk. Corbin was coming off a standout season in Arizona, with a 3.15 ERA in 200 innings. He struck out 11.1 batters per 9 innings, the highest rate of his career, and had one of the best sliders in baseball. That he was a lefty and made 30-plus starts in back-to-back years only upped his value. But that came with obvious concerns. He had missed all of 2014 after undergoing Tommy John surgery in his left elbow. He bottomed out in 2016, his ERA spiking to 5.15, and was relegated to the Diamondbacks' bullpen.

The Nationals had to decide if he was the pitcher from 2018, or if that version was an aberration. They also had to project how he might age across a long-term contract. Rizzo wasn't afraid to extend lengthy deals to starting pitchers. He signed Scherzer for seven years and $210 million in 2015. He extended Strasburg for seven years and $175 million a year later. The Nationals' front office viewed any one season as a trap. Corbin was an All-Star in 2013. He struggled in the seasons after his injury. Now he was back to his All-Star self, thanks to a reimagined pitch mix, but they had six years of data to survey.

They were confident Corbin would age well because he relied on low-90s heat, a slider and changeup, not an overpowering fastball. They were encouraged by the steady improvement after his surgery. They liked his athleticism, and that he was once a standout high school basketball player. That showed in his smooth delivery, his defense, and even on film of him at the plate. The last step for Rizzo was gauging Corbin's character. His dinner pitch had doubled as an entrance exam.

"I was interviewing him as much as he was interviewing me. I wanted to see who he was, I wanted to see if he was the kind of guy that would fit into the clubhouse. And into our style," Rizzo recalled later. "If he wasn't about that, he would've probably went to a glitzier place."

They next saw each other on December 7. Lerner and Jen sat in the front row of the Nationals Park conference room. Courtright lingered by a side door, glancing at his iPhone, and Corbin and Rizzo were on the small stage. Scherzer, Strasburg, and Gomes even came to see their newest teammate introduced.

Lerner was later grabbed by two local radio hosts on his way out. They asked him about Harper, naturally, and the owner made his first public comments on the matter: "I don't really expect him to come back at this point. I think they've decided to move on."

When pressed on the ten-year, $300 million offer in September, and whether it was still on the table for Harper, Lerner doubled down: "We'll have to sit down and figure it out," he told 106.7 The Fan. "If he comes back, it's a strong possibility that we won't be able to make it work. But I really don't expect him to come back at this point. I think they've decided to move on. There's just too much money out there that he'd be leaving on the table. That's just not Mr. Boras's MO, to leave money on the table."

The quotes went viral right away. Lerner had gone entirely off-script, frustrating many in the front office, and reality had come into focus. The Nationals were not finished after landing Corbin. They brought back first baseman Matt Adams on a one-year, $4 million deal in mid-December. They followed that by signing Aníbal Sánchez for two years and $19 million, investing around $95 million in their rotation for 2019. Then came the additions of second baseman Brian Dozier, for one year and $9 million, and starter Jeremy Hellickson, for one year and $3 million, before spring training.

But the Corbin deal signaled the Nationals' most important intentions. They'd spent more on their starters than five teams would on their entire rosters for the coming season. The Harper money was spread elsewhere, and Washington had all but moved on.

2

The Little Things

February 14, 2019

The reminders were everywhere at the Nationals' spring training facility in West Palm Beach. Photos of Harper dotted the hallway by the clubhouse, the stairwell leading to the executive offices, and even the windowless media room. During an early workout, when the pitchers and catchers were still getting acquainted, Sam Hunt's "Body Like a Back Road" blared through a group of speakers. That was one of Harper's many walk-up songs while playing in Washington. It didn't pass without a round of jokes.

"Ooh, Bryce!" someone yelled from the outfield. "Break the news! He's coming back!"

"Come on!" shouted another player. "Who can get that song out of the rotation?"

This all began in the early hours of February 14, in the kind of morning that soon blended into dozens just like it. It began with coffee, pots and pots of coffee, to shake off sleep before the first drills of the season. It began with Max Scherzer charging past those Harper photos, red helmet pushed onto his head, as if he were pulled by the loud *thwack*s from the batting cages, of wood colliding with leather, and rust meeting kinetic energy.

But it really began with the league still dangling on Harper's free agency. The Nationals were not exempt from that, no matter how much they spent throughout the winter, or tried to distance themselves from Harper and a market that dragged at his feet.

The ten-year, $300 million offer was not the Nationals' last attempt to bring Harper back. The second, during a December meeting, was not made public until the *Washington Post* reported it on April 1. The destination was Ted Lerner's winter home in Palm Springs. Lerner, the Nationals' founding principal owner, saw Harper as a second son. The December meeting included the two of them, Harper's wife, Kayla, Rizzo, Boras, and Lerner's wife, Annette. Harper later admitted that he thought a deal was coming. But the numbers never aligned.

While they deliberated, and Annette told Ted to make it happen, Boras peeled off for a phone call with Ted Towne, the Nationals' assistant general manager in charge of finances. They talked for close to an hour, until Towne's phone died. The offer reached Harper a few days after he left Palm Springs, and he was disappointed. It was for twelve years and $250 million, a much lower average annual value, and the deferrals grew.

Both contracts had big payment deferrals, a hallmark of the Lerners' negotiating style, and Harper wanted his money now. He wanted a lifetime contract to avoid free agency in the future. He wanted to break records. But the Nationals wanted to pay him over decades, this offer made that even more clear, and they were unwilling to budge. So that was that.

Thirty spring training sessions soon started without him. In West Palm Beach, Nationals manager Dave Martinez stood by his office and greeted everyone with a stiff handshake. A wisp of smoke blew off his styrofoam coffee cup. Adam Eaton paced into an empty clubhouse, a harsh sun peaking in, and yelled, "Well, here we go again!" Sean Doolittle walked by new teammate Aníbal Sánchez, a veteran starter from Venezuela who greeted him in Spanish.

Doolittle, a reliever from New Jersey, smiled and stumbled through his best shot at *"Bien, y tu?"* They laughed before heading to the practice fields. It was like the first day of school, wrapped in excitement, the only time of year that optimism can't be dented by a bad bounce, slight misstep, or any of the inches that make baseball a test of patience and will. There would be time for that later. Plenty of it.

For now, for the first time in close to a decade, the Nationals went forward without Harper. His old locker was stuffed with whatever Ryan Zimmerman and Howie Kendrick couldn't fit in theirs. He was stuck at his winter home in Las Vegas, where he once grew into a generational talent, waiting impatiently for his phone to ring.

Then Harper kept waiting. Then he waited some more.

When his name came up, and it often did, "Harper," "Harp," or "Bryce" floated through quiet side conversations. The Nationals wanted to turn Harper into a nonstory. But it didn't help that labor issues were the focus of many questions, and Harper was the focus of that problem. His free agent sweepstakes seeped well into the spring, as did those for Manny Machado, Dallas Keuchel, Craig Kimbrel, and Mike Moustakas. And the list of team-less veterans only started there.

Most of the league expressed interest in cheap, young talent, with years of club control, and left those over thirty in the cold. The Nationals' approach—spending, building around experienced pitchers, signing 36-year-old catcher Kurt Suzuki, plus many other veterans—was a total outlier. There were murmurs of collusion, that not enough clubs were trying to win, that there could be a major overhaul when the collective bargaining agreement was renegotiated in 2021. Players felt that owners used the future, and the concept of "tanking" to win later, as an excuse not to spend. The evidence was in the market trends.

Scherzer, the Nationals' player union representative, spoke for twenty minutes about this on the first day in Florida. It felt like a pivot point for the sport, one that's had trouble attracting younger generations and was exploring ways to do so. An experimental pitch clock, designed to shorten games, was gone as soon as it came. Scherzer basically refused to use it after his first spring training start. Now the market was entirely flat, and players were angry, and coverage was dominated by their unrest.

The NFL and NBA turn set free agency periods into television specials and social media blowouts. Baseball, on the other hand, was in a months-long lag that left some of its best talent on the couch.

"When there are too many teams that are not trying to win, that poisons the game, poisons the fan experience, and it creates bandwagon fans," Scherzer said, twice telling reporters to get their notebooks back out to jot down his thoughts. "I'm very appreciative to have an ownership group that has been aggressive in free agency and continues to make moves and push financial resources onto the table to be in a win-now mode, and do whatever it takes to win. We're not seeing that across the league."

The thirty-four-year-old nodded to the moves for Corbin, Suzuki, Yan Gomes, and Sánchez; to adding Brian Dozier at second; and to bringing back Adams. Rizzo was not afraid to sign older players. He embraced experience and, by midsummer, would have the league's oldest roster. Scherzer was in favor of that, too. And now he could do nothing but wish Harper well.

He respected Harper and always had, but a handful believed a parting was necessary. Some felt Harper set a poor example for young outfielders such as Soto and Robles. Harper, like many players, had a habit of not always hustling out of the batter's box. One prominent, unnamed veteran told Thomas Boswell of the *Washington Post* that Harper's departure would immediately improve the Nationals' fundamentals.

That was the main goal of Martinez's second spring training as manager. The Nationals were going to emphasize *the little things*, as silly as it sounded, and practice baserunning, basic fielding, and hitting the cutoff men. Everything would tie back to the basics. They could still have fun. Third-base coach Bobby Henley would still run the Circle of Trust every morning, still commission goofy skits during it, still set up a relay race that ended with two cabbages smashed into the pavement. Music would still blare during batting practice. But Martinez told his coaches to remember those words—*the little things*—and bring them up whenever necessary.

Days began at 6:00 a.m. and often stretched well into the evenings. Martinez started at his desk, in front of a white board with fifty-eight magnets on it, one for each player in camp. They moved around as the season inched closer, reflecting a few rounds of cuts, an evolving forty-man roster, and, finally, the team that opened the year. The clock across the room ran a few minutes fast, helping him stay on schedule, and a pile of mail never stopped growing. A letter from Japan asked for an autograph. Fans sent his old Montreal Expos cards to be signed. He was their connection to the Nationals, who left Montreal for Washington in 2005, and smiled at himself in those red-white-and-blue uniforms, thirty years younger, eager and so naïve. He answered whatever he could, whenever he had a few free minutes, but otherwise stood by the field to implement his new approach.

Coaches ran full-team defensive drills that spurred another three-word phrase. If the players faltered, if they sailed a throw, if they messed up a *little thing*, Martinez yelled, "Do it again!" The first instance was met with light laughter. This wasn't Little League. Yet some players came around, following Martinez's lead, and it wasn't long before "Do it again!" was an expected reaction to miscues.

"We're going to stick to this," Martinez told reporters in mid-February. "I told the guys, 'We're not just going to do this for the first few days of camp. We're going to do this every day.' "

The veteran who spoke to Boswell felt Harper didn't fit within this culture. He instructed Boswell to "write it," as was printed in a February 15 column, and those two words became a running joke in the clubhouse. They affirmed what a few thought, yet wouldn't say themselves. Harper was a feared hitter and liked by most of his former teammates. But the Nationals were moving in a different direction. Their plans no longer revolved around a megastar. Then they were on the field in Fort Myers, Florida, for an exhibition with the Boston Red Sox, when the news finally broke.

A light breeze pushed off the Caloosahatchee River and into JetBlue Park at Fenway South. It was the last afternoon of February, and Opening Day was in less than a month. Scherzer had just tossed three scoreless innings against the Red Sox, and the press box announcer leaned into his microphone. His voice crackled over the old speakers, cutting in and out, saying Scherzer was available for his poststart interview by the visiting clubhouse. But a small group of reporters were caught between Scherzer and their computer screens.

Harper had signed with the Philadelphia Phillies, and specifics were trickling out. It was for thirteen years, $330 million, and, most curiously, no opt-outs along the way. That only underscored Harper's distaste toward the free agency process. He never wanted to go through it again. He was committed to Philadelphia, ready to raise a family there, resting years of speculation of where he'd land. And it was with one of the Nationals' division rivals.

Scherzer stood in a dim hallway and tried to predict Harper's contract. Cell service was spotty beneath the ballpark's bleachers. But soon a reporter read the details while Scherzer nodded along, running the numbers in his head, crunching them against his guesses. His eyes grew wide at the total money. They grew even wider at the lack of opt-outs. He then thought for a moment before drawing a line to labor discussions: "Obviously a thirteen-year deal, that's good for the game. To be that young and to be a free agent, you know, teams are flush with money, and it's good to see teams spend it."

Two days later, on top of a dugout in Clearwater, Florida, Harper was officially introduced as a member of the Phillies. The front office, ownership group, new teammates, and local press dotted a section of their spring training stadium. Boras sat to Harper's left. A cardboard cover of *MLB The Show 19*, a popular baseball video game, already showed Harper in a pin-striped Phillies uniform. On the other side was that first *Sports Illustrated* cover, because The Chosen One had met his destiny, and Harper hit the right notes in an opening statement.

He thanked the organization for making a big investment in him. He thanked Boras for having guided him since Harper was a kid. He went on about Philadelphia, about how he loved visiting Citizens Bank Park with the Nationals, about how he couldn't wait to settle in, find a home, plot a life with his wife, Kayla, and stay there for good.

"We're going to do everything we can to win and play hard and play well," Harper stated, a tan collar popping out of his jersey, his eyes shaded by the brim of his hat. "That's what it's all about. That's what I want to do. We want to bring a title back to DC. . . ."

Wait.

What?

He motored through the mistake and kept with his vision: parade buses down Broad Street, maybe even boats, whatever the city wanted once the Phillies won it all. Yet bringing a title "back to DC" was no longer his dream. He'd left that to everyone else.

3

"How long until we land?"

March 28, 2019

What immediately became routine was Dave Martinez making a bullpen move, and that move not working, and Martinez later walking into his postgame press conference, bordering on anger, sometimes shaking to fend it off, to explain a problem he could not fix.

The harsh truth was that Washington had one reliever, Sean Doolittle, who could get outs with any consistency. Putting in the others was like walking to the mound, covering it in gasoline, then tossing a match on before innings, and leads, burned down. But Martinez had to paint this as a solvable issue, game after game, until his reasoning blended into vague clichés.

Take March 28, Opening Day, Washington against the Mets at Nationals Park. The Nationals trailed, 1–0, when a critical spot arrived in the eighth inning. The left-handed Robinson Canó was up with a runner on second and two outs. Martinez had three lefties in the bullpen—Doolittle, Tony Sipp, and Matt Grace—and Sipp had been signed by Rizzo, two weeks earlier, for this very situation. Sipp, thirty-six, made a living as a matchup specialist. He rushed through a truncated spring training to be ready. But Martinez went with Grace, Canó poked an inside sinker to left, and Martinez soon slumped into a leather chair, his soft eyes squinted, to unpack the year's first loss.

"He made a great pitch," Martinez said of Grace, and the manager may have even believed it. This was just his least favorite part of the job. He never wanted to sell himself, or be a public face, or do anything but play. Martinez fell in love with baseball because his father, Ernie, once fell in love with Roberto Clemente. Ernie was from Puerto Rico, as was Martinez's mother, Lillian, and Clemente was the family's hero.

They hung his photo in their Manhattan home. When Martinez went to the park, whenever it wasn't snowing or pouring rain, he'd try to mimic Clemente's swing. It didn't matter that Clemente was a righty and Martinez hit from the other side. He still tucked his chin on his front shoulder, cocked his hands behind his back ear, and unloaded on each pitch as if he were inside Three Rivers Stadium in Pittsburgh. Then he'd jog to the outfield and stain his clothes with grass.

Ernie wasn't around much while Martinez grew up. Ernie was a long-distance truck driver, and Martinez remembers him often leaving before sunrise and returning after dark. But Martinez watched Ernie closely and saw he never complained, never took off, never broke from a schedule that kept him alone with headlights and long highway strips. Martinez spent most days with his doting grandmother, who cooked him rice and beans, pozole, and spoke nothing but Spanish. They hung out in a little kitchen, and Martinez tried to keep up, until he'd sneak off to pick through Ernie's baseball cards.

At twelve, when he outgrew the cold-weather competition, Martinez moved in with an uncle in Winter Park, Florida. Ernie wanted him to play in front of scouts and have a chance to get recruited. Martinez became a standout at Lake Howell High School. He earned a spot at nearby Valencia Community College, thrived there, too, and he was drafted by the Cubs in the January phase of the 1983 draft. He was only nineteen years old. So, while he bounced around the minors, from Geneva, New York, to Davenport, Iowa, then to Winston-Salem, North Carolina, then back to Iowa again, Ernie was there whenever possible.

The game was their bond. If Martinez was in a slump, and his confidence low, Ernie picked up tape from the nearest store, took his son's socks, and rolled them into makeshift baseballs. He'd tell Martinez to take a bat home from the field. When they got back to their motel, in the shadows of some no-name town, they'd flip the mattress against the wall and start a familiar drill. Ernie knelt on the carpet and flipped the sock balls in Martinez's direction. Martinez took half swings, getting his timing back, and sent the balls bouncing off the walls for hours. He worked out kinks without damaging the lights or cheap artwork.

He hit .139 in 116 plate appearances as a rookie for the Cubs. It was weird for a big leaguer to travel with a parent, even if that big leaguer was twenty-one, and Ernie stopped coming on trips. But when the struggles returned, and Martinez felt lost, Ernie's voice popped into his head: Grab a bat. Don't let your teammates see. Ask the medical staff for tape—hell, fake a minor injury if you have to—and turn your room into a personal cage.

Martinez had to get creative without Ernie there to flip for him. That led to screwing tall lamps apart to use the bottom half as a tee. It worked, most of the time, except when he grew so frustrated that a full swing shattered a lamp into pieces. He rushed to the landline and dialed Ernie's number. Ernie told him to calm down, to take a breath, go to the front desk and admit he lost control. The receptionists didn't believe Martinez was a ballplayer trying to find his rhythm. They just told him not to worry, as if that were possible, and to get some sleep.

He carried *that* routine throughout his whole career—16 seasons, 1,918 games, nine teams, 1,599 hits and a .276 batting average. And when it was over, when his body told him it had to stop, it was really over. Done. At least that's what Martinez told himself in 2001. He was thirty-eight and aching. He was tired of the moves, of rushing to the next opportunity, of being that reliable, veteran outfielder who was adored by every teammate. He wanted out for good.

Most guys retire and can't pull away. They get into coaching, the broadcast booth, anything to keep a dying connection alive. They miss the competition, the road, being loved, unconditionally, by fans who view the world through wins and losses. Yet Martinez wanted to watch his kids grow up. He wanted to stop missing birthdays. He wanted to see Josh play youth soccer, and Jagger start football, and help Dalton dive into baseball, just like his dad. Martinez did that for five years, leading a normal life, losing himself in the drumbeat of a family schedule and carpool lines. Then Joe Maddon called.

Maddon met Martinez during the Cubs instructional league in 1983, when Martinez was just a skinny prospect and Maddon a young coach. Maddon told Martinez that he liked how Martinez played, and that started their long-distance friendship. So when Maddon became the Rays manager in 2006, and was piecing together a staff, he knew Martinez lived close to their spring training facility. Maddon invited him to be a guest instructor, and Martinez figured that would last a few weeks before he was back to being a dad. But he was there again in 2007, with no intentions of coaching full-time. That changed, too, without Martinez knowing it.

Another spring training wound down when Martinez walked into the Rays' facility. The team was about to head north for its season opener against the Yankees. Martinez noticed his bags were packed and figured it was a nice gesture from the clubhouse staff. But then an equipment manager offered a handshake and congratulations.

"For what?" Martinez asked.

"You're going to be the first-base coach until George is back," he was told.

"No, I'm not. Nobody told me that."

"Maybe you should go to talk to Joe."

Martinez went straight to Maddon's office to see what was up. George Hendrick, the regular first-base coach, was going to miss time with an injury. Maddon needed Martinez to fill in. Martinez didn't want to travel. Maddon promised it was only for a couple months. Martinez agreed, the players loved having him around, and he realized how much he missed the clubhouse, the small talk, the rhythms of each game, and the season they fit into. He stuck out the year, and, despite that, planned to go home.

But Andrew Friedman, then the Rays' general manager, would not let him. They met for an hour at a Starbucks in Tampa Bay, discussing Martinez's season and his place in the Rays' future. Martinez didn't think he had one. Friedman was set on convincing him otherwise.

"Congratulations," Friedman began, and Martinez, by that point, was wary of that word. "You're the new bench coach."

Maddon was a skilled tactician and comfortable with the media. Martinez was the perfect complement. He spent all his time with the players, instituting a disco ball in the clubhouse, a neon sign they turned on after wins, and encouraged first baseman James Loney to play his saxophone for the team. He defused problems without Maddon ever seeing them. Martinez paced around the outfield, using a bat as a walking stick, cracking jokes with veterans and patting rookies on the back. He was once them, facing pressure, straddling the thin line between confidence and losing his mind, but it was more than that. Sixteen years offered every experience Martinez could need.

There was December of 1984, when Martinez took a winter league assignment in Puerto Rico. He was a Cubs prospect, looking to improve, and thought it'd be fun to play in his native country.

But the Puerto Rican press was hard on him. They asked him to answer questions in Spanish, Martinez only knew a bit of the language, and once that got out, he was showered with boos. He had only been there a few days. The worst of it was a six-foot piece of barbed wire being chucked in his direction during his first game. He committed to learning Spanish and, a winter later, told Puerto Rican teammates to never use English around him. It taught him the importance of diverse communication.

Then there was 1992, when Martinez was twenty-seven, and he found a first baseman's mitt on the chair by his locker. Martinez and the Reds were facing the Giants at Candlestick Park in San Francisco. Martinez had exclusively played the outfield across seven seasons. But with first baseman Hal Morris injured, Reds manager Lou Piniella needed Martinez in that spot. Martinez thought his teammates were pranking him. Yet there his name was on the lineup card, starting at first, and Martinez took a sharp grounder off his foot in the first inning.

"I thought you said you could play first base," Piniella barked at Martinez in the dugout.

"No, you said I could play first base!" he shouted back. He wound up making 137 starts at first throughout his career. It taught him the importance of flexibility.

Then there was August of 1996, when Martinez was roped into a fistfight between teammates Frank Thomas and Robin Ventura. Ventura yelled at Thomas because he would not stop yelling at the umpires. Martinez led by example, never saying much, but soon found Thomas charging his way in the White Sox clubhouse. Thomas was six feet five, 240 pounds, and the team's best player. Martinez was five feet ten, 160 pounds, and a journeyman outfielder. It did not stop Martinez from wrestling Thomas to the carpet. That taught Martinez when to intervene.

This all made him effective and elastic as Maddon's bench coach.

And it's why his name surfaced when the Nationals needed a manager in 2013. They had fired Davey Johnson after missing the playoffs that year. Martinez flew to Washington and met with Rizzo and top members of the ownership group. But Martinez's pitch included too many references to Maddon, to "we," to what they did together, and not what he'd do on his own. The Nationals saw a coach, not a manager, and felt Martinez was not ready to break off.

He stayed in Tampa and later moved with Maddon when he was hired to manage the Cubs. The Nationals went with Matt Williams, he lasted two seasons, Dusty Baker followed him, and he didn't make it any further. The Nationals were flipping through managers like television channels.

Between 2006 and 2017, from when the Lerners bought the team to when they fired Baker, the Nationals had eight different managers, counting interim John McLaren for three games in 2011. None of them made it three full seasons. Martinez's second shot came four years after the first, after he won a title as the Cubs bench coach in 2016, and after the Nationals fired Baker despite 97 wins in 2017. Rizzo was against the Baker decision, one ownership made, but quickly lobbied to bring in Martinez for another interview.

This time, Martinez was confident, talking less about Maddon, and more about what *he* learned in Chicago's title run. His vision was to blend analytics with an old-school approach. He described his relationship with players as a defining strength. He wanted to learn from the front office, and build an experienced staff, and his voice stayed calm, his diction smooth, while he swerved from one topic to the next.

That didn't mean he liked pitching himself. That would never feel right. His agent did all the talking while he played. Martinez liked it that way, removed from the process, waiting with a few packed bags before jetting to another chance. But now he felt ready to push away from Maddon and run his own team. Rizzo reached out a few days after the interview, wasting no time, and the job was his.

"This is a half a dream come true to me . . . ," Martinez said at his introductory press conference on November 2, 2017. "This is just an ongoing thing that they've started years ago, and to continue in the successes that they've had and to get to that next level, which is win a world championship here in Washington."

Before a pitch was thrown in 2019, and before he was defending Grace on Opening Day, Martinez had to reset the Nationals' culture. He tried in 2018, ahead of his first year in charge, but his efforts backfired. He brought camels to spring training to say the Nationals would get over the hump. The gimmick was panned on social media and led to angry letters from PETA. He finished one day of workouts with a golf-chipping contest. The response was that the team wasn't focused enough. These were Maddon's antics, even if Martinez was always behind them, and kept him tied to his mentor. He tried using a purple-tinted disco ball after wins. He played music out of a speaker in his office. But any fun felt manufactured, and the results didn't help.

The Nationals were stung by injuries to start 2018, Harper took three months to get going, and they were trading key pieces by mid-August. Reliever Shawn Kelley was released on August 1 after showing up Martinez from the mound. Kelley was pitching the end of a blowout, and didn't want to, so he spiked his glove and glared at Martinez after allowing a homer. Rizzo rushed down after the game and charged at Kelley. He had to be held back by Adam Eaton, who wedged himself between the two, and Kelley was packing his locker by the end of the night. Reliever Brandon Kintzler was traded the same day because he was the suspected anonymous source who called the Nationals clubhouse "a mess" in a Yahoo! Sports story. Rizzo then met with reporters in the dugout that afternoon and delivered a sharp message to the remaining players: "If you're not in, you're in the way."

But a sell-off still began in less than three weeks. The Nationals were 7½ games back in the division on August 21. They first traded Daniel Murphy to the Cubs and Matt Adams to the Cardinals. They finished the month by sending Ryan Madson to the Dodgers and Gio González to the Brewers. All four of those teams had a shot to make the playoffs. The Nationals, though, were left shaving their payroll and looking ahead. They finished 82-80, their worst record in seven years, and Martinez's future was questioned.

His bullpen management was subpar. The team had a lot of injuries, especially early on, but were listless at full health. Yet Martinez didn't lose his players. They kept playing for him, even when their playoff odds dwindled to zero, and even once the roster was thinned to a shell of itself.

That's what the organization saw, too. They held on to Martinez, despite the faint calls for his job, and he didn't spend October watching the postseason. That would have been one kind of torture. He chose even worse.

He went everywhere with an iPad that had each of the Nationals' 162 games loaded onto it. He hunted in Wisconsin, fished outside Salt Lake City, lay in the hammock at his farm outside Nashville, and still carved out time, every day, to relive all the mistakes. There were his mistakes, mostly with the bullpen, such as leaving relievers in too long, or not striking the right balance between analytics and his gut. Then there were his players' mistakes, such as taking the wrong plate approach, the wrong baserunning approach, or lapsing on defense.

Martinez took hand notes and texted his video team with requests. He needed specific situations put on loop. He wanted to see Wander Suero's cutter against lefties, Eaton's at bats when Trea Turner was on first, Juan Soto's two-strike stance, and so on. The research left him irritated and itching for spring. The diagnosis was poor fundamentals and, even simpler, bad baseball.

He got to West Palm Beach in early February and called for a staff meeting. That's when he told the coaches about correcting *the little things*. Mistakes were met with yelling "Do it again!" into quiet mornings. But there were still far too many of them once the regular season began.

Grace allowing that single to Canó, and Grace pitching in the first place, was only the beginning. The bullpen was a complete mess from the start. Trevor Rosenthal, signed to pitch the eighth inning, couldn't control a high-90s fastball. Harper returned to Washington on the first Tuesday of the season and was loudly booed, but the game was a disaster for the Nationals. In the bottom of the first, in his fourteenth at bat of the season, Turner squared to bunt and saw a Zach Eflin fastball running toward his face. He tried to get out of the way, falling backward, but couldn't avoid danger. The pitch struck the wooden bat handle, jamming Turner's right index finger against it, and he sprawled into the dirt before receiving immediate medical attention.

The shortstop screamed, "Damn it!" and went straight to the trainer's room. An X-ray revealed a fracture, and a six-to-eight-week recovery window, while the Nationals limped to an 8–2 defeat. It was capped by Harper blasting a 458-foot homer off Jeremy Hellickson, flipping his bat toward the Nationals dugout, then rounding the bases while Phillies fans took over the storm-slicked park. It felt like a test of Murphy's Law.

"We lost one of our good players and we lost. We got to come back tomorrow, and we got to get better," Martinez said, and that became a regular refrain. But the Nationals did not get better. Not for more than a game or two at a time. When the bullpen blew another late lead in New York that Saturday, in Game 17 against the Mets, it had allowed 17 total runs in the eighth inning. Rosenthal pitched again in the series finale, an eventual win, but still couldn't find the plate. He'd made four appearances, thrown 38 pitches, allowed 7 runs, and recorded 0 outs. His ERA was an incalculable "infinity."

At home, with his press conferences packed with cameras, Martinez remained coy. But on the road, with a small group of traveling reporters, he often expressed confusion about whom to pitch. His starters were sharp. His relievers were the opposite. So he'd sit in the visiting manager's office after games, turn his palms toward the ceiling, and shrug. There were no right answers.

"We have to come up with something. We have to figure something out for him," Martinez said of Rosenthal before the Nationals trained to Philadelphia on April 7. They split the series with the Mets but left in doubt. Martinez already sounded desperate to fix the $8 million reliever. Rosenthal's control issues forced Martinez to overuse others, and so early in the season, when all arms should have been fresh. "We tried to tweak something with his mechanics, but we've got to keep working on it. It's tough because up here you've only got so many guys in the bullpen. You need everybody. I tried to give guys off today that have been pitching quite a bit. These guys have got to pitch. But we're going to need Rosey. We really are. So we've got to get him right."

The team's potential came in quick flashes. They soon staged a dramatic win over the Phillies, with late homers from Victor Robles and Juan Soto, and capped a weeklong trip with a 16–1 blowout. They were 6-5, with all those games in the division, and headed home to light competition. Rosenthal even got his first out, 48 pitches into his season, and looked as if he might ease into form. But any success was short-lived.

The Nationals dropped two of three to the lowly Pittsburgh Pirates, played too close with the San Francisco Giants, then tripped through a road set with the Marlins in Miami. The Marlins were one of the league's worst teams. Their lineup was a collection of should-be minor leaguers. Their rotation had little to no experience. Yet they beat the Nationals, twice, and that's when the injuries piled up. Anthony Rendon was scorching hot before he was hit in the left elbow by a 95 mph fastball. He joined Turner on the shelf, and three days later, Zimmerman hurt his right foot during a win in Denver. Then Juan Soto went to the injured list with back spasms in early May.

Their replacements—Carter Kieboom, Jake Noll, Andrew Stevenson—had to take red-eye flights from Fresno, California, to join the team. That's where the Nationals AAA team had relocated to before the season, creating a mess of delays and lost luggage. Players mockingly called it the Midnight Express. One team official cracked that the Nationals should reserve one seat on each United flight from Fresno for the rest of the season. It was common for a young guy to show up, his face sunk by fatigue, and start right away because numbers were so thin.

And there was Martinez, staying upbeat, spreading optimism wherever he could. He tried to keep the clubhouse loose with post-win celebrations. But smashing cabbage after an April victory, when so few were going the Nationals' way, felt like camels and golf all over again. The excitement only lasted until the Nationals were beat down the next day. Turner was in a cast and doing one-handed hitting drills. Rendon's elbow was swollen and movement was tough. Zimmerman stared down a long rehab—at least weeks, maybe months—and Soto moped for the first time in his career.

The twenty-year-old was tired of his back tightening up whenever he sprinted or swiveled. Martinez told him not to let the bitterness show. Yet there had been a jolt away from the manager's usual steadiness. He assured the Nationals were fine, that they'd turn it around when healthy, that there was no reason to panic or make any drastic moves. Yet firing pitching coach Derek Lilliquist felt like a drastic move.

That came on May 2, before a three-city road swing, after a win the relievers actually excelled in. But the decision was made before the Nationals took the field that night. Lilliquist was just unaware until a victory wore off and he walked into Martinez's office. The bullpen's ERA was 6.02, a historically bad pace, and many felt Lilliquist had not properly prepared it for the season. The team was told while stuffing clothes into their bags. Rizzo held a last-minute press conference and noted that Lilliquist, though opposed to the assessment, took the news like a "true champion."

Lilliquist left the clubhouse through a side door to avoid lingering reporters. Some players, specifically some relievers, felt responsible for Lilliquist losing his job just a month into the year. They knew and liked Paul Menhart, Lilliquist's replacement, who'd been with the Nationals for more than a decade. But that didn't soften the reality. It was the front office's turn to make a public statement. The long-held belief is when coaches get ousted, and cracks begin to show, the manager isn't too far behind.

"At this point, we wanted a new voice and a new face, somebody to relay the message in a different way," Martinez said while his voice clutched with emotion. "As you guys know, Derek's a good friend of mine. So this is tough."

The team went back to Philadelphia and lost, then won, then fell again, 7–1, with a starting lineup of Wilmer Difo at third, Adam Eaton hitting third, catcher Kurt Suzuki behind him, Stevenson in left, Noll at first, and Kieboom playing shortstop. It looked like a spring training order. It played like one, too. There was little chance of progress without Rendon, Soto, Turner, and Zimmerman, and still, somehow, Martinez expressed confidence before his team bused to Philadelphia International Airport.

They boarded their Delta charter plane, reclined in their first-class seats, and downloaded movies and TV shows for the short flight to Milwaukee. But there was a problem. The engine needed a new part, and since Philadelphia is not a Delta hub, it would take a while for it to get there. The players poured drinks, dealt cards, figured it would be an hour or so before they left. Then that hour passed, then two, then three became four, and four became five, and they were still sitting on the plane. Pitcher Joe Ross passed out around 6:30 p.m., when they first got on, and later woke up rubbing his eyes.

"I slept great," Ross told no one in particular. "How long until we land?"

"We haven't even taken off yet," answered Eaton, and Ross figured he was kidding. Yet they hadn't budged. Once 9:00 p.m. arrived, laptops and iPads were lit by the new episode of *Game of Thrones*. Once midnight came, everyone started to wonder why they couldn't just come back in the morning. The Nationals tailored their entire travel schedule to advice from leading sleep specialists. But this, with a game the next night, in another time zone, no less, felt fitting.

They deplaned after eight hours and headed for the team hotel. Dozens of UberXLs were ordered. Players scrambled off the pavement, jammed into the cars, wanting nothing more than their king-size beds.

Martinez let his disbelief turn to twisted laughter. He came into the year with big plans for this team, for himself, for what they could accomplish after flatlining the previous summer. Now they had already fired a coach, sunk to 14-19 with that loss to the Phillies, and couldn't even fly without everything going wrong. He figured right then, under the harsh lights of the arrivals terminal, that the season couldn't get any worse. But of course it could. And of course it did.

4

19–31

May 24, 2019

Juan Soto and Victor Robles didn't like waking up early. Soto, twenty, preferred to sleep through alarms, bang the snooze button a few times, then roll out of bed to eat lunch instead of breakfast. Robles, twenty-two, is the exact same way. The center fielder is a ball of energy at the field, often yelling his teammates' names in the clubhouse, or mimicking people's walks as they pass him. Just don't ask him to do much before noon. But now they were in the Lotte New York Palace lobby, yawning, because they were expected at MLB Network in Secaucus, New Jersey, on May 21. And it wasn't even 9:00 a.m.

They were two stud outfielders from the Dominican Republic, and two reasons to believe that Washington could excel without Harper. Soto was coming off one of the best nineteen-year-old seasons in history. Robles burned opponents with his speed and gap-to-gap defense. That's what attracted the network to their story, as a colorful pair, both ready to smile and rib each other nonstop. They rode in a black SUV, through midtown Manhattan traffic, with two members of the Nationals' public relations staff. They took a bit to warm up and shake the sleep from their eyes, but were soon excited by the television sets.

Soto and Robles took photos with a plaque for Roberto Clemente. They laughed at each other's dress clothes, Soto in a pressed button-down, Robles's golf shirt tucked into khaki pants. They went to Studio 42, dedicated to Jackie Robinson, and pointed to the big cameras, bright lights, and the makeshift field. Then Robles noticed all thirty teams listed on the back wall. He scanned the metal circles, scanned them again, and quickly recognized the order.

"Are those the standings?" Robles asked in Spanish.

"Yeah," answered the producer assigned to him. "Someone comes in every day to change them, so they are up-to-date."

Up-to-date showed what Robles didn't want to see. The Nationals were 19-28, in fourth place in the division, and stumbling into four games with the Mets at Citi Field. They got swept in Milwaukee after the engine debacle. From April 26 to May 6, the day of the series opener with the Brewers, the Nationals had more players leave a game with injury or hit the IL (eight) than they did wins (three). Then they split with the Dodgers in Los Angeles, thanks to a game-winning grand slam from newcomer Gerardo Parra, and went 3-3 at home before heading to New York.

A loss to the Mets on Monday, the night before Soto and Robles did TV, brought a new twist on defeat. Corbin was roughed up for three innings, before relievers could even enter, and the bats went quiet. Turner, Rendon, and Soto were active again, and that was good, but it wasn't enough to hide the glaring issues.

The bullpen had yet to improve under Menhart. Closer Sean Doolittle was already up to 20 appearances, a concerning workload, and Rosenthal was on the injured list with what the team called a "viral infection." He got sick during a trip to Denver, in the days before he was sidelined, but it read like a fibbed condition to help him reset in the minors. The other options weren't faring much better. Free agent reliever Craig Kimbrel was still available, for any club willing to pay him, but ownership didn't want to spend over the competitive-balance tax threshold. It was set at $206 million and they were already close. Reinforcements would be unproven and cheap.

The offense, still inching back to full strength, was hot for one game and ice-cold the next. The Nationals dropped eight of Scherzer's first ten starts. Aníbal Sánchez, their fourth starter, was 0-6 and out with a strained left hamstring. Jeremy Hellickson, their fifth starter, was even less effective.

Robles watched from the side while Soto shot a segment. Soto told the host his childhood heroes were Robinson Canó and Manny Ramírez. He dug into the carpeted box and swung a Wiffle ball bat. He then put his hand over his eyes, as if he'd rocked a home run, and everyone in the studio laughed. But Robles was quiet until his turn came. Players avoid standings, no matter how they look, because the season's too long for a day, week, or month to stick out. Peeking is how you go crazy. Especially in May. Yet Robles didn't have much of a choice, staring at the Nationals logo beneath those of the Phillies, Braves, and Mets. It was hard not to. It kept staring right back.

The week was odd from beginning, once the Nationals train caught fire on their way to New York, they didn't reach the hotel until well past midnight, and, in the first game at Citi Field, Adam Eaton and Todd Frazier stole headlines with a petty fight. Or maybe this was just on-brand for Washington.

They started the series with a loss, falling 5–3, when the Mets jumped all over Corbin. That's when Eaton and Frazier provided perfect material for the city tabloids. They became enemies while playing together with the Chicago White Sox in 2016. They had chirped across the diamond in 2018, when Eaton was with the

Nationals, Frazier with the Mets, and Eaton believed Zack Wheeler had brushed him back with inside fastballs. Now, less than a year later, in the third inning of a critical series, Frazier screamed in Eaton's direction while jogging off the field.

He heard Frazier, from maybe a hundred feet away, and whipped his head around. Frazier was already being held back by teammates. Eaton couldn't make out what Frazier was saying. Frazier declined to discuss the incident in a postgame interview. Then the local media rushed to get Eaton's thoughts, like passing gossip through a middle school hallway.

Eaton told reporters Frazier was "very childish," and, as a man with a mortgage, he did not want to deal with him. The first social media reaction asked why Eaton, a multimillionaire, was still paying off a mortgage. Frazier later snapped back with, "Pay off your mortgage. I don't know what to tell you." Eaton clarified that he didn't have a mortgage, and it was just a figure of speech to say that while he was an adult, Frazier had trouble acting like one. There was a lot of mortgage talk.

The two players squashed the feud by chatting in the outfield before the next game. The news cycle filtered it out. Later that night, with Washington begging for a lift, Soto parked a Wheeler fastball into the right-field seats. That came in the second inning, bringing hints of life, but no lead was large enough. The bullpen soon reminded the Nationals of that. Reliever Wander Suero blew an advantage in the seventh, Tanner Rainey did the same in the eighth, and the Mets won in the ninth, 6–5, when Amed Rosario legged out an infield single.

Citi Field exploded once Rosario crossed first ahead of Trea Turner's wobbly throw. The Nationals dropped their heads and walked toward a quiet clubhouse. Turner was playing with a bent index finger, and would for the rest of the season, but didn't pin the end on that. No one wanted to hear excuses. It would have been a bad time to offer one. Rosario is fast, Turner did all he could, the Nationals fell because their bullpen couldn't finish games. That was the story. Rinse, repeat.

"Mostly the seventh, eighth innings start happening, or when those runs start coming in, we, I mean, you definitely see a drop," said catcher Yan Gomes after the loss. "We were still tied and you kind of saw a drop in our . . ."

Gomes stopped short of finishing his thought. But he didn't have to. He'd already described the biggest problem facing the Nationals, a talented team until pressure rose. They had Scherzer going on Wednesday, he went pitch-for-pitch with Jacob deGrom, and the Nationals again carried a slim lead into the eighth inning. But Kyle Barraclough put two runners on and forced Martinez to bring in Doolittle with four outs to go. The lefty then hit Carlos Gómez with a pitch, loading the bases, and Juan Lagares smacked a low-and-in fastball into the left-center gap. Robles sprinted toward it from center. Soto closed in from left. Yet they both pulled up short, just before the warning track, and the ball bounced between them for a double.

It rattled against the wall and three Mets scored. Doolittle paced off the mound and shook his head. He glanced at the dugout, wondering if Martinez would pull him, yet stayed in until Rajai Davis blasted a 3-run homer. Doolittle allowed 5 runs without getting an out. It was the worst appearance of his career. To that point of the season, through 48 games, he was the only reliever Martinez could count on. His four-seam fastball, thrown about 92 percent of the time, was basically all the bullpen had. But this outing left him frozen by his locker, staring at the ground, then his iPhone, waiting for questions to come.

"It was shocking. That's a good word for it," Martinez said, and it felt as if whenever he was here, behind this old wooden desk at Citi Field, there was nothing good to say. "He's the best, the best we have."

"I'm really frustrated," Doolittle admitted, his eyes blank behind a pair of round glasses, his voice hovering above a mumble. "I'm disgusted with myself, I let the team down, and it hurts."

"No one likes to lose. Everyone hates losing. Everyone in here hates to lose," Scherzer told reporters, stepping toward the center of the room, making it impossible for teammates to ignore him. Howie Kendrick stopped buttoning the cuffs of a dress shirt and listened. Doolittle noticed Scherzer's sharp tone. "You don't have time to feel sorry for yourself. You got to come out tomorrow and just compete. There's nothing else you can do.

"When you face adversity, this is when you reveal yourself." Scherzer was getting louder by the word, and challenged everyone in earshot. "Whether you have the mental fortitude to come and block out all the negativity that's probably going to surround us right now."

The Nationals showed up the next day looking to avoid a sweep. That was all they could do. The bus pulled into Citi Field just before 10:00 a.m., and players dragged suitcases behind them. There was whispered frustration that neither Soto or Robles had dived after Lagares's double. It was the first sign of visible fractures, however small, and one player summed up what a handful thought: "If they ran into each other, that'd be one thing. But they didn't take the initiative to make the catch. You have to with the game on the line."

The TVs were turned off for a change. There weren't any games to show, and talk shows were filled with similar noise. The analysts wanted Martinez fired. They suggested the Nationals trade key veterans—Scherzer, Doolittle, maybe Anthony Rendon, who'd be a free agent at year's end—and start building for 2020. No one wanted to hear it. The players kept their headphones on, dipped into sudoku, or fixed on crossword puzzles to pass the time. But there was soon a break from the typical pregame routine.

Of all the managers he'd been around, as a player and a coach, Martinez may have learned the most from Bobby Cox. Martinez played for Cox with the Braves for one season before retiring. Cox was old-school, down to the core, and always left the clubhouse to his veterans. Martinez then made that his style. He doesn't yell after losses, doesn't flip tables, doesn't show much emotion in front of his guys. There was that time in August of 2018, when he snapped at Wrigley Field and smashed a coffee maker to pieces. But Martinez did that alone in the manager's office. Otherwise, across fourteen months in Washington, he'd kept his cool and let the players own their space.

He had Scherzer, a thirty-four-year-old Ryan Zimmerman, enough leaders to handle whatever came up. They could meet if they wanted. Martinez never made them. Yet they felt a pressing need to clear the air before the finale with the Mets. They brought Martinez and the whole staff into the room, and everyone got a turn to share what he thought was wrong. Martinez had introduced the concept during spring training, as a team-building exercise, and he'd used it again during that May skid in Milwaukee.

Now, on the last day in New York, the veterans did it on their own. A wall clock ticked toward first pitch. A few relievers owned their poor performance. Other guys promised to improve. When the circle was complete, and everyone had had a chance to talk, Martinez stood and looked around. If this was a turning point, something critical, the moment they chose to fight instead of fold, none of them knew it yet. All Martinez did was show his players what they'd missed.

"Listen to yourselves. You're all saying the same stuff," Martinez told his players. "You still trust each other."

Then they went out and lost again.

Martinez had stayed up until 2:00 a.m. the night before in his hotel room, rewatching Doolittle's meltdown. The manager mapped out a late-inning bullpen plan and didn't sleep until it felt just right. But he wouldn't see it unfold from the dugout. He got ejected in the eighth for arguing with home-plate umpire Bruce Dreckman. Martinez was defending Kendrick, who disagreed with a check-swing call, and seemed to beg for Dreckman to toss him.

And for a moment, with Martinez stuck inside, it seemed as if his players might use his anger as fuel. They pushed ahead by scoring 3 runs in the eighth. But the advantage disappeared, and quickly, once Suero entered from the bullpen. He had pitched so much in the first six weeks of the season—22 times—that the relievers had a running joke. Whenever a phone rang, whether they were in the clubhouse, the bullpen, or eating at a restaurant, they all told Suero to warm up. So here he was again, trying to hang on with a tired arm, but instead hung a cutter onto Carlos Gómez's bat.

Gómez cracked a 3-run homer over the left-field wall and spread his arms while rounding second. It capped a week that went from bad, to awful, to, in the end, a full-on nightmare for Washington. When it had started, four long days ago, the Mets were wading through their own pile of issues. They'd been swept by the Marlins in Miami. Their manager, Mickey Callaway, was at risk of losing his job. Their general manager, Brodie Van Wagenen, called a Monday press conference to give Callaway a shaky vote of confidence. *Their* season, not the Nationals', was slipping away.

That gave the Nationals a springboard to leap on. It was right there. But all they did was run a losing streak to five games and tumble into crisis. They were 19-31, their World Series odds down to 1.5 percent, and the calendar had yet to hit Memorial Day. They were already 10 games back of first place in the division. The only National League team with a worse record was the Marlins, and the Marlins were trying to lose.

A reporter asked Martinez who should get the blame, the implication being that it might soon fall on him. His voice was hoarse from yelling at Dreckman. He wanted to pack his camouflage bag and bust out of these cinder-block walls. He just had a few more answers to push through.

"Things are going to change. Things are going to change," he repeated. "And I know that. So we got to keep pounding away, keep playing baseball. There's good players in that clubhouse, really good players. We'll turn things around."

The Nationals got back on two buses, and they drove to Grand Central Terminal, and then they boarded a private Amtrak charter bound for home. They settled in for a three-hour ride, dining on room-temperature pizza, while the takes splashed across the internet. But most players avoided their phones, even for harmless text messages, because the opinions were everywhere.

Friends sent articles the players didn't want to read. Family asked how they were doing. The *Washington Post* published a column under this headline: "Who cares about Dave Martinez? In a lost season, Nationals face tougher decisions." It had been two weeks since Jim Bowden, a former Nationals GM and now a columnist for *The Athletic*, wrote, "Dave Martinez is one of the worst managers I've seen in the big leagues in a long time." The four losses in New York only left everyone piling on.

Martinez didn't use social media or have a Twitter account. But he knew what they were saying and that his chances were limited. He scootered to Nationals Park the next morning, a bit earlier than usual, and told his staff to head in. Rizzo had asked them to gather for a discussion about next steps. They weren't getting fired. The players had aired their frustrations, and Rizzo wanted to do the same.

"We've been here a year and a third. Whatever we're doing, we've got to change it, because we got to do something different," Rizzo told Martinez and his staff. Then they went around the office and asked each other, *What can you do?... What can you do differently?... What can you do better?* Rizzo later described it as a "bullshitting session" with no raised voices, no finger-pointing, just a group of "baseball grunts" searching for answers.

They settled on mandatory batting practice, more infield drills, making the basics a priority as they were back in spring training. That was Rizzo's directive until results improved, and he had one last thought to share.

"Whatever happens when we leave this room, we have to be ultrapositive," Rizzo remembered telling them. "Because everyone, when this door opens, everyone's going to be looking at us. And we can't crack. We have to be ultrapositive and do things with a smile on our faces. Because if we panic, we're done. And if we're going out, let's go out on our terms. Let's get this thing turned around. It's not turning around tomorrow. We're not turning around tomorrow. This thing is going to be a slow, painful process."

When the meeting ended, and the coaches scattered to the field, Rizzo and Martinez stayed behind. Rizzo didn't ask Martinez to make promises for the future. But Martinez did anyway, looking Rizzo straight in the eye, telling him, in the privacy of a one-on-one conversation, that everything would be okay. He gave Rizzo his word.

5

Posting

June 19, 2019

As Yan Gomes sat by his locker at Nationals Park on June 19, leafing through a stack of scouting reports, he heard commotion rumble through the clubhouse door. It was a lazy afternoon, nothing out of the ordinary, just a bunch of guys hoping it wouldn't rain. But then Gomes looked up to see Max Scherzer pressing a white towel to his face, the towel soaked in blood, and Scherzer cursing his way to the trainer's room, hiding a crooked nose.

"Fuck, man! Fuck!" Scherzer barked, and who could blame him? The Nationals had been on a tear since returning home from New York in late May. They took three of four from the Marlins, swept a two-game set against the Braves in Atlanta, then won back-to-back series with the Cincinnati Reds and the Chicago White Sox. Improvements still needed to be made, up and down the roster, but the Nationals were no longer dead in the water. They were beginning to tread, if only lightly, and have a bit of fun.

That began with health, and better performance followed. Scherzer had allowed just 4 earned runs in his last five starts, nudging himself into the early Cy Young conversation. Stephen Strasburg was regularly pushing into the seventh inning. Patrick Corbin sifted through a rough patch that quickly dissipated. Even Aníbal Sánchez, after such a bad start, was synced into a groove. The offense clicked behind Rendon, Soto, and Kendrick, who'd kept the order breathing when the meat of it was out. Rendon looked like a potential MVP candidate. Soto made a slight tweak, adjusting his timing and hands, and took off.

In San Diego on June 9, with the Nationals trying for a series split, Kendrick dug into the box against Padres reliever Craig Stammen. The Nationals were down in the eighth, 2–1, and Martinez needed Kendrick to spark the lineup. They were at risk of wasting a dominant day from Strasburg. But Kendrick ripped a 2-2 curveball off a digital scoreboard in left field. Tie game. Then Trea Turner skied a sinker out to center, and Adam Eaton pulled a sinker over the fence, and Rendon lifted one into the first row of seats in right-center.

Petco Park was quiet aside from the faint announcements of last call. The damage was back-to-back-to-back-to-back home runs, totaling 1,639 feet, tucked into four minutes that buried the Padres and made two statements: The Nationals could hit. They also had a knack for coming from behind.

"I don't think I've ever seen that," Martinez said after the win. It had happened nine times in history once the Nationals clobbered Stammen. They did it in 2017, when Martinez was still in Chicago, and now he watched from the dugout steps as each ball flew through a cloudless sky. "I liked the first one, for sure. That put us ahead. And then it was wow . . . wow . . . and *wow*."

"So I went and looked at the exit velocities, and he hit his the softest—I have no idea how it went out," Turner cracked with a smirk, referring to Rendon's shot. Rendon sat a few feet away, opening a forty-ounce beer, and shook his head at Turner. Rendon was up to 12 homers on the season, almost halfway to a career high, and he'd played just 51 games. He often left teammates wondering how he made such hard contact, how his hands moved so fast, how he took great pitches and flicked them into a gap. Sort of like Turner suggesting that Rendon's latest homer, a high-arcing one, should have run out of steam.

"Play the wind!" Rendon countered, a smile spreading above his goatee, his voice singing in too high a pitch. The tension from New York had faded into afternoons such as this, when it was okay to laugh and joke and jack the clubhouse music to full volume.

But now, just ten days after leaving San Diego, Scherzer's blood was a stark reminder: the Nationals had not lost a series in three weeks. But they were still digging out of a hole, from starting 19-31, and needed just about everything to go right. They were chasing the Phillies, Braves, and Mets in the division and were 7 games back of first place. Their bullpen remained a loud question mark. They couldn't afford to lose their ace, for any amount of time, and that's when Scherzer had a freak accident.

He was taking batting practice when third-base coach Bobby Henley told him to lay down a few bunts. It was supposed to be a harmless drill. There were four hours until a game against the Phillies, weather permitting, and Scherzer squared while Henley wound up. But Henley's lob was high and tight, Scherzer's effort was half-hearted, and the ball bounced off the bat and into his face. A pair of sunglasses jumped onto his forehead. Scherzer spun around, bent in half, and reached for the bridge of his nose. A jagged cut spat blood onto his fingers. Henley yelled for Paul Lessard, the club's head athletic trainer, and bench coach Chip Hale gave Scherzer that Gatorade towel.

Tests at a nearby hospital revealed a broken nose. A CT scan indicated no brain damage. A steady rain fell back at Nationals Park, and play was postponed for a second straight night. A doubleheader was scheduled for the next day, with starts at 1:05 and 7:05 p.m., and Martinez was unsure if Scherzer could go. He was supposed to face the Phillies in the second game. The risk was that a line drive could put him in serious danger, or the pain would make it hard to focus, or his breathing might be restricted by the fractured bones. But Scherzer was already texting friends that he would pitch, as if there were never a doubt.

J. C. Field didn't know much about the University Missouri when he transferred from Pima Community College in 2005. A sturdy catcher from Tucson, Arizona, Field had impressed Division I coaches and knew the competition would be a lot tougher in the Southeastern Conference. But that was it. That, and the sophomore Max Scherzer that everyone was talking about.

Scherzer spent his freshman year begging to get in games. He was recruited to Missouri from nearby Parkway Central High School, where he was a three-sport athlete in football, basketball, and baseball. He was a quarterback and wide receiver, a scrapper on the court who used his elbows as a weapon, and shone on the mound with a violent delivery.

The hometown Cardinals picked Scherzer in the forty-third round of the 2003 draft, and he chose college to up his stock. But the problem, at least early on, was the Tigers' experienced rotation. There wasn't room for a nineteen-year-old wearing training wheels. Scherzer had to wait and wait, and he wasn't good at that.

In the summer of 2005, a few months before Field got to campus, Scherzer searched for a way in front of scouts. He wasn't called by the premier leagues in Cape Cod, Massachusetts, or Alaska. But a spot was open in the Northwoods League, in La Crosse, Wisconsin, because the Loggers had a few pitchers leave for Team USA. The catch was that Scherzer had to trek there to try out.

He arrived at a high school gymnasium with nothing but a mitt and light duffel bag. He told Rich Russell, the Loggers' catcher, that he wasn't ready to throw too hard. Scherzer figured his heat might kiss the low 90s, if he got really warm, but he was going to take it easy. Then Scherzer's fastball attacked Russell's glove like a missile. Russell had trouble tracking it against the white walls. Scherzer made the team, started right away, and scouts soon knew a well-kept secret.

That's what Field had heard before meeting Scherzer at fall practices. Scherzer joined the Loggers midseason and became the league's best pitcher. The tail on his fastball was ridiculous. A year earlier, when he was still new to Missouri, a few upperclassmen had challenged Scherzer to eat three Chipotle burritos in one sitting. And he did it, toppings and all.

"There were some times where I had to pat him on the butt a little bit," Field recalled years later. "I had to kind of get into him. He was the type of personality where you continue to challenge him and continued to push him, that's when you're really going to see the real Max."

That's what would drive Scherzer into a Hall of Fame–caliber career. He was at his best when challenged, when told he can't do something, when given a chance to prove anyone, or everyone, wrong. The burritos were only a start. He constantly told Missouri position players that he was a better hitter. He nagged Tim Jamieson, the Tigers' manager, to give him a shot at the plate. He was known for pinning a $10 bill to the bulletin board in the locker room, a call to any pitcher who dared face him. The bet was for two pitches. If Scherzer hit either for a homer, they owed him another $10. If he didn't, they kept the money.

When Scherzer was drafted by the Arizona Diamondbacks in 2006, with the eleventh overall pick, he didn't feel they were valuing him correctly. So he and his agent, Scott Boras, devised a creative plan. You could wait almost a full year then, then decide between signing or reentering the next draft. Scherzer didn't want to leave first-round money on the table. But he did want to show the Diamondbacks what they'd miss if he did. Scherzer joined the Fort Worth Cats of the American Association in the spring of 2007. The independent league had teams in El Paso, Texas; Pensacola, Florida; Sioux City, Iowa; and six other small towns. It was full of college players gripping one more chance.

Boras made sure Scherzer's starts were flooded with scouts. The Diamondbacks showed up and raised cameras alongside their competition. Scherzer pitched 16 innings across three appearances, struck out 25, and gave up a lone run. On May 31, 2007, just hours before the deadline to sign, the Diamondbacks blinked. Scherzer agreed to a four-year major league contract worth $4.3 million in guaranteed money. It came with a $3 million signing bonus plus incentives. He rolled the dice, risking a top 10 draft slot, and he won.

Scherzer carried that reputation to the minors, then the majors, then from Arizona to Detroit when he was traded to the Tigers in 2009. The stories followed him wherever he went. Once, in June of 2007, Scherzer had a no-hitter through seven innings but had reached his pitch limit. Héctor de la Cruz, managing the Visalia Oaks in the Diamondbacks' system, came to the mound and asked for the ball. But Scherzer refused to hand it over. De la Cruz pleaded, saying he was under strict orders to keep Scherzer fresh, mentioning his wife and kids, and that he couldn't lose his job. Scherzer relented, after some pleading of his own, and left the field while shaking his head.

That was typical behavior. Scherzer ignored a teammate at a charity golf tournament because he was so intent on winning. His preparation was so detailed, stretching for pages, filling entire afternoons, that catchers showed up hours earlier for his starts. When Scherzer signed with the Nationals in 2015, for seven years and $250 million, he told Wilson Ramos that their brains had to meld.

That's what Scherzer demanded from those around him. He brought it every day.

Scherzer asked for a ride back to Nationals Park after getting X-rays on June 18. He heard the game was canceled, again, but wanted to speak with Martinez. The manager was lounging in his office, feet up on the desk, when Scherzer charged in and stated his case. His breathing was fine. He could see out of his blue eye and brown eye. It may have looked bad, with a green-and-maroon bruise above his right cheek, but the pain had already eased. Earlier that day, when he was sitting in the trainer's room, Scherzer told Lessard that if this had happened in a game, in the heat of a start, he would have stayed in. A day to recover was a no-brainer.

Martinez was required to push back. But he could see Scherzer was fixed on "posting." Of all that made Scherzer great—the tailing fastball, his off-speed pitches, his ability to mix six options like a video game—it's his desire to post, to pitch whenever called upon, that set him apart. He often uses the word when discussing his legacy, and he wanted to be remembered for always taking the ball. He'd made 30 or more starts in each of the last ten seasons. He led the league in innings pitched in 2018, with 220⅔, and often finished outings by emptying the tank. That's another one of his catchphrases. It means throwing his hardest pitches once his energy sagged.

He doesn't discuss most of his methods with reporters, such as how he grips his pitches, or how much he runs in a training regimen that leaves him sprinting through the outfield between starts. He feels that doing so, even at a surface level, would give a competitive advantage over opponents. He's leery of anyone studying as hard as he does. He imagines Freddie Freeman, the Braves' best hitter, opening the newspaper to find a grain of intel that could tilt their next matchup. Call it insane paranoia. Scherzer still won't deviate.

But he is clear on the root of his dominance, the reason he's won three Cy Young trophies and been in the mix for three more. It all goes back to posting. It runs on a constant stream of information. It depends on his taking every chance to carve through teams and learn their countermoves. That's why he couldn't bear sitting for a broken nose. He stood across from Martinez, between a leather couch and blue stadium seats, and went through his delivery. He dialed up the speed, as if he were on an actual mound, to show that nothing was off. Martinez smiled and told him to get some rest.

"I'm pitching," Scherzer stated before he left. "Expect me to pitch tomorrow."

The plan was for Scherzer to wake up and let Lessard know how he felt. If he was fine—and of course he would be—he would go through his normal start-day routine. Martinez wouldn't hear from him. They never talked before Scherzer pitched, and Martinez didn't rush for an update that morning. He figured no news was good news, and he was right, and the Nationals won the first game behind Corbin and a Gerardo Parra home run.

That evening, with Washington eyeing a doubleheader sweep, Scherzer took the field to a huge ovation. He kept his head tilted down while crossing the right-field line. He began his usual warm-ups, bursting into a light jog, then tossed with bullpen catcher Octavio Martinez. His face was shaded by distance and the red brim of his hat. But when he turned toward television cameras, in the middle of a light throw, it took seconds for the images to flood social media.

Most noticeable was the black-and-blue mark above his right cheek, shaped like a flattened oval, spreading into tints of light green. The area around his right eye, where the ball smacked into him, was shaded a dull maroon. The left side had specks of the same colors. His teammates passed him on the field, in the clubhouse, and whispered to one another about how crazy he was. And that was the point.

When the Nationals skidded to 19-31 in May and stood at the fork of two fates, the math was pretty simple. They had to win at a crazy clip to save their season. They adopted Martinez's favorite saying—"Let's go 1–0 today"—and that reflected in their banged-up stars. Turner returned before his broken right index finger could grip a bat or a ball. He weighed his options, asked the medical staff if he could injure it further, and assessed if his performance would help or hurt. Surgery was not required in June. The clean fracture was expected to heal properly. The pain worsened with time, when a bone spur developed in Turner's knuckle and his tendon scarred into the top of his finger. But he kept his head down and never complained.

The shortstop had played in every game since he was activated, a stretch of 29 straight, and wouldn't sit again for months. Neither would Rendon, who returned before the swelling on his left elbow subsided. Neither would Soto, who couldn't stand caving to the lingering back pain. The Nationals soon printed shirts that read DAY OFF? FUCK THAT!, with the expletive written in special characters.

And here was Scherzer against Philadelphia, gritting his teeth in the first, getting out of it when Rhys Hoskins looked at a third-strike slider. The Nationals took the afternoon game, 6–2, because Corbin breezed through the Phillies. Now Scherzer did the same, striking out 10 in 7 innings, and closed the night with his patented theatrics.

Washington led by one in the seventh when César Hernández tagged Scherzer with a leadoff double. He was at 102 pitches, and the tying run was in scoring position, but Martinez didn't hook him. This was Scherzer's inning. He still had to empty the tank. He struck out Brad Miller swinging with a 97 mph fastball at the belt. He struck out Andrew Knapp with a 96 mph fastball at the hands. He had one batter left, All-Star catcher J. T. Realmuto, and lasered his glare at Kurt Suzuki's mitt. Scherzer's bottom lip quivered. Suzuki put down the sign for a 1-2 slider, Scherzer spun one just below the zone, and Realmuto waved through Scherzer's 117th pitch.

Scherzer saw Realmuto whiff, spun around, and, in the same

motion, smacked his glove with an open palm. Hernández had never moved off second. The crowd had chanted, "Let's go Max!" filling the stadium with noise, and Scherzer screamed those first two words right back. His chest rose with heavy breaths while he ducked into the dugout. He went through a line of high fives, whacking every hand he saw, and the Nationals held on for a tight victory.

"I wanted to pitch. I didn't feel any p—" Scherzer began after the game, letting the next three letters hang in the air for good. He isn't a liar. The broken nose hurt, and there was blood to prove it, but he never considered skipping the start. "I knew I could post tonight."

While he spoke, describing the last twenty-four hours, detailing, beyond logic, why this was always the outcome he saw, it was hard not to notice a new addition to his locker. A red North Carolina State football helmet was at his feet. It belonged to Turner, an NC State grad, and came with a note taped to the wall behind Scherzer's right shoulder: "If you bunt tonight . . . PLEASE do us all a favor and wear this."

The Nationals were clicking, on and off the field, and had learned something about themselves. They were 18-7 since the Mets had swept them in New York. They were healthy, they were talented, and those were the keys to the sudden turnaround. But now came signs of an essential trait, of what they needed to make a reviving month count. They were tough.

6

"The best worst deal"

July 31, 2019

They spent too much time together each July, once the calendar flipped, the trade deadline neared, and weeks whittled into a matter of days. Then the front office became outright sick of each other, stuck in a conference room by Rizzo's office, searching for the "best worst" deals to elevate this roster. They ignored a wall-mounted TV that played on mute. They were aware of the outside world—the Nationals' 42-41 record by the end of June, their climb up the standings—but kept their focus on the task at hand. There were holes to fill, and there wasn't much time.

The club helped Rizzo convince ownership to spend. They were 31-10 since flatlining in New York. That kept pace with the Braves, who were just as hot, and solidified a spot in the wild-card race. A new worry was Scherzer tweaking his back against the Tigers in Detroit. He felt lingering pain once they returned from a two-city trip, and it proved a tricky diagnosis for the medical staff. But beyond that, and the dilemma it soon spiraled into, Rizzo was zeroed on the deadline.

He always splits his blueprint into one-, three-, and five-year plans, including current contracts, potential trade and free agent targets, and whom the club expects out of its minor-league system.

Foresight is a must. Yet flexibility, especially at this point of the season, is the only way it all worked. That's why Rizzo took a long view in July, considering the team and resources, and assessed what was missing. That was pretty easy with this team. There was a potential need for rotation depth, despite that Erick Fedde and Austin Voth were doing fine in place of the injured Jeremy Hellickson. Even with Ryan Zimmerman returning on June 28, after missing two months with plantar fasciitis in his right foot, the bench could have used a sound utility player. But the obvious problem was the bullpen. Still.

Rizzo tried to patch that with a series of low-cost moves. He'd signed lefty Dan Jennings to a minor league deal in mid-April, and Jennings lasted eight appearances before he was released. Rizzo signed Javy Guerra to a minor league deal on May 20, and Guerra hung on as a long reliever. Rizzo signed Jonny Venters on May 30, after the lefty had returned from three-and-a-half elbow surgeries and flopped with the Braves. Rizzo then brought in forty-two-year-old Fernando Rodney on June 1, making him the league's oldest player, and Rodney was called up from the minors a few weeks later. Veteran castoffs George Kontos and Kevin McGowan were getting tryouts in Fresno. But the bridge between the starters and Doolittle was still a revolving mess.

The Nationals released Trevor Rosenthal on June 23, eating $9 million and hoping another eighth-inning answer would emerge. Ownership never authorized Rizzo to make a real push for Kimbrel, who signed a three-year, $43 million contract with the Cubs on June 6. Kyle Barraclough, who was acquired to pitch the seventh, spent most of June on the injured list with right radial nerve damage. That was another "go figure it out in the minors" condition.

It got so dire that, in late July, Rodney was asked to pitch three times in two days. He blew a save in the third appearance and wound up throwing 63 pitches in a thirty-hour stretch. Rizzo had to make something out of nothing, and it wouldn't be the first time.

Anyone close to Mike Rizzo, or close enough to cheers a Coors Light with him, has heard his Frank Thomas story. His friends tell it in his rambling cadence and thick Chicago accent. Rizzo's son, Michael, can recite it line by line.

It was Rizzo's father, Phil, who told Rizzo there was a place for him in baseball. The work suited Rizzo, a blue-collar kid, the son of a truck driver and major league scout. But he wouldn't stick it as a player. The Angels had cut him after three seasons in the minors. That's when Phil told him to try scouting, too, if he was willing to build a reputation from the ground up. It wouldn't happen overnight, with one trip or a single player found. He had to earn what came in the spring of 1989.

Rizzo was a twenty-nine-year-old amateur scout for the Chicago White Sox, and had just been reassigned to a new area. He was leaving the Upper Midwest, all the cold towns and leafy highways, where he had yet to sign a major leaguer. He was heading to the Southeast, a clear promotion, to scour Alabama, Mississippi, Georgia, and northern Florida. He would have settled for anything, a small victory, a scrappy infielder or a pitcher with promising stuff. Then he saw Frank Thomas play.

Thomas was a two-sport athlete at Auburn University, playing tight end and first base. He entered the 1986 MLB draft and was passed over by every team. He then played football for two years, since that's what his scholarship was for, but quit after suffering back-to-back injuries as a sophomore. Baseball became his focus. That's what he'd wanted all along. He towered over his teammates with his six-foot-five frame and belted home runs. But some doubted his defense, speed, and ability to hit for contact. Many evaluators, including the league's official scouting bureau, did not consider Thomas a first-round pick. Rizzo's assessment skewed in the opposite direction.

When the White Sox met ahead of the 1989 draft, Rizzo rated Thomas as the best amateur in the country. He received a few sideways glances, and a lot of pushback, but didn't waver. Larry Himes, the general manager who'd drafted Rizzo before hiring him to scout, offered the easy rebuttals. Al Goldis, then the White Sox scouting director, did the same. The other scouts sold their players and dug at Thomas's flaws. They asked about his glove and whether he did anything but swat homers. Rizzo maintained that Thomas was a slugger, a pure slugger, and that the White Sox would regret not taking him with their first pick. The room filled with shouts until, finally, a massive decision was made.

The White Sox soon selected Thomas seventh overall. Himes and Goldis let Rizzo negotiate Thomas's contract, a rare task for a scout, and Thomas spent seventeen years of his Hall of Fame career in Chicago. Now everyone knew Rizzo had a keen eye for talent. And now Rizzo knew he wanted to be a GM.

"My goal was always to run my own team, run my own franchise, to build it the way I wanted to build it and do it on my terms," Rizzo recalled. "My first year as an area scout, you're a long way from being a GM at that time, but I still had my plans."

He hatched them while driving the long roads between games. He thought back to his first year in pro ball, after he was drafted in the twenty-second round by the California Angels. He was a Single A utility man and his team, the Salem Angels, won the Northwest League. But the next season he played for the Peoria Suns, another Single A club, and they finished in last place. So what was the difference? What did the Angels have that the Suns didn't? What mattered in the clubhouse? What didn't? He used those experiences to project his own franchise, the one he'd run once he found a trove of prospects for the White Sox, Red Sox, and Diamondbacks.

That took another decade on the road, bouncing between different areas, putting thousands of miles on a Mercury Grand Marquis. The Red Sox bought their guys a new Mercury every two years, making them the envy among scouts. Rizzo carried a thick binder overflowing with notes and neon Hi-Liters. The Thomas signing was one small break. The next came in 1999, before his fortieth birthday, when the Diamondbacks hired him as their scouting director.

Rizzo kept piling up names in the coming years. He helped find future Cy Young winner Brandon Webb in the eighth round in 2000. He signed off on Justin Upton, the first overall pick in 2005, who quickly debuted for the Diamondbacks at nineteen years old. Rizzo keyed on Max Scherzer at the University of Missouri, despite concerning mechanics, and urged the Diamondbacks to select him early on. Rizzo still had his share of misses. The hits were just a lot louder.

That all led him to the Nationals in 2006, as an assistant general manager under Jim Bowden. The Nationals had been in Washington for two seasons after moving from Montreal. The city was without baseball since 1972, when the Senators relocated to become the expansion Texas Rangers. Summers were quiet, for decades on end, and Washington revolved around the Redskins, Capitals, and a grassroots basketball scene. Then came the Nationals, with uniforms and all, plopped right into RFK Stadium and a town begging for the sport.

It took years for Washington to get baseball back, for its mayor, Anthony A. Williams, to push the league and the city to renew their vows. But humble beginnings would have been an overstatement. The Nationals were much lower than that. The first corporate offices were in two double-wide trailers outside RFK. That was it.

Employees relieved themselves in Porta Potties and dined on pizzas delivered to Parking Lot 4.

"Major League Baseball gave us nothing, it was below an expansion franchise," recalled Mark Lerner, whose father, Ted, headed a family that purchased the Nationals on July 24, 2006. They paid $450 million. The official announcement promised immediate improvements to RFK Stadium, including "a wider variety of improved concession choices, cleaner concourses and professionally trained customer service staff to cater to the fans' needs."

Rizzo was promoted to general manager in 2009, after Jim Bowden was fired in the wake of a federal probe into the Nationals' international operations. This was the punctuation mark of a rough honeymoon. In the inaugural season, before the Lerners bought the club, the Nationals were actually 13 games above .500 in July. Then their slide began, and they bottomed into the first of three consecutive last-place finishes. The early results gave a blink of a brighter future. But it remained hard to see.

The next spring training opened with around 80 players. Dave Jageler, then in his first season on the Nationals' radio broadcast, later described it as a "tryout camp for outcasts." To fit everyone, the clubhouse in Viera, Florida, was outfitted with makeshift lockers in the middle of the room. There were a dozen no-names competing for rotation spots. The farm system was nonexistent. That team, led by first-year manager Manny Acta, was projected by some to lose 120 games. So it was maybe an accomplishment that it only lost 91.

Then it got worse, and even worse yet, before trouble brewed in the Dominican Republic. In February 2009, Esmailyn "Smiley" Gonzalez, a nineteen-year prospect, was revealed as a twenty-three-year-old named Carlos Alvarez. The scandal rocked the Nationals' Dominican academy, where Gonzalez was a budding shortstop. They had signed him for $1.4 million, but his fake age led to an investigation, which led to suspicion that Bowden was skimming signing bonus money into his own pockets, which led to his resignation on March 1.

The season was just a few weeks away, and Rizzo was in the Dominican Republic, head shaking, when the academy was shut down. A crowd of teenagers hopped on their bikes and whizzed past him, pedaling away from the now-shuttered facility. Rizzo was named interim GM, weighed against candidates in the coming months, then hired as Bowden's full-time replacement in August of that same year.

He'd negotiated a huge deal for first-round pick Stephen Strasburg that summer, and was familiar with how the Lerners operated. He also knew, better than anyone, how much work was needed to win Washington over. The team kept losing, and losing, and cratered to 103 losses in 2009. The offense had Ryan Zimmerman before a steep drop-off. The pitching staff was somehow thinner. Yet the repeated failure could be rationalized. It led to high draft picks, and that led to Strasburg and Bryce Harper, and that brought juice to their new ballpark.

The Nationals moved to the Southeast waterfront in March of 2008, and many saw it as their first step toward legitimacy. The project was expected to cost the city more than $1 billion. A *Washington Post* poll later found that two-thirds of DC residents opposed using public dollars to finance it. Yet the city government seized land from twenty-three property owners to make room for the forty-one-thousand-seat ballpark. Leases in the neighborhood had been cheap, since that area, right by the Anacostia River, was known for high crime rates and vacant lots. But it was about to get hit with a rush of corporate gentrification.

Nationals Park brought chain restaurants, trendy bars, and high-rise apartments to a typically low-income neighborhood, even if the stadium seats were slow to fill. One of its main attractions upon opening was a clear view of the U.S. Capitol. But that soon disappeared behind a clump of cranes and half-built buildings. Longtime residents were priced out of their homes. The ballpark experience, with its expensive parking, expensive food, and expensive merchandise, was not for them. It targeted suburban families, young professionals, and, really, anyone who could afford to watch a bad team. Both money and patience were a must.

Then Strasburg and Harper added winning to the equation. Strasburg's debut, on June 8, 2010, was a national television event. And when Harper debuted a season later, a sensation at nineteen, the Nationals were vaulted to their first playoff appearance. It came even earlier than expected, and was tainted by a quick exit against the Cardinals, and the decision to shut down Strasburg in early September. Yet it told Rizzo that he could start building a contender every year.

Some tries were better than others. They all ended too fast, with fired managers and just the faint promise of another chance. The mix of talent and chemistry was never quite right. Rizzo was aggressive at trade deadlines, always trying to finish the puzzle, often searching for the right relievers. He preferred to crash that market in-season, when he can remove some variance from the equation. One of Rizzo's favorite sayings is that a player is reflected on the back of his baseball card, and the numbers tell a story once a sample's big enough. But the volatility of relievers can complicate that logic.

That's why each July brought a remodeling of the Nationals' bullpen. Rizzo built his cores around strong rotations, homegrown hitters in Harper, Zimmerman, and Rendon, yet always seemed to be a reliever or two short. He had made two quick bullpen moves the previous off-season, and added Tony Sipp in the spring. But Rosenthal and Barraclough fell well short of expectations by July. Sipp had, too, and battled age and injures for the first four months of the year.

Now Rizzo had to figure out how to best replace them. He had to figure it out fast. The deadline was closing in, relievers were wanted around the league, and the only cause for comfort, if there was one, was that this conundrum was familiar.

So they were glued to their phones, to their laptops, to scouting reports on their iPads, and video of potential trade targets. That's how the conference room looked on July 31, with hours until the trade deadline, with a TV set to MLB Network and the take-out piling up. Soon, at 12:05 p.m., the Nationals would begin a game against the Braves. The front office put it on, and maybe glanced at the score, but Plan A had become Plan B, and Plan B was formed that morning, and the whole group took on Rizzo's mood. And he was tense.

The bullpen was the driving concern behind his shopping list. But Scherzer's health had become another. Scherzer sat out the All-Star game in Cleveland, had his next start bumped back, then went to the injured list on July 13. Dave Martinez had told reporters they just wanted to give the ace extra rest. Yet it wasn't even close to that simple. The initial diagnosis was a "mid-back strain." A week later, it changed to "inflammation in the bursa under his right shoulder blade." Martinez denied a misdiagnosis by the training staff. Scherzer had to use Google and WebMD to learn more about the condition. Shawn Kelley, Scherzer's former teammate and now a reliever with the Texas Rangers, had just dealt with scapulothoracic bursitis and texted encouragement. He promised Scherzer that a cortisone shot took five or six days to kick in, and Scherzer clung to that timeline. But it still took more than a week after the injection for Scherzer to finally return.

He did so against the Rockies, in a series finale on July 25, and gave up 3 runs in five strenuous innings. Something was clearly off. That was confirmed the next morning, once Scherzer woke up with new tightness in his upper back. He underwent an MRI at the ballpark, and it revealed a "mild rhomboid strain" below his right shoulder. That was the third announced injury in sixteen days.

"I felt like I was back to one hundred percent, throwing a bullpen, stepping on everything. We kind of thought we were through this," Scherzer said in the dugout that day. He'd received a stem-cell injection and, at the very least, was out for the next two days. But his tone made the reality clear: The recovery was going to take much longer. "And the fact that it kind of reoccurred, now we got to start thinking: What did we miss? Everybody, myself included, what did we not do to make sure this was completely gone? Nobody is at fault. Now we just have to try something maybe a little bit different."

This all created a hole in the rotation, with Scherzer out, Voth sidelined with shoulder tendinitis, and Fedde and Ross, the two depth options behind Voth, getting completely shelled. Ross gave up six earned runs in a lopsided loss to the Dodgers on July 27. Two nights later, Fedde allowed nine earned runs in 3⅔ innings against the Braves, and Rizzo, having seen enough, made a last-minute plunge into the starters market.

The Nationals nearly struck a deal for Reds lefty Alex Wood. They figured Wood could fill out the rotation with Scherzer injured, moonlight as a fifth starter down the stretch, then join the bullpen as a swingman for the postseason.

It filled multiple needs with one move. But the Reds balked in the final step, the night before the deadline, because they had just acquired starter Trevor Bauer in a three-team deal. The Reds felt Bauer made them competitive in the NL Central race and wanted

Wood for the remainder of the season. That returned the Nationals' focus to the top available relievers.

Rizzo sent Kasey McKeon, the club's director of player procurement, to scout Will Smith and Sam Dyson during a July 22 game against the Cubs in San Francisco. Smith and Dyson were the relievers everyone wanted, and Rizzo always liked having an in-person account to use in decision-making. Yet McKeon's report did not center on either pitcher. He was enamored with Drew Pomeranz, who had a miserable 6.10 ERA through 17 starts with the Giants. Now the lefty's fastball-curveball combination was thriving after a move to the bullpen.

McKeon was there for his first relief appearance, and Pomeranz breezed through two scoreless innings. McKeon then left his seat behind home plate and called Rizzo right away.

"Hey, man. Pomeranz just came out of the bullpen and was lights out," Rizzo recalled McKeon saying. "We got to get this guy."

That led to conversations between Rizzo and the Giants front office. Rizzo wanted Pomeranz more than any other pitcher. But sensing a growing market for Pomeranz, and Rizzo's obvious interest, the Giants kept asking for more. They were stuck between buying and selling, even if logic said sell, giving them an edge in negotiations. They didn't need to move Pomeranz before July 31. The Nationals had a lot more urgency and were left directing it elsewhere.

They had been in on closer Shane Greene, who had 22 saves and a 1.18 ERA for the Tigers. The thirty-year-old righty was on just about everyone's radar, made evident once Rizzo and the Tigers engaged in negotiations. The Tigers would only trade Greene if the Nationals included Luis Garcia in a return package. Garcia was an eighteen-year-old shortstop and the Nationals' second-ranked prospect. The Tigers would also have considered a deal if Carter Kieboom was involved.

Kieboom, the Nationals' top prospect, had struggled in April and May. He played 10 games in the majors, hit .128, and made 3 errors at shortstop. But Kieboom was only twenty-one years old, and Rizzo wasn't giving up on him. He was an insurance policy at third base if Anthony Rendon left in free agency after the season. Rizzo told the Tigers that the kids were off-limits. So they told him Greene was, too.

That again forced Rizzo to adjust his approach. If the Nationals acquired Greene, they would have likely exhausted their remaining funds. Yet with Greene out of the picture, Rizzo turned his focus to White Sox closer Alex Colomé. The thirty-year-old righty was in the middle of a strong season. He finished July with a 2.18 ERA in 41⅓ innings. Colomé had a low strikeout rate for a back-end reliever, but the rest of his statistics checked out. That he was right-handed, and could complement the left-handed Doolittle, made him that much more appealing to Washington.

The sides were close to a deal on July 30, but that fell through, too. The White Sox upped their demands at the last minute. The Nationals were willing to trade anyone but a small group of promising prospects. In the final hours of that Tuesday, the Nationals thought they'd add Wood to their rotation, Colomé to their bullpen, and those felt like major improvements. But they were back to square one by the next morning.

One solution was to fill a gaping void with multiple pitchers. The issue, from Opening Day on, was the seventh and eighth innings. Rosenthal and Barraclough made sure of that. Martinez had tried the two of them, Justin Miller and Tanner Rainey, and was now flipping between Fernando Rodney and Wander Suero ahead of Doolittle in the ninth. None of it worked.

Rizzo even considered trying an "opener"—a reliever for the first inning or two of games—to take pressure off the bullpen. But the Nationals didn't have the personnel for it. In Atlanta on May 30, when they were just starting to improve, Martinez was asked how difficult it was to manage his relievers. His answer came with a smile and spoke volumes.

"We brainstorm every day," he said through laughter. "I wake up with brainstorms."

That was no different for Rizzo on July 31, when *his* brainstorms met a shrinking list of options. The Nationals liked lefty reliever Jake Diekman from the Royals, but he landed with The Athletics four days prior. They checked in on the Diamondbacks' Andrew Chafin, another lefty, but Arizona was asking for too much. That exhausted Pomeranz, Wood, Colomé, Diekman, and Chafin as options. The Nationals could not give what the Giants wanted for Dyson or Smith. So the whole front office dug deeper.

The Braves game began. The Nationals and Braves traded homers in the second. A light crowd cheered Soto around the bases. Aníbal Sánchez faced Mike Soroka, a Rookie of the Year candidate, and the Nationals had trouble with Soroka's sinker-slider mix. That played on a TV that Rizzo and his staff paid little attention to. Rizzo, in the end, wanted two righties and a lefty before the 4:00 p.m. deadline, and needed them to be cheap.

It made for a stressful day. Everyone was running on next to no sleep. But this is what Rizzo lives for, why he became a scout in the first place, with the chance to scrape the margins for the right fit. Then three names surfaced while, outside in the ballpark, the Nationals staged a comeback:

Daniel Hudson, Blue Jays
Hunter Strickland, Mariners
Roenis Elías, Mariners

Rizzo stared into video of each pitcher. He reviewed notes from his analytics team, weighing internal data against outside metrics, and considered which minor leaguers to part with. The Nationals approach was to find the "best worst deal" for their club. They knew they had to part with something, since they were trying to compete now, but tried to hedge any future regret.

That's where a team of analysts helped Rizzo zero on expendable prospects. The process was rooted in traditional scouting, such as that Pomeranz tip from McKeon, but Rizzo used all kinds of information to craft moves.

Hudson was not on their radar until around 11:00 a.m. on July 31, roughly five hours before the deadline. He was signed to a minor league deal by the Angels on February 9, cut before the season, then joined the Blue Jays on a one-year contract. He was thirty-two years old, and a two-time recipient of Tommy John surgery, but had a 3.00 ERA in 48 innings in Toronto. He showed a knack for stranding runners in high-leverage situations. So Rizzo got in touch with Ross Atkins, the Blue Jays' general manager, and offered pitcher Kyle Johnston for Hudson.

Assessing Elías proved a bit trickier. The Nationals needed a lefty because Sipp and Matt Grace weren't cutting it. But Elías, a thirty-year-old with the Mariners, was having trouble in lefty-lefty matchups for the first time in his career. He was, in an odd twist, having much more success against right-handed hitters. Rizzo had to decide if he could count on Elías's reverting to his usual stats. Rizzo also knew that Jerry Dipoto, the Mariners' GM, was often looking to acquire future assets. So Rizzo got in touch with Dipoto and offered two minor league pitchers, Taylor Guilbeau and Elvis Alvarado, for Elías.

Then there was Strickland, Elías's teammate in Seattle, who had a special spot in Nationals history. He was with the Giants in 2014 and faced the Nationals in the NLDS. That's when Bryce Harper hit a towering homer off him at AT&T Park, and lingered at the plate to watch it land. Strickland never let go of that image, of Harper showing him up, of what he thought was a young player disrespecting the game. About three years later, in May of 2017, Strickland reared back for a fastball and threw it right into Harper's front hip. Harper sprinted toward the mound and chucked his helmet about twenty feet wide of Strickland, and the benches cleared in a full-on brawl.

That was just one instance of Strickland's anger getting the best of him. Another, in June of 2018, came when he punched a door and missed two months with a broken hand. He was mad about a blown save. But Rizzo weighed that against what he now saw in Strickland. The thirty-year-old had missed most of the season with a strained right lat muscle. Rizzo put scouts at his minor league rehab appearances in July, up in Tacoma, Washington, and they reported normal velocity and a sharp breaking ball. Rizzo was already in touch with Dipoto, with the Elías talks in motion, and offered left-handed pitcher Aaron Fletcher for Strickland.

The Nationals landed Hudson as Howie Kendrick pinch-hit against the Braves in the sixth. They landed Elías while going down one-two-three in the seventh. They landed Strickland in the eighth, right after Matt Adams rocked a homer, and that was it. Three deals were agreed upon in forty minutes. The Nationals fell in the tenth, once Doolittle gave up a solo shot to Josh Donaldson, but bullpen reinforcements were on the way.

Hudson was called in from the bullpen in Kansas City and told he was headed to Washington. Strickland was on the Mariners' team bus in Arlington, Texas, on the way to a game against the Rangers, when his brother texted him the news. Strickland hadn't heard from Dipoto or his agent. He yelled over to Elías, who sat a few rows back, and Elías was just as confused. But they were soon plugged right into an NL East arms race.

The Braves went all in for their bullpen at the deadline, adding Greene from the Tigers, Chris Martin, and Mark Melancon, who cost $14 million. They led the Nationals by 6½ games in the division after their extra-inning win on July 31. The Nationals' haul, on the other hand, was colored with uncertainty, such as if Hudson had really improved, or if Elías could retire lefties, or if Strickland had the right personality for a tight-knit clubhouse. It was a far cry from Wood and Colomé. But Rizzo insisted, in the span of a few breaths, that he wasn't pushed by the Braves and felt confident in each move.

"It was a busy, productive day for us. I think we've upgraded our bullpen," Rizzo said in the press conference room at Nationals Park. "These aren't the sexiest names in the trade market, but we think we got good-quality, reliable guys with some moxie and some experience."

Within the tight parameters from ownership, that's what Rizzo came up with: quality on a budget, reliability, some moxie, and some experience. Or so he hoped. Two big trucks filled the tunnel once Rizzo made his way back to Martinez's office that afternoon. The GM squeezed past and swatted at a cloud of exhaust fumes. Players hugged Javy Guerra and Michael Blazek, who were released to make room on the twenty-five-man roster. The rest had to catch a flight to Phoenix. Hudson, Elías, and Strickland were meeting them there, and Rizzo had his team for the pennant race.

7

Insurance Plan

August 17, 2019

Dave Martinez stood on the dugout steps at Chase Field and screamed an order in Spanish. Then he flipped to English and yelled it again. Roenis Elías had just retired the first two batters he faced with the Nationals. The Diamondbacks had a lefty due up in the next inning, Washington led by two runs, and so Martinez decided to leave Elías in for one more batter. The catch was that Elías had to hit, something he'd done only six times in his career, and that's when the bilingual directions began.

"Don't swing!" Martinez repeated in Phoenix on August 2, begging the reliever to watch three pitches to avoid getting hurt. "Do! Not! Swing!"

But Elías didn't listen. He swung and missed at a sinker. He swung at another sinker, on the next pitch, and fouled it off. And after he swung a third time, at a sinker way off the plate, he looked up to see a chopper bouncing over the mound. He sprinted out of the box, thinking he could beat the throw, yet slowed a few steps from first. He felt a pull in his right hamstring and grabbed it. It was exactly what Martinez had feared, a fluke injury, and the manager stayed quiet while Elías limped off the field.

The Nationals won that game, 3–0, and there was a lot to like. Hunter Strickland worked a perfect seventh, Fernando Rodney did the same in the eighth, and Sean Doolittle matched them to close it out. The Diamondbacks finished with one hit. It came off Joe Ross, who dominated 5⅓ innings, and the bullpen didn't allow a base runner. Yet the Elías incident dampened the mood.

Martinez danced through a postgame press conference, trying to keep the focus on the victory, saying Elías felt a cramp and they'd know more in the morning. Not fifteen minutes later, at a locker he had yet to break in, Elías mentioned a pulled hamstring. A reporter pressed Elías for specifics. There were competing stories—cramps or a pull—with varying potential effects on the new-look bullpen. Elías quickly backtracked and left his status up in the air.

The weekend only got weirder from there. Stephen Strasburg was named National League pitcher of the month for July after going 5-0 with a 1.14 ERA. But the Diamondbacks were all over him in Phoenix, continuing an odd trend from earlier in the year. They scored 6 runs in five innings on Strasburg at Nationals Park on June 15. They were one of just a few teams to have any measure of success against the thirty-year-old righty. And somehow they found even more.

Strasburg allowed a career-high 9 runs in 4⅔ innings on August 3. It looked as if the Diamondbacks knew what was coming, and Strasburg soon admitted that they basically did. Every hit was a rocket into the outfield. By the ninth, when the Nationals trailed 11–4, Martinez waved the white flag. He was already down one reliever in Elías. He didn't want to tax others in a game the Nationals couldn't win. So he looked down the bench, spotted Gerardo Parra leaning on the railing, and asked Parra to pitch.

The game finished with Parra taking and leaving the mound, then moving to third base, then second base, all while infielder Brian Dozier got the final outs. Parra later joked that it was a huge opportunity for him to debut at three different positions. Martinez knew where Parra was coming from.

It was the second time in franchise history that two position players had pitched in the same game. The first came in 1990, when the Nationals were still the Montreal Expos, and manager Buck Rodgers asked a skinny young outfielder to throw. He gave up 2 runs on 2 hits and 2 walks. His name was Dave Martinez.

That led Martinez into a fit of laughter while evaluating Parra and Dozier. He described the 11-run defeat as "fun," and it was hard to argue with that. But the Nationals had begun deflecting any issues with the same fact. A loss? *Best record in baseball since May 24.* Scherzer's injury? *Best record in baseball since May 24.* The still-evident cracks in a reconfigured bullpen? *Best record in baseball since May 24.*

Yet Martinez was well aware of a developing reality. The Nationals could joke about their makeshift relievers for a few hours, dull the frustration over Elías's injury, dodge the implications, and sort them out later. Then they'd need two real relievers to carry the bullpen. They needed Doolittle and Daniel Hudson up to that task.

You don't become a one-pitch reliever by accident.

You shine as a slugger in southern New Jersey, shine some more as a first baseman at the University of Virginia, shine because you whack homers often enough, and far enough, that there's belief you could do it in the show. You're selected as a first-round pick in 2007, by the Oakland Athletics, and hope like hell that the shine doesn't wear off. But it does. Injuries chop you down, one after another, until you're stuck between baseball and the rest of your life. You consider graduate school. You fret. Then you try pitching, since you'd done it in the past, and somehow wind up in the trainer's room at the Oakland Coliseum, in June of 2012, with a major league GM telling you—no, yelling at you—to throw your fastball and nothing else. *That's* how you become a one-pitch reliever.

At least that's how it went for Sean Doolittle.

While Doolittle shouldered the biggest workload of his career, with 46 appearances at the trade deadline, he threw his fastball around 90 percent of the time. The approach is entirely antithetical to conventional strategy. The best pitchers rely on deception. They keep hitters guessing. They mix a number of pitches—a fastball, maybe two, then their off-speed—to turn each at bat into a chess match. But that was never Doolittle's path forward.

It was June 16, 2012, a normal afternoon in Oakland, when Doolittle was set on this track. He was a rookie trying to maximize a last chance with the Athletics. Doolittle was once on the fast track as a hitter. The A's drafted him in the first round in 2007 to play outfield and first base. He made their Arizona Fall League team in 2008. In 2009, after a strong spring training, he started the year as the Triple A cleanup hitter.

He felt that he was knocking on the door. But his body had other plans. Right-knee tendinitis led to his first surgery in October of 2009. The fraying was so bad that doctors had to reattach the patella tendon to the knee. The second came in July of 2010, when they cut out the sliver of a tendon and shaved his kneecap. That put him in line to return at the beginning of 2011. He was in extended spring training and was told to play two more games before joining the Athletics in mid-May. It would have been his debut as a position player. Then he strained his right wrist and went straight back to the shelf.

Doolittle describes those as "really dark days," when he often considered starting life after baseball. He had his agent research how to enroll in a grad program at Virginia. He was ready to move on. But there was one more way for Doolittle to extend his career. When he signed his first contract with the A's, their general manager,

Billy Beane, noted that he came with an insurance policy. The Braves had selected him as a pitcher out of high school. He then pitched at Virginia—relieving as a freshman, starting as a sophomore and junior—making him a quasi-two-way prospect.

"How would you like to start a throwing program?" asked Keith Lippman, then the A's' farm director, in the spring of 2011. "It'll give you something to do other than sitting in the training room and, you know, doing all your wrist rehab. But it'll also get us closer in case we have to activate your insurance plan."

The insurance plan was a full transition to the mound. Doolittle faced live batters that next fall in Arizona, during an Instructional League game, and was flagged down by Bob Welch in the parking lot. Welch, a former Cy Young winner with the Dodgers, told Doolittle he had a "special fastball." Welch urged him to throw it, to trust it in all counts, and make it the dead center of his arsenal. That was the first time someone had expressed such interest in the pitch. The second was after that June game in Oakland.

Doolittle had been in the majors for eleven days, and was stumbling through the fifth appearance of his career. He allowed a leadoff double, struck out the next batter, issued a walk, and notched another strikeout. Then, with Will Venable up, he came set and looked at catcher Kurt Suzuki's sign. Suzuki wanted a curveball. Doolittle threw one, leaving it smack in the middle of the plate, and Venable lined it into the right-field corner for a double. The Athletics' lead evaporated. They later came back to win, but that didn't get Doolittle off the hook.

He was doing cool-down stretches in the trainer's room when Beane charged in. Beane, the Athletics' general manager and the architect of *Moneyball*, hated the curveball decision. He offered the same advice that Welch had. It was just angrier, and in a burst, and definitely not a suggestion. Beane wanted to see Doolittle's four-seam fastball, almost exclusively, and so that's what Doolittle showed him.

"It was the hardest thing for me, to stand on the mound and think that everyone knew I was throwing a fastball," Doolittle recalled a half decade later. "I had a lot of anxiety earlier in my career with that. But I figured out that it could actually play in my favor."

The Athletics signed Doolittle to a five-year, $10.2 million extension in 2014, and he was named an All-Star that summer. His constant flow of fastballs had obvious benefits. The pitch's spin axis, or its side-to-side movement, creates the illusion that it rises while nearing the plate. That's physically impossible, and Doolittle knows it, but he uses the mirage to get bad swings at the top of the zone. He actually likes that hitters know what's coming, and trick themselves into swinging on his terms. And because of the 10 percent chance that he will throw a secondary pitch, either his slider or changeup, they have to keep that in the back of their heads. That's where he finds deception. He can still play chess.

But the style also offers a rail-thin margin for error. He has to have pinpoint command. If his velocity wavers, and dips into the low 90s, the command has to be that much better. The movement of his fastball is essential, and it depends on sound mechanics, and everything goes wrong if his mechanics are even a hair off. That's what happened in May, when the Nationals were swept by the Mets in New York, and Doolittle was rocked for 5 runs without recording an out.

Doolittle followed that nightmare in New York with a rough outing against the Marlins. In just two appearances, and in the span of one full inning, his ERA ballooned from 1.71 to 3.68. So when he left Nationals Park that Friday, after the Nationals edged out Miami in spite of him, Doolittle replaced sleep with self-study.

The thirty-two-year-old loaded his iPad with videos of himself from April and May of 2018. That's when he last felt great about his mechanics. He stared at the screen as night became morning, blaring Metallica into his headphones, and didn't finish until he'd listened to the band's first three albums in full.

That took ninety minutes. Ninety minutes of starting clips, stopping them, slowing down, zooming in on his legs and hands, and checking the tiniest nuances. Doolittle is a relentlessly thoughtful athlete. That goes for liberal political opinions that often clash with a baseball clubhouse. That goes for his love of reading and independent bookstores, such as the Book Table in Oak Park, Illinois; Tattered Cover in Denver; or Left Bank Books in St. Louis. And that goes for poor performance, his process to fix it, and how harrowing it is to be a closer who can't close.

He was stumped in bed until noticing a problem with his toe tap. His delivery was fine until he touched his front foot to the dirt before throwing. Then it fell out of sync, his release point sagged, his spin rate did, too, and batters teed off. He knew that fatigue was creating bad habits. He had 5 multi-inning appearances to that point of the year, led the National League with 19 games finished, and was frequently used when Martinez would have preferred not to. The other options were just too shaky to rely on.

Before the Nationals' next game, Doolittle rushed in with his findings. He compared notes with pitching coach Paul Menhart, video coordinators, and the strength-and-conditioning staff. Everyone landed on the same tweak. The toe tap was eliminated. He wasn't perfect throughout the summer, with the Nationals marching up the standings and handing him leads. He gave up 2 runs and took a loss in San Diego on June 7. He allowed 3 hits and a run in a save against the Marlins on July 3. He finished July by yielding a run in back-to-back appearances.

Then August came, Martinez kept calling his number, and the fatigue roared right back.

It happened again at Citi Field in Queens, the park Doolittle and the Nationals couldn't conquer. It was his personal springboard to self-doubt. The Mets had won 13 of their last 14, and 6 in a row, heading into the series with Washington on August 9. It was a Friday. The stadium was absolutely rocking.

The Nationals were atop the wild-card standings, 2½ games up of the Mets, and still eyeing the Braves in the division. They carried a 3-run lead into the bottom of the ninth. It was the sixth time this season they were tied or ahead of the Mets in the eighth inning or later. But once Doolittle entered, and eight Mets came to the plate, each of those six instances had ended in a loss.

The unraveling looked like this: J. D. Davis whacking an inside fastball for a double. Wilson Ramos whacking an inside fastball for a single. Todd Frazier whacking a down-the-middle fastball for a 3-run homer. Joe Panik whacking a high fastball for a single. Amed Rosario whacking a low changeup for a single. Michael Conforto whacking a high-and-inside fastball for a walk-off single that sailed over Adam Eaton's reach in right. Ball game. Everything was whacked.

Doolittle retired 2 hitters, gave up 4 runs, and ducked into the clubhouse with a re-rattled brain. A scout who watched the Nationals all year, as part of his assignment from an American League team, offered a blunt assessment over text: "The Nationals are absolutely fucked if Doolittle doesn't figure it out." Martinez faced constant criticism for trusting his relievers beyond reason. This was another of those times.

"It wasn't like I came in here looking to exorcise any demons or anything like that," Doolittle explained in the clubhouse. It felt like a twisted instant replay, the manager defending his guy in one room, his guy feeling defenseless in another, everyone processing the fresh shock. Then Doolittle paused because, yeah, maybe those demons had crossed his mind. "Walking off the field with that same sick feeling . . . it was kind of surreal."

He was out there two days later, facing the Mets, fighting his issues at game speed. He got the last three outs of a 7–4 victory. His fastball hovered around 94 mph. He retired the side in order—with a lineout, strikeout, and groundout—and was pointing in the right direction. The offense was keyed by Asdrúbal Cabrera, who was signed as a utility player that week and delivered a 2-run double in the seventh. Cabrera, like Gerardo Parra, was released and jobless before the Nationals gave him a call. Now he gave Doolittle the bounce-back save opportunity he needed.

But the progress came and went. The Brewers visited the next weekend, with that series beginning on August 16, and the opener funneled into Doolittle's hands. He worked a quick ninth, needing just 15 pitches, but Martinez was taxing him, and the next night showed that it was finally too much. The Nationals fell behind 5–0, sprung ahead 11–8, and, by the ninth, needed just three more outs from Doolittle.

He got one.

The Brewers crushed him, much as the Mets had eight days earlier, and his velocity was concerning. Christian Yelich sent a 92 mph fastball into the left-field seats. Keston Hiura followed with a double, on another 92 mph fastball, and Mike Moustakas scored them both when he homered to center. That tied the game. The Brewers nudged in front when Ryan Braun belted a low-and-inside fastball out to left. The radar gun blinked 90 mph, well below Doolittle's average, and he made another slow walk into the dugout. It would be his last for a while. The Nationals lost in 14 innings, 15–14, and it was entirely his fault.

"I'm still searching for answers, to be honest, I don't know," Doolittle said, voice hushed, eyes glued to the clubhouse carpet, after his sixth blown save of the year. "We keep trying to go back to the drawing board, we're watching film, we're looking at the metrics. I'm doing extra dry work before games. We've changed up a lot of my routine in the weight room, my maintenance and stuff. I just . . ." He stopped and shook his head. His rant had run out of gas, too. "I don't know. It just wasn't coming out tonight."

Two lockers away from the recorders and camera lights stood Daniel Hudson. He buttoned a dress shirt and glanced at the small crowd around Doolittle. There were logical calls for Doolittle to lose the closer's role. The argument was built on his results, on how tired he looked, on the evidence, the mounds of it, saying this workload wasn't sustainable. But it was compounded by how well Hudson was pitching.

Sometimes Hudson wondered how the hell he was even here. He, like Doolittle, was once rolling in the right direction. He impressed across 44 starts for the Diamondbacks in 2010 and 2011. He was twenty-four years old, everything in front of him, until a random pain shot into his forearm. He'll never forget the feeling, because his life was never the same.

The pain soon crept up to his elbow. He needed Tommy John surgery and missed most of 2012, all of 2013, then most of 2014 while recovering from a repeat of the procedure. He was making his first rehab start after the first surgery in Jacksonville, close to rejoining the Diamondbacks, when he knew. Tests soon confirmed his worst fears. Another Tommy John surgery totaled two and a half seasons before pitching in the majors again. One was tough to handle. Recovering from two, in the span of two seasons, was unprecedented.

But he chose one last push before calling it quits. He became a reliever, starting only three games since the surgeries, and bounced from Arizona to Pittsburgh, then Pittsburgh to Los Angeles, then to his off-season home in Phoenix last winter, waiting for a call. The phone was quiet for months, the market not so hot for an aging righty with a time-bomb elbow. Christmas passed. So did most of

January. Hudson figured he would get a minor league deal, a chance to latch on in camp, but even that wasn't happening.

On January 28, 2019, with spring training less than two weeks away, he threw for fifteen scouts at Hamilton High School in Scottsdale. He saw them lift radar guns and was nervous about the readings. I'm thirty-two, he thought, and still here begging for a shot in the middle of winter. It went well enough for the Angels to sign him on February 10, three days before he was expected to report, but he was cut before the season. That's when he was scooped up by the Blue Jays on a low-cost deal. And that was another improbable step, in a career chock-full of them, to joining the Nationals in a pennant race.

"I gave retirement some thought, but I wouldn't to be able to look myself in the mirror five years down the road if I didn't give it another shot," Hudson reflected. His original return from the Tommy Johns came on September 4, 2014. Now, a few weeks from the five-year anniversary, he replaced a closer that kept spiraling.

Hudson had only two saves in Toronto before the Nationals dealt for him. He had only nine in his other four years as a reliever. He really had no interest in being a closer. Too much pressure. Not his thing. But he had yielded 1 earned run in his first 8⅓ innings with Washington. He had just collected a 4-out save against the Reds, when Doolittle needed a rare night off, and was bumped into a bigger role.

By the morning, about twelve hours after Doolittle had folded against Milwaukee, he was placed on the injured list with right-knee tendinitis. It seemed like a funny diagnosis given the obvious wear on his arm. Yet lingering knee pain led to another lapse in mechanics, and that led to a less effective fastball, and that all put him at risk of burning out. Mechanical tweaks to help his knee made his fastball less effective. He was already up to 54 appearances, 7 short of a career high, and the Nationals had 40 games remaining.

He had never pitched this much, or this late, in a season without getting some break for some injury. So Martinez shut him down.

"I was pretty beaten up mentally, by that point. That was rock bottom," Doolittle recalled. "It took a lot out of me to go in there and say I needed a break because I'm not right. That was so hard to do. They couldn't have been excited about hearing that. We're in a playoff push. But I needed it."

"When he does come back, he's our closer," Martinez said after the decision was made. "And I reiterated that to him. He's our closer, but we got to get him right. We need him for the duration. We need Doolittle to pull this off."

Those comments were echoed, almost verbatim, by Hudson in the coming days. The best version of the Nationals had Doolittle pitching with games on the line. That was the company line. It was boosted when the Nationals traveled to Pittsburgh, held a late lead, then saw it disappear once Wander Suero and Hudson entered. Strasburg tossed seven scoreless innings on 94 pitches. Martinez still went to the bullpen, figuring it was rested, and that decision backfired.

Hunter Strickland was unavailable after breaking his nose in a weight-room accident that afternoon. It was another major letdown from the bullpen, the one part of the Nationals that hadn't clicked. Doolittle could only watch, leaning back in a folding chair, filling his downtime with a science fiction novel by Octavia E. Butler.

He spoke with a few reporters on the first day of the weeklong road trip. He owned his mistakes, outlined a recovery plan, accepted that he had to earn his job back. He repeated that the Nationals deserved better from him. When his teammates went out to stretch, around 4:00 p.m. on a cloudless Monday, he hung back in the clubhouse and sank into a brown leather couch. He squared his attention on a crossword puzzle, rubbing his temples, and looked intent on staying there awhile.

"I just needed a break. I'm stumped on a couple of them," Doolittle said once he put the puzzle in his locker and rested a blue pen on top. "A lot of times I put it down for a little and pick it back up and figure it out."

8

Baby Shark

August 20, 2019

Max Scherzer calls August the "month of hate."

The season was about five months old. Most players, himself included, were dealing with minor or major injuries. It was weird if someone didn't wake up in pain, peeling himself out of bed, pretending, against reality, that he was ready to play that night. The players had been on the move since early February, away from their wives and kids, arriving in cities on hours of airplane sleep.

So it was common, by this point of the calendar, to have no clue what day of the week it was. Any start of a series was a Monday. Any day game was a Sunday. Any travel day was a Thursday. Or maybe those were Sundays, too. It was hard to tell. Players forgot birthdays, holidays, let the missed calls and unread texts pile up like firewood. They were conditioned to leave the field, find bus times on a worn whiteboard, then walk like robots toward their next destination. The monotony could cripple. The pennant race was still in the distance, and only inching nearer, making August ripe for small arguments and clubhouse tension. And that's what made it the month of hate.

"We are set up to not get along, if you really think about it," explained second baseman Brian Dozier, kicked back in a rolling chair by his locker at PNC Park in Pittsburgh. He was trying to get comfortable. He was trying to think of a name for his fantasy football team, settling on the Monstars, a squad of superpower players from the basketball movie *Space Jam*. He was trying, really, to ease his boredom until first pitch rolled round. This was his eighth year in the league, and 124th game of this season, and he still had no clue how.

"Let's put it this way," Dozier continued in his slow, southern drawl, as if he were plucked off a back road in Fulton, Mississippi, and handed a bat. "Everyone here has friends, like real-life friends, and most of us have significant others, kids, a family who loves us and is counting on us. All of that. But now you spend every waking hour of six months with your teammates. You can start to resent a guy just because he isn't who you'd rather be around. You look to your left and see his big head instead of your wife. I've watched it happen. It ain't pretty."

But it was clear, even in August, that the Nationals had found another sort of market efficiency: they liked each other. There is no way to quantify chemistry, its effect on results, or if it has a tangible effect at all. That's why, in the age of advanced analytics, it is often supposed that being a good person, and fitting into a room, is squeezed out of the winning formula. It's not that teams are trying to fill their rosters with jerks. It's just that clubs that run on numbers, and numbers alone, may overlook the benefit of everyone getting along.

Rizzo is the first to admit he prioritizes talent before anything else. A nice guy doesn't fit if he can't play. But Rizzo does consider the person he's bringing into the mix, conducting background research on their makeup, quizzing past teammates and coaches to get the full picture. That doesn't always show in his decisions. Yet it certainly did with this team.

It was in the first game of that doubleheader on June 19, before

Scherzer pitched with his broken nose, that Gerardo Parra switched his walk-up music to "Baby Shark." The Giants released Parra on May 3, and, for six days, he was a light-hitting thirty-two-year-old without a job. But once Dave Martinez saw that Parra was available, he told the front office that he wanted the veteran outfielder. One Nationals executive later described Martinez as "pounding the table" to sign Parra. Martinez knew Parra was a respected veteran, and thought that, with the season slipping, his club had to loosen up. Rizzo listened and gave Parra a chance.

When Parra arrived on May 11, at the start of a series with the Dodgers, he whistled at Anibal Sánchez from the clubhouse doorway. They were buddies from their native Venezuela, and now embraced in a falling-down hug. Parra did the same with Rizzo, nearly tackling him to the carpet in Los Angeles, and he and Sánchez could not stop laughing. They soon tag-teamed the Nationals' entire culture. Their first act was blasting "Sondito," a frenetic techno song by Hechizeros Band, after each win. Then they encouraged hitters to dance after each home run, and even got Strasburg, shy and stone-faced, to break it down after smacking one in mid-July.

The next gimmick was a set of sunglasses they stumbled upon in Detroit. During a late-June series there, Parra and Sánchez left the team hotel, felt a light breeze, and decided they'd walk to Comerica Park. That's when they saw a giveaway table set up by Bubly, a sparkling-water brand, and were drawn to free shades. The frames were clear. The lens were each a shade of some wacky color. Parra picked out a pink pair. Sánchez went with orange. They began wearing them in the dugout, and no one questioned it. Martinez joked that he felt left out. Howie Kendrick even joined in for a few games, wearing a pink pair, too, then set them down when he had to hit.

But it was "Baby Shark" that took on a life of its own. When it first played at Nationals Park, a scattered crowd rustled with confusion. That was a quiet afternoon on June 19. The song's high-pitched melody was out of place, with each "Doo, doo, doo" feeling like a punch to the ears. Parra later explained that his daughter, Aaliyah, loved it, and he thought a change might break a weeks-long slump. And since it worked, leading to two hits, a homer and a nice barehanded play in that game, he had no choice but to keep it.

His next at-bats led to light shark clapping among fans. Some teammates followed suit from the dugout. Then, all of a sudden, this became a unified, viral, ballpark-wide routine. Whenever Parra came to the plate, whether in the early innings or a big spot, thousands of fans chomped their hands together. The song was now the Nationals' unofficial anthem, and hypnotized the stadium from Baby Shark, to Mama Shark, all the way down to Grandpa Shark and a refrain about hunting in the ocean. Players sported red shirts with PARRA SHARK stripped across the front. Others wore headbands covered in cartoon shark teeth. The song made them laugh, and it further eased the dugout, and it was a reminder—a loud and piercing one—that they were playing a game, just baseball, and supposed to have fun. Parra was rarely seen without the shirt on, bouncing between the clubhouse and the field, bubbling with a raw optimism and contagious laugh. He then spread his favorite saying among his teammates.

Through eleven years in the majors, and hundreds of interviews in his second language, Parra had nailed down a way to explain the game's unpredictability. Two words could sum up a bad slump, a hot streak, an odd statistic, or even the weirdest plays. Parra would curl his lips a bit, squint his brown eyes, and say, "That's baseball." That was it. If he stayed happy, and that made his teammates happy, and that helped everyone go home happy, regardless of the results, he'd do anything to sustain that.

He didn't think much else about being the energizing bench player. He never calculated the reaction he'd get to "Baby Shark" or wearing rose-tinted sunglasses, or honking the horn of his bright orange scooter to announce his arrival each day. He just did it. It all poured out of his heart. His favorite part of playing was smiling—not to mention winning—and, in a way, he brought both to Washington.

Adam Eaton described the Gerardo Parra effect this way: Imagine the Nationals have a must-win game. Their confidence is shot after a rough start to the year. So they sign a pitcher who's been in Japan for the last half decade, maybe longer, and bring him in to pitch. He doesn't know the stakes. He doesn't know that the Nationals have been losing, who's on the roster, whether there have been years of bad playoff luck, or five straight World Series titles. He just throws, and he dominates—"Because of course he'd shove," Eaton added—and the Nationals ride his arm to victory.

Then they step back and wonder where this pitcher came from.

"That was Gerardo for us," Eaton finished. "We needed someone who didn't know what was going on. There is a tendency to start feeling a little sorry for yourself when you're injured and not winning and the hits aren't falling or whatever. Gerardo came in with a smile and was like, 'Why's everyone so tight?' "

"This never was about me," Parra said in August, right as Sean Doolittle walked by him wearing his PARRA SHARK shirt and the matching headband. "This was always about these guys and this team. I'm just being myself."

He just helped everyone do the same, locating their goofiest selves, letting loose in the public eye of the dugout. The post-home-run dance parties were maybe his biggest gift to the club, even if he immediately deflected credit to Aníbal Sánchez for starting them. When told this, Sánchez cracked, "Gerardo doesn't lie about anything serious. But that is him being a liar." Either way, in a season that was once angling into the ground, the Nationals wound up dancing their way into the fall.

While Doolittle's latest struggle stood out against Milwaukee, that game began a historic run of offense. Once the Nationals beat the Pirates in Pittsburgh on August 19, 13–0, they'd scored 13 or more runs in four of their last five contests. Their 62 runs in that stretch was the highest five-game total of the season, for any team, and the most since the Yankees in 2007. And each home run was celebrated accordingly.

The Nationals tied a club record with 8 homers in the series finale with the Brewers. They blasted 4 more the next night, burying the Pirates, and the dugout turned into a dry rave. Eaton got it all going in the first inning. After he homered, with a roped liner to right, he entered a line of clapping teammates. Shouts of "Hey! Hey! Hey!" could be heard from the top of a near-empty PNC Park.

Eaton moved a red helmet to his right hip, then his left, and it looked as if his legs were pogo sticks bouncing off the concrete floor. Parra and Sánchez waited at the end, as they always did, for a quick finale and group hug. Eaton's routine was to then call over Howie Kendrick to be his racing partner. The two veterans—thirty and thirty-six years old—sat on the wooden bench and acted as if they were putting sports cars into gear. This came from their mutual love of big trucks and fast vehicles. About ten seconds later, once they had jammed their feet against invisible gas pedals and were short of breath, the whole group melted with laughter. Then they waited for the next home run.

When it was hit by Matt Adams, stretching a first-inning lead to 4–0, he rolled out his signature move. Ali Modami, one of the Nationals' batting-practice pitchers, was already waiting for Adams once he rounded the bases. Modami held the secret role of Martinez's good-luck charm. Since May 24, the start of Washington's turnaround, he'd been walking the lineup card to home plate before each game. That was usually a job for a manager or bench coach. But Martinez rotated, the Nationals won on Modami's turn, and Martinez told Modami to carry the lineup card until they slowed down. And more than two months later, they had yet to slow down.

Now Modami was ready for his other duty. Adams, a six-foot-three, 230-pound first baseman, hopped onto Modami's back while everyone cheered. Modami sprinted through the dance line and delivered Adams to Parra and Sánchez. Trea Turner smacked a solo homer in the second and, on cue, knelt to the ground and struck the pose made famous by Olympic sprinter Usain Bolt. This was Turner's way of dancing without, well, dancing. He admitted to having no moves. His teammates mobbed him, anyway.

The last shot of the blowout came from Asdrúbal Cabrera, in the top of the ninth, and he punctuated it with a string of salsa steps. Cabrera, Parra, and Sánchez are all from Venezuela, and this was a chance to bring a flavor of their culture to Pittsburgh. Cabrera's homer gave the Nationals a franchise-record 16 homers across their last three games. It also gave him 10 RBI in 7 starts for Washington, production that helped him take Dozier's starting spot at second.

The lineup, from Turner at the top, to Cabrera behind the heavy hitters, down to Victor Robles and the catchers toward the bottom, was gelling. Max Scherzer returned that Thursday, in the series finale in Pittsburgh, and threw 71 pitches in 4 innings. The main takeaway was that he didn't reinjure himself. There was, in sum, a lot for the Nationals to be excited about, and the dancing wasn't out of place.

"You see the unity in all of them, it's been a lot of fun. And the only thing I ask is that we do it in the dugout," Martinez said after the offense exploded against the Pirates. "We don't show any other team up, and we want to be ourselves, and they've been doing that."

Back in April, during the Nationals' first trip to Philadelphia, Juan Soto and Robles jacked late homers to stun the Phillies. Robles's was in the ninth, tying the game with two outs, and he and Soto then joined in a loud celebration. They exchanged three quick hand slaps before revving invisible chain saws. Martinez didn't mind the fire. His two youngest players were just having fun. But the manager did have one problem.

He told Soto and Robles to take it off the field. That became one of Martinez's few rules, Parra came a month later, and the dancing came about a month after that. Soto and Robles had an outlet for their unchained energy. Shier players such as Strasburg, Adams, and Turner were pulled into the fray. The Nationals were full-on social media catnip.

Johnny DiPuglia noticed a stark difference between this team and those of the recent past. It wasn't just the dancing and what cameras caught. DiPuglia arrived from the Red Sox in 2009 to head the Nationals' revamped international operation. That centered on the Dominican Academy, after the scandal shut it down, and scouting players all over Latin America. He helped discover Soto, Robles, and to restore the club's image in the islands. Then he made a point to check in on the assimilation process.

That's why DiPuglia popped in throughout the year, needling anyone he saw, flashing the World Series ring he won with the Red Sox in 2007. When he did visit, he felt a deep Latin influence on this clubhouse. Spanish-speaking players made up 25 percent of the league when the season began. The Nationals' roster reflected that by August, with eight or so Latin players in the clubhouse on a given day. DiPuglia heard it whenever he walked in.

Spanish bounced off the walls, from Parra to Soto and even Dozier, a near-fluent speaker after teaching himself through conversations and Rosetta Stone. Reggaeton and Mexican pop hummed out of a speaker by Sánchez's locker. DiPuglia had never before seen American players cede the room, much less the music, to Washington's pack of Latin Americans. Not like this.

He compared the Nationals, the league's oldest team, to a bunch of teenagers at Dominican Summer League. To explain the cultural gap, and what Latin players face in America, DiPuglia used a simple analogy: Soto and Robles were like inner-city basketball players at a suburban private school. They grew up with a different version of the sport. There was a lot more flair in the Dominican. The game in America, with its unwritten rules, with a tradition of buttoned-up respect, tried to suppress that. But this now felt like a safe space.

"When you have all of those kids, everyone's speaking Spanish and you have the music going, a lot of the Americans sometimes aren't very happy about it. And they accepted it, and part of them became Latinos, too," DiPuglia noted of Scherzer, Strasburg, and Washington's other leading veterans. "It was one of the most unbelievable things I've ever seen."

So here those Nationals were in late August, with Spanish being shouted across the visitor's clubhouse at PNC Park. Venezuela was playing Curaçao in the Little League World Series. Parra, Aníbal Sánchez, Adrián Sanchez, and Cabrera were rooting for their country. Venezuela's coach was Adrián Sanchez's longtime friend. Soto and Robles became Curaçao fans, if only to get under the others' skin, and cheered when a twelve-year-old from Curaçao dribbled a single on the overhead TVs.

Parra lounged in a leather recliner, his sandals off, and switched over to high-pitched English: "Robles, baby, don't do that! Don't do that to me! Venezuela!" Roenis Elías, his hamstring still healing, made a joke in Spanish that made everyone crack up. Parra's eight-year-old son, Gerardo, looked at them like heroes, his eyes glossed with admiration, his tiny metal bat scraping the floor. Then Venezuela got a strikeout, ending a Curaçao threat, and the Venezuelans erupted in cheers.

"Hey!" yelled Anthony Rendon after emerging from the bathroom. "What the hell is going on in here?"

"I'm not here, I'm not here," he continued, warding off reporters before any came his way. The MVP candidate had a wide grin on his face. This was his routine, a balance of serious and shtick, calling attention to himself before deflecting it elsewhere. His tone was sarcastic, its default mode, and he kept telling the Latin players to calm down. “Y’all are crazy, we have a game tonight! And stop with all that dancing. You’re going to hurt yourselves.”

Parra’s joy had become one of the Nationals’ defining traits. The steadiness of Rendon, their unwilling superstar, was another.

9

"What the hell is going on in there?"

August 25, 2019

If he had it his way, if he made the rules, Anthony Rendon would play in an empty stadium and make it home for dinner every night. There would be no interviews, no cameras in his face, nothing aside from a job to do before sundown, just like everyone else. Janitors don't get articles written about them. Teachers aren't plastered all over the local news. That's why Rendon hates the spotlight. He can hit a baseball better than most other people on the planet. He is one of the best defensive third baseman of his generation. But that's what he is paid to do. Why, he asks, does that make him any more special than the next guy?

He was always like this, growing up in Houston, gathering attention he didn't want. His father, Rene, could have been a traveling, professional pool player. He was a legend around southeast Texas, stacking cash with his cue stick, owning the green felt the way his son would own the local diamonds. Yet Rene turned that down to raise his boys, Rendon and his brother, David, teaching them the value of family and hard work.

Rendon's first swings were with a stick and pine cones in the family's backyard. Rene went right to the store, bought his five-year-old a glove, and Rendon soon started tee-ball. The key was Rene being there to see it.

When Rendon was nine and playing for the Houston Thunder, a local travel team, Willie Ansley took an interest in the quiet kid. Ansley had a minor league run with the Astros in the early 1990s. He was a top prospect then, and a former first-round pick, but never made it past AAA. Now he coached the Thunder and saw a lot of potential in Rendon. Rendon already knew the basics, how to generate power, how to use his wrists to whip the bat through the zone. Ansley asked Rendon if he wanted private lessons, outside their packed schedule of games, and that's how a swing was born.

Front foot open six or so inches, knees bent, hands resting, and wagging slightly, between the chest and belly button. The front foot lifts while the pitcher winds up, just a hair off the ground, before planting in the same spot a millisecond later. That gives the hands, and those lightning-quick wrists, a chance to read the pitch and react to whether it's heat or off-speed. That's what Ansley taught Rendon before he could write his name in cursive. And little has changed in the two decades since.

His first stance, the slight step, and finish were almost identical to his approach in 2019, as a twenty-nine-year-old with a growing MVP case. Once Rendon had the foundation down, and was working to polish it, Ansley sought ways to keep challenging him. The coach put a metal pole behind Rendon's back leg to keep his mechanics tight. If Rendon didn't go straight to the ball, he would smack the pole and a loud sound would ring in his ear. But it didn't take long before he swung as if the pole wasn't there.

Then there was that one tournament, in the summer of 2004, when Ansley accused Rendon of trying too hard to crank homers. Rendon had lofted a bunch of pop flies to the warning track. He quickly denied Ansley's theory, grinning at his coach, insisting nothing had changed. Yet a confession arrived at a showcase the next weekend.

He went 14 for 14 across a day of games. Every one of the hits was a lined single or double. The air under his drives had disappeared. Rendon had listened to Ansley and, without a word, proved that he could hit however he wanted. Ansley recalled leaning over to an assistant and saying, "I'm not sure he'll ever get out again."

"It was sort of like playing a video game, even when he was that young," Ansley added to the memory. "You could tell him to do something, and he was so coordinated that he figured it out right away."

But if there was a problem with that ability, with how smooth it made Rendon look in action, it was that people noticed. He didn't mind the scouts and coaches latching on. He needed their attention to achieve his goals. It was the media, and the idea of being glorified, that bothered him. Coverage wasn't crazy at his two high schools in Houston, or even during his three years at nearby Rice University. It just picked up once he didn't slow down.

In 682 at bats across three collegiate seasons, Rendon finished with 176 walks against 76 strikeouts. He had a supernatural feel for the strike zone. He was a doubles machine. The Nationals drafted him in the first round in 2011, sixth overall, and he rocketed through the system. He was an everyday player by twenty-four, splitting time between second and third. He arrived that year by leading the league with 111 runs scored. That piqued the interest in his story, in how he learned to hit, and that's when Rendon's personality showed.

He evaded the press as if it were a game of hide-and-seek. If he had to address them—and his success often forced him to—he sidestepped questions with dry humor. In July of 2014, during his first full season in the majors, he told the *Washington Post* that he didn't watch baseball because "it's too long and boring." That actually wasn't a joke. The NBA is much more his speed.

A breakthrough moment came three seasons later, when Washington trounced the Mets, 23–5, at Nationals Park. Rendon went

6 for 6 with 3 home runs and 10 RBI. It was a historic performance, on many levels, and he was grabbed by Dan Kolko for a TV interview after the game. Kolko, the on-field reporter for Mid-Atlantic Sports Network, tried to get Rendon talking about himself. He teed up Rendon with a question on contributing to the lopsided victory. The third baseman didn't bite.

"It's definitely fun to be a part of, to be out here obviously, but it was a long game," Rendon offered. The cameras kept rolling.

Kolko took another shot toward the end of the interview. "You don't like talking about yourself, but I'm going to have to do this to you. You went six for six with three home runs and ten RBI today. You're the thirteenth player in the history of Major League Baseball to have ten RBI in a game. How do you react to that?"

"Oh, our pitching was, you know, just amazing," Rendon answered through the slightest smirk. "They kept them down to five runs, so, as long as we scored six, all we had to do is win."

"Can I do anything to get you to comment on your offensive day today?" Kolko asked with a smile, knowing full well what came next.

"No." And with that, and another smirk, Rendon darted into the clubhouse. Reporters found a semicircle of chairs around his locker. He'd set them up so the cameras and recorders wouldn't get too close. If it seemed as if he loathed self-promotion, and would do anything to avoid it, then Rendon was projecting how he felt. That just got more complicated when his contract negotiations picked up.

Back in the spring, before this season began and his bat caught fire, Rendon was nearing his final year before free agency. He wanted his agent, Scott Boras, to explore a long-term extension with the Nationals. Rendon was comfortable in Washington. He was a fixture at the Nationals Youth Baseball Academy, where he loved the kids and made a silent donation of $150,000 in 2018. He promised the kids that he'd consider sticking around.

The organization had sold Rendon as one of the league's most underrated players. His numbers stacked up with those of the household names. In wins above replacement, an all-encompassing statistic that measures player value, Rendon trailed only Mike Trout, Mookie Betts, José Ramírez, José Altuve, Francisco Lindor, and Christian Yelich between 2016 and 2018. Trout, Betts, Altuve, and Yelich had each won an MVP award in that stretch. But Rendon was overshadowed in his own market by Bryce Harper and Max Scherzer. He was overshadowed by Nolan Arenado in conversations about the league's best third basemen. And Rendon was fine with those shadows until money was concerned.

Rendon watched a number of franchise players sign big extensions before the season. When he first did an interview on his negotiations, in West Palm Beach on February 20, he mentioned that he and the Nationals had been talking for a year. He stated that Boras worked for him, and not the other way around, to make it known that he, the player, would dictate the next steps. Boras is known for bringing clients to free agency. That's the only way a bidding war can drive up the price. But Boras's job here was to work with the Nationals on a deal. If it happened, great. If it didn't, Rendon would move on.

Six days later, Arenado signed an eight-year, $260 million extension with the Colorado Rockies. That made him the league's highest-paid position player in salary per year. Boras always planned to pitch Rendon as a better all-around player than Arenado, and therefore demand a more lucrative contract. He didn't care that Arenado had won every annual award, including All-Star appearances, Gold Gloves, and Silver Sluggers, ahead of Rendon. Boras didn't care that Rendon presented as the anti-superstar, his worth lowered by a lack of TV appearances and social media clout.

Arenado's statistics sagged when he played away from Coors Field, the Rockies' hitter-friendly ballpark. Rendon was consistent across the board, no matter the stadium, and Boras's comparison started there. That's what the agent cared about. Now he had a financial baseline to work with.

But the Nationals soon made an offer that fell limp. A person with knowledge of the figures described them as "not close" to what Rendon and Boras wanted. One Nationals official privately noted that they didn't equate Rendon to Altuve, who had signed a five-year, $151 million extension with the Astros in March of 2018. Arenado's money was in a totally different class. Yet Rendon was ready to bet on himself, on 2019, on what he could do between then and the end of a critical year. He felt little need to sit in a room and convince the Nationals to spend more on him. He could do that on the field.

"I don't care. You guys know my personality. My identity is not in this game," he said in the spring of how a slow market, and Bryce Harper's flatlined free agency, would affect his approach to extension discussions. The suggestion was to sign and avoid the stress. The response was vintage Rendon: "If this game is taken away from me at any time, I'd be fine going back to the house and living a happy life. If that happens, it happens. I'm going to play as long as I can, but my identity is not in this game. This game doesn't define who I am as a person."

Harper began his contract year with the Nationals by making a rule with reporters. He wasn't going to talk about free agency. He offered a statement at the start of spring training, explaining his reasons, and that was it. Questions would center on baseball, and the season at hand, or he'd respectfully decline.

Some players felt that hung an eerie cloud of silence over Washington's clubhouse. Everyone knew Harper could become a free agent once the year ended. Everyone knew the Nationals wanted to keep him if possible. But since Harper was quiet on the subject, reporters were left asking teammates and coaches about his mood or feelings toward the franchise. The line between what they should and shouldn't say was thin. The exercise became a regular source of discomfort.

Rendon, though evasive as ever with the media, drew no such parameters. He would talk about free agency if asked. He might even offer a window into his thinking. He gave a frank assessment to the *Washington Post* in late June: "At this point, if they present something and both sides are happy, then cool. If not and it doesn't happen, then no hard feelings." He followed a month later with an extensive radio interview on the popular *Grant & Danny Show* on 106.7 The Fan. He told the hosts, Grant Paulsen and Danny Rouhier, that he, Boras, and the front office hadn't talked for a while. Boras had visited Nationals Park a few weeks earlier, watching a full game with founding owner Ted Lerner, but the meeting didn't lead to any traction.

The conversation wound in a bunch of directions, with Paulsen and Rouhier nudging Rendon to drop hints. They painted Boras as the ultimate decision-maker, and Rendon shot that down. Paulsen declared that there was no way Boras would let Rendon sign before free agency, with all the teams that would want him, and Rendon debunked that theory, too. Then he backed it up with his own desires:

"I don't know. I still think it's up in the air. I mean, we haven't heard from the front office in a few weeks or a month now, and we haven't had an offer, I don't believe, in a little bit longer than that. But I mean, if you're giving me the opportunity, and saying I'm this close from going to go car shopping, from multiple lots, instead of staying in one lot, I mean, what would you do?"

Those words spilled through airwaves to form a brewing reality. Rendon was all but heading to free agency. There was a chance for the Nationals to dissuade him, but that meant meeting high demands that could only grow. Rendon's *Grant & Danny* appearance was on a Tuesday, timed perfectly to Rizzo's live weekly spot the next morning. It was July 31, and he was supposed to discuss the approaching trade deadline, but Rizzo was instead pressed on Rendon's comments.

The general manager walked a tightrope of diplomacy. He was

unhappy with Rendon's indicating that talks were stagnant, yet vowed to never negotiate contracts through the media. But he did throw one jab before hanging up the phone.

"He better call his agent, because we got a counterproposal from his agent on July fifteenth," Rizzo told the hosts of *The Sports Junkies*. "So he better be in contact with him."

Now Boras was mad that Rizzo had questioned his communication with Rendon. The agent flew to Phoenix the next weekend, where the Nationals played the Diamondbacks, so he and Rendon could get on the same page. It would have been normal for Rendon to lose focus, to wilt, if only for a moment, beneath the weight of it all. He and his wife, Amanda, were raising a one-year-old daughter. Another baby was on the way. Not knowing where they would live in a year, or in a few months, was enough to twist even the calmest person into a ball of stress.

But Rendon never let that show. He just kept hitting, and hitting, until, one day, he seemed incapable of doing anything else. It's hard to pinpoint when that was. Maybe it was early, April 3, when he tagged the Phillies with a single, double, a homer and, for good measure, worked a walk. Maybe it was July 29, when he lifted the Nationals over the Braves with a game-winning grand slam. Maybe it was thirteen days after that, August 11, when he pestered the Mets by spraying four singles into one afternoon.

Or maybe he was born this way. His teammates took notice of how collected he stayed, of his ability to turn pressure into dust. Nothing rattled Anthony Rendon, and so nothing would rattle them.

Victor Robles lay flat on his back in his locker at Wrigley Field, headphones on, wanting no one to bother him before he had to grab a glove or bat. A reporter wanted an interview and muttered his name. No answer. The reporter tried again, a bit louder this time, and Robles didn't flinch a muscle. His head was buried by a rack of hanging uniforms. Octavio Martinez, the Nationals' team interpreter, walked over and patted Robles on the leg, like a mother waking up a child for school.

Robles sat up, separating the shirts with his face, and rubbed his eyes with two fists. Everyone around him looked just as tired. Washington had played the evening before in Pittsburgh, with the first pitch at 7:15 p.m., and didn't land in Chicago until well past midnight. They rolled up to the hotel around 1:00 a.m. Then they were at the park a few hours later on Friday, August 23, readying for a day game with the Cubs.

The league should never have approved such a tight turnaround. The Nationals protested as soon as the schedule came out, sending emails, pleading for a change, but nothing came of it. Now they had to make do. The Cubs didn't care about the Nationals' slashed-up sleep. The result wouldn't, either. Dave Martinez canvassed a room full of writers before leaving Pittsburgh, pointing his right index finger in every direction: "Can you play tomorrow? . . . Can you play tomorrow? . . . Who can hit around here?" Then he sat in another office, in another time zone, and wrote the same order on his lineup card:

Trea Turner, SS
Adam Eaton, RF
Anthony Rendon, 3B
Juan Soto, LF
Howie Kendrick, 1B
Kurt Suzuki, C
Brian Dozier, 2B
Victor Robles, CF
Aníbal Sánchez, P

They each told Martinez they wanted to play again, one by one, giving him no choice but to test their will. Even Suzuki, a worn-down catcher at thirty-five, chose to get right back behind the plate. He regularly caught Scherzer, who started the night before against the Pirates. He regularly caught Sánchez, too, and wasn't going to change that for a bit of rest. The Nationals had eliminated that option long ago.

Sánchez soon dominated the Cubs for 8⅓ innings, finishing two outs short of a complete-game shutout. He added two singles and an RBI. The offense stayed sharp, plating 9 runs, and didn't stop there. They paced the Nationals on Saturday, in a 7–2 win, setting up the chance of an improbable sweep. It was even sweeter because Wander Suero, Tanner Rainey, Hunter Strickland, Fernando Rodney, and Daniel Hudson combined for 4⅔ scoreless innings out of the bullpen.

The Cubs were contending in both their division and the wild-card hunt. They had added Craig Kimbrel in June and star outfielder Nicholas Castellanos at the trade deadline. They entered the weekend with the league's fourth-best home record, 44-19, and had dropped just one series here all year. They were a good club, and the Nationals were smacking them around at Wrigley, and that was a statement in itself.

Twelve months before, in the twilight of a lost season, the Nationals took their final breath in this building. They led the Cubs by 3 runs in the ninth. Ryan Madson was on the mound, David Bote was at the plate, and the Nationals hung by a thread at the bottom of the pennant race. They were still alive, if you twisted the math a certain way, until one swing made sure they weren't.

Bote lifted a two-out, two-strike, walk-off grand slam against the stars of a late-summer Sunday night. The Cubs leaped onto the field in shocked celebration. The Nationals limped off it, shocked themselves, and were shoved out of the playoff picture. That's when

Martinez ducked into the visiting manager's office, slammed the door behind him, then sprang out of his chair to beat up the coffee maker. But here, on another Sunday in Chicago, in an August that felt much brighter, was the difference a year makes.

Rendon got August 25 started with a solo homer in the fourth. He beat a crosscutting wind, jolting the ball with more than enough muscle, and jogged around the bases while the dugout prepared a runway. Rendon's dance was subdued as he raised his arms like a puppet, as if they were starched still, before pushing onto his toes. Strasburg picked through the Cubs' order, striking out 10, and exited with the score tied, 2–2, after six. He'd stranded two runners on base to keep it that way. Then Juan Soto nudged the Nationals ahead with an RBI single, then Cabrera upped the deficit to 3 runs, then the bullpen blew the lead across the seventh and eighth.

The Cubs used homers off Strickland and Rodney to force extra innings. There were shades of *here we go again*. But after Wander Suero worked a scoreless ninth, and Hudson worked a scoreless tenth, Howie Kendrick came in on a wild pitch in the eleventh. That put Washington in front for good, and Rendon had a chance to pad the cushion. He already had 3 hits in the game. Tyler Chatwood challenged him inside, throwing a fastball on his hands, and Rendon poked it into left-center for a single.

Turner scored from third without a throw. Rendon pulled into first, lifted his right foot in the air as if he were kicking in slow motion, and lowered it to the ground before settling on the base. His teammates hung over the dugout rail and pressed their thumbs and pointer fingers together. Rendon returned the gesture, giving three finger taps in his lime-green batting gloves, and a section of traveling Washington fans did the same.

This "Baby Shark" clap had been developed for each time a player notched a hit. A single got a small clap, just that subtle joining of thumb and index finger. A double made it grow, with wrists pressed together and hands smacking at the bench. A triple was a full-on clap, like the ones in the stands, as if two arms were needed to devour a toddler. And a homer, well, the players were too busy dancing to worry about that.

"Reee-lent-less," F.P. Santangelo, the Nationals' color commentator, said on the TV broadcast after Rendon's knock. "They get a couple of punches to the gut, no big deal. We'll just keep pushing."

The Nationals wouldn't leave Chicago quietly. They had won 5 straight games, 7 of their last 8, and 12 of 14 to build a 4-game lead over the Cubs atop the wild-card standings. They were a season-best 16 games over .500 at 73-57. They still had the best record in baseball since May 24.

Parra and Sánchez blew toy whistles in the clubhouse while waving everyone close. Martinez wore shark glasses, the lens winged by plastic fins, and clapped to the music. "El Sonidito" blared through a single speaker, its bass thumping so hard that the floor vibrated and walls shook. The players joined in a conga line, gripping the shoulders of the guy in front of them, snaking past pillars and couches that tried to get in their way. But nothing could. Not the Cubs. Not themselves. Not even their bullpen, shaky as it still was, because the rest of the team could compensate.

Family members waited in a stairwell leading up to the clubhouse entrance. They laughed at the noise, the shrill screech of Parra's and Sánchez's whistles, the chant of "Hey! Hey! Hey!" that had become so familiar. Eireann Dolan, married to Sean Doolittle, looked at a few other wives and asked what everyone had wondered for months now: "What the hell is going on in there?"

"I credit these guys for sticking with it. Because they could have easily went south when things were going bad, and they didn't," Martinez said in his office. A new coffee maker was safe across the room. He'd purchased it himself, after battering the old one last

August, so some other manager could unleash his anger on the plastic and glass.

All Martinez could do now was lean back and reflect. He extended his press conference to thank those who came to cheer Washington on. His voice caught with emotion when saying this club never quit. His eyes watered at the mention of resilience. Then they lit up to discuss Rendon's MVP candidacy, now equipped with 29 homers and a .329 average. Martinez gave a simple summary: "I'll make a case for him right now"—the manager hovered above his chair, as if just the thought of Rendon could peel him off his seat—"MVP, Gold Glove, my man Anthony!"

Martinez went on like this, dripping with pride, drawing thick lines between the past and how they had closed the month of hate. Martinez says his players are his kids. Seeing them win, and have fun doing it, is like watching a ballet recital or peewee soccer game. Seeing them fail, as they did throughout spring, makes him anxious and sad. His favorite days are when he can walk locker to locker, a smile planted on his face, telling each player, Good job, and I'm proud of you. He was doing it a lot lately.

"Fuck." Martinez sighed as the room emptied around him, as if he'd forgotten, in a heap of feelings, how much work remained. "We can't stop here."

10

"Boom"

September 3, 2019

It was bundled into ten seconds, maybe less, just long enough for Ryan Zimmerman to turn Nationals Park into a kaleidoscope of the past, present, and future. The sequence began as they always had, with Zimmerman's front foot lifting into the air, his front knee bending with it, and a pitch hurtling in while he squinted at its seams. He ran the image through his brain, taking a millionth of a moment, and recognized fastball. It was a hard one, thrown 98 mph by Mets closer Edwin Díaz, and Zimmerman twitched his arms, hips, and light-brown bat into motion.

The Nationals trailed the Mets, 10–4, when the ninth inning began on September 3. The Mets had scored 5 runs in the top of the frame. The end had become a formality, just three outs needed so everyone could go home. Most of a scattered crowd had already, skipping onto the last runs of the metro, or beating highway traffic with school and work tugging them to bed. But the Nationals' offense had other plans.

The deficit was shaved to 4 runs, and the bases were loaded, once Zimmerman dug in. The Mets had one out. Zimmerman was in a trying season, maybe the most trying of his fifteen-year career, because his body wouldn't cooperate. Again. Somewhere along the line, after he was named Rookie of the Year, became an All-Star and one of the league's best third basemen, injuries hijacked his life and legacy.

In 2014, his throwing shoulder had been inflamed, triggering surgery and a move from third to first. In 2015, his first bout with plantar fasciitis kept him out for nearly half that season. In 2018, a pair of injuries to his calf and oblique limited him to 85 games. And now, in 2019, he'd missed two months when the plantar fasciitis returned.

This all came after Zimmerman signed a six-year, $100 million deal in 2012 to spend his prime with the Nationals. He just spent most of it trying to get back on the field. Fans mumbled that he was stealing money. The social media managers called for him to be traded or, at the very least, locked out of the lineup for good. He went from franchise player, the organization's first draft pick, the one who'd stuck through those bleak summers at RFK Stadium, to the brunt of continued frustration.

But with Edwin Díaz's fastball humming in, and a miracle comeback in his hands, Zimmerman could still shift his script. If the game had robbed him of sleep, of time, of months wondering if the pain would stop, this was the least it could offer. His forearms jerked and his bat whipped through the zone. He glanced at the right-center gap and took off running. A double was bound for grass, then the dirt warning track, then landed past a diving Michael Conforto, by a matter of inches, and bounced off the wall.

Cabrera jogged home. Rendon did, too. Zimmerman coasted into second, his chest rising with heavy breaths, and spun toward the dugout. He clenched two fists and yelled. He ripped off his gloves as if they were stinging his wrists. He stared at his teammates, his pupils ablaze, his eyebrows flirting at the bridge of his nose, and the crowd roared, getting louder yet, until it calmed and Zimmerman exhaled.

It was fair, in that moment, to think of all Washington and Zimmerman had coiled through. And it was maybe even more fair, once the moment had subsided, to wonder how many of these were left.

Before the Lerner family bought the team, before they named Mike Rizzo the general manager, before there was a new stadium and anything to market or sell, there was Ryan Zimmerman. He was twenty years old, wide-eyed and wound by a dream, when the Nationals selected him fourth overall in the 2005 draft. They were just months into their first year back in Washington. This kid from the University of Virginia, raised a few more hours south in Virginia Beach, was their very first building block. He was expected to handle expectations.

They sent him to the minors because that's what teams do, wary of fast-tracking prospects and stunting growth. But Zimmerman was never really a prospect. His 67 games in the system—4 with the Savannah Sand Gnats, another 63 in Harrisburg—were for convention's sake. He was called up in September of 2005, once rosters expanded to forty players, and was a big leaguer from that point forward. His first home at bat ended with a double ripped through the right-center gap. About 29,000 people were there to see it. RFK sat about 45,000 for baseball games.

When Nationals Park opened in March of 2008, Opening Day was a citywide celebration. President George W. Bush threw out the first pitch. The stadium filled to capacity. Beyond the left-field fence, the fresh blue seats, a neighborhood that heard excitement rumbling like an oncoming train, was the Capitol, lit like a candle, shining bright in the dark sky. But it was Zimmerman who made the night unforgettable.

He came up with two outs and the bases empty in the ninth inning. The Nationals were live on ESPN's national telecast, for a change, and the score was tied. Then Zimmerman clocked a 1-0 fastball into the first row above the wall in left-center.

The Nationals spilled from the dugout to surround home plate. Zimmerman leaped into their arms, mobbed by Willie Harris and Nick Johnson, Austin Kearns and Paul Lo Duca, and this feeling, the feeling of playing hero in the end, became routine. Zimmerman would do this eleven times for Washington, earning the nickname Mr. Walk-Off, but this one meant a bit more.

They lost a lot that season, and for seasons to come, but Zimmerman was a reason to wage hope against reality. This was how Barry Svrluga described his outsize influence in the next morning's *Washington Post*:

> "The biggest part of those at-bats is keeping your emotions in check," Zimmerman said. But he couldn't as he rounded first, thrusting his right arm into the air. New ballpark, new era—same result from Ryan Zimmerman, the player given the task of carrying the Nationals forward, this year and beyond.

Beyond, for Zimmerman, was staying patient while a core grew around him. He was there to welcome Stephen Strasburg in 2009. He was there, a year later, when the Nationals signed Jayson Werth as another veteran cornerstone. He was there for Bryce Harper, in August of 2010, as a special guest at the teenager's introductory press conference. He was no longer alone.

Once Harper debuted in 2012, the nucleus was Harper, Werth, Zimmerman, and shortstop Ian Desmond on offense, with Strasburg, Gio Gonzalez, and Jordan Zimmermann on the mound. But that's the same year Zimmerman's shoulder acted up. He received a cortisone shot, spent two weeks on the injured list, and finished the season on a three-month tear, keying a playoff push with 25 homers and 95 RBI.

Yet he still needed off-season shoulder surgery to repair a sprained right AC joint, shave down a bone spur in his collarbone, and handle fraying in both his labrum and rotator cuff. That's how screwed up his arm was. The initial rehab was set to take eight weeks. He was cleared on schedule and, as if little were wrong, whacked 26 home runs with a .275 average in 2013. But his throwing motion dropped to three-quarters, numbering his days at third. Then the injuries kept piling up.

His career soon read like a sign-in sheet to the trainer's room: a broken thumb and strained hamstring in 2014; a full-time move to first in 2015, due to an arthritic right shoulder, before plantar fasciitis knocked him out of 40 games, before an oblique strain ended his year in early September; a rib-cage strain and a left-wrist contusion in 2016; a stretch of good health in 2017—finally—before 2018 was marred by an oblique injury, which was rumored to be compounded by a calf injury, which Zimmerman insisted was not true.

He was ridiculed in 2018 for what he did, or didn't do, in the leadup to the season. He took just two spring training at bats because of lingering discomfort in his calf. Fans then blamed a slow start and oblique strain, suffered in early May, on his not being physically ready to compete. Zimmerman denied that correlation, answering constant questions on the matter, even sparring with reporters over allegations that he'd covered up injuries.

But there was little else to ask him about. The spring training narrative trailed him from start to finish. That came after appearing in 156 contests, 6 fewer than a full season's worth, across 2014 and 2015, and just 115 a season later. He was cursed or made of glass—or both—so it was hard to blame him, really, for being down during the Nationals' trip to San Diego in mid-June of 2019.

The plantar fasciitis was back. He'd been out for more than a month and mostly stayed home to work with a personal trainer. But he itched to be around the team, in the clubhouse, anywhere except watching the losses, and then the wins, tick by from his couch. He joined the West Coast swing to see the Nationals' medical staff and enjoy the Southern California weather. He and his wife, Heather, took their two young daughters to the San Diego Zoo. He jokingly introduced himself to coaches once he arrived for light batting practice. But every second at Petco Park was a reminder of what he was missing.

"It's been really frustrating. It's probably one of the more frustrating things I've gone through," he admitted, and that was saying a lot. "Just because the rest of my body feels so good. I felt good this year up until the point where the heel started acting up, and there's nothing you can really do to prevent something like this."

And the complicating layer, as if one were needed, was Zimmerman's contract situation. His initial agreement included an $18 million club option for 2020, meaning the Nationals could choose to pay it or make him a free agent after this season. They'd known, for years now, that Zimmerman was no longer worth that kind of money. He knew it. The mailman, the teachers at his daughters' school, the next-door neighbor's dog walker—everyone knew he was gone without a restructured deal.

But Zimmerman was open to lowering his price. He began expressing this in 2018, toward the end of *that* stressful season, telling reporters he wanted to stay. Rizzo's public stance rang the same, that they'd discuss the details when necessary, that Zimmerman was and always should be a staple in Washington.

It is just never so simple. No one had to tell Zimmerman that. He had played for seven managers in fifteen seasons. He'd had friends hang it up because the game moved on. He'd watched the nameplates cycle above each locker, the faces blending into a blur, the roster turning over, from one day to the next, as if the front office were trying on sunglasses at a drugstore.

There was no reason that, in the history of baseball, he'd be the one player immune to what business demands. Rizzo's job was to chase championships. Zimmerman's job was to man first base for the Washington Nationals until further notice, as long as he had a parking spot and security let him in. Then loyalty had a limit. Then it was up to Zimmerman, the one holding this fading chance, to stretch that limit while he could.

He did peel his eyes off the dugout, did stop breathing so heavily, did center his focus on the basepaths, and the 180 feet in front of him, once Díaz toed the rubber and the game resumed. That's about the distance that separated Zimmerman, leading off second, from scoring the tying run. That was it.

The Nationals still trailed the Mets, 10–8, after Zimmerman's double halved the deficit on September 3. Díaz was spiraling. He had nothing but that single out. Up stepped Kurt Suzuki, Washington's thirty-five-year-old catcher, and Zimmerman had a clean view of the matchup. Suzuki swung through a first-pitch slider that was low and off the plate. Then Díaz tried two more, pounding the exact same spot, and Suzuki laid off to get ahead.

An inside fastball sent Suzuki sliding out of the way. That put him in control, 3-1, but Díaz pushed back. He spun another slider that Suzuki missed. He wiped the sweat from his brow. Suzuki fouled off a high 100.2 MPH fastball. He fouled off the next heater, clocked at 99.3, which would have been ball four. But when Díaz came with a third, challenging the speed of Suzuki's bat, checking to see what he could get away with, the answer was loud and clear.

Suzuki swung as if the location had been whispered into his ear. Zimmerman turned toward the left-field seats, giving the ball a quick glance, then shot his arms into the chilly air. It was a no-doubt, moon-shot, three-run, walk-off home run. Suzuki took a few steps up the line and pointed at the dugout. Before it emptied out, before that blast was gone, and before it splashed into Katie Atwater's waiting hands, the Nationals had had a near-zero chance of coming back.

Teams were 274-0 when leading by 6 or more runs in the ninth this season. Now that record was 274-1. And now the team that had made it that way, a team that wouldn't die, waited to smother Suzuki with hugs and punches at home plate.

But one player was missing. Max Scherzer was nestled with the Nationals' video team, in a windowless room off the home clubhouse, and had no interest in looking at a TV, or his iPhone, or anything that could have told him what had just happened on the field. If he did, if only for a split second, if temptation tugged his eyes to a screen, he would have seen the biggest comeback in the ninth inning or later in franchise history.

He would have seen Suzuki embrace Trea Turner, since Turner's mental error had helped the Mets build a yawning lead in the ninth, before Suzuki made that error a nonissue. Scherzer would have seen Suzuki stop midstride, spread his arms into a perfect *T*, and wait for Turner to dump a cooler of yellow Gatorade onto his head. Yet Scherzer didn't look. He could only hear the noise and wonder what had caused it. Noise was good, he knew that much, but his part wasn't finished.

After an uneven start, scattering 4 runs in 6 innings, Scherzer had gone to break down tape of himself. He was unhappy with the life of his fastball, the sharpness of his breaking pitches, the tiny details that had lagged since his return from injury. His attention was off the game. He counted it as a loss, once the Mets scored 5 runs in the top of the ninth, and figured he'd study a bit before showering.

But that's when he caught light cheers, then louder ones, then a series of full-on screams.

Anyone else would have sprinted down the hall, poked his head into the dugout, checked on the commotion for peace of mind. But Scherzer isn't anyone. He believes, down to his very bones, that change is what changes good luck. He believes in superstition. He wasn't watching when the rally began, so he couldn't start in the middle, or ever, and bear responsibility if it fell short. He just missed a hell of an ending and could live with that.

"It's one of the wins of the year!" bellowed Charlie Slowes on the Nationals' radio network. "And if you walked out of the ballpark when the Mets scored five runs in the top of the ninth inning . . ." Slowes paused for a beat to welcome his partner, Dave Jageler, into the call. Then they yelled the next three words together.

"You! . . . Blew! . . . It!"

The Nationals Park interview room is next to the Lexus Presidents Club. A large window separates the room from long bars, longer buffets, clumps of white-clothed tables for the highest-spending fans. Most nights, whether the Nationals win or lose, they are gone well before Martinez meets the media. Maybe a few hang around, hanging on his every word, only heading home once the last drops of alcohol run dry. But now Martinez stepped through the interview-room door to find dozens of people behind the glass. They pounded on it with closed fists. They chanted his name.

He sat down, folded his hands in front of the microphone, shrugged, and raised his eyebrows. A silence lingered. Martinez wasn't sure where to start. So he went with the first word that came to him when Suzuki obliterated that baseball.

"Boom."

The crowd let out a cheer.

No one asked a question.

"Boom," Martinez repeated, his brain still fluttering, and the cheers got even louder. "What do you want me to say? A win is a win is a win. The boys fought."

In close to two years on the job, Martinez often fell back on this type of phrase. *The boys fought. The boys battled. The boys* this, and *the boys* that, and if *the boys* had done anything else, it would have been headline news. He was slammed on social media for it after losses. He was needled after wins. But if there was a benefit to staying on message, no matter the reaction or result, it showed once it turned into truth.

There were stories to weave into his retelling of the comeback. In the ninth, when the offense was just getting started, Cabrera asked Martinez why he wouldn't stop smiling. Martinez told the veteran he saw no choice but to stay positive. Cabrera laughed and made his way to the on-deck circle, a little more relaxed, before slapping a single. The manager felt for Turner after he forgot how many outs there were in the top of that inning, allowing the Mets to ding Daniel Hudson for three additional runs. But that made Turner's RBI double even sweeter in the bottom half. That's what made Martinez most proud.

"One more thing, twenty-sixth man right there!" Martinez pointed to the fans who'd stuck around. "Thank you! Thanks for hanging on. It was long but we did it. Thank you."

What they'd done, in that grand scheme of it, was win one game in stunning fashion. It did not count any extra in the standings. It would be an ancient artifact by morning. The schedule offers little opportunity, if any, to dwell on a victory or defeat. But it wasn't worth saying that to the Nationals on September 3.

Because what they'd really done was prove something to themselves. Maybe there was magic in Scherzer's restraint. Maybe the offense had some magic, too. Maybe Martinez was right, that this club couldn't quit, that it only improved when it was supposed to fail. He had been preaching it for months, bending wary ears, begging his players to believe in the power of believing. Now they had concrete reasons to.

"Let's be honest, I don't think we thought it was going to happen, either," Zimmerman, ever the pragmatist, said by his locker in the back of the clubhouse. "A lot of us have been around baseball for a long time. Once it starts going, the pressure shifts obviously squarely on their shoulders. Stuff like that is not supposed to happen. It's a crazy sport. Crazy things happen."

They do. They were. The swelling group of reporters moved from Zimmerman's locker to Suzuki's, flicking their camera lights back on, fighting for position with their recorders and notebooks. Zimmerman sat on the edge of his leather rolling chair. He rubbed his calves and slid on red flip-flops. He glanced over at Suzuki, cracked a half smile, then went for a late dinner in the players' cafeteria.

It was nights such as this—when everything went right, when time stretched like elastic—that Zimmerman wanted to last forever. He could only get this feeling here, in Washington, in a game that had yet to spit him out. And the best part was that he got to come back tomorrow.

11

"Big fucking scare"

September 15, 2019

Dave Martinez stood on the top step of the Nationals' dugout, just as he always does, and lasered his focus on Aníbal Sánchez's pitching mechanics. It was the sixth inning on September 15, a Sunday matchup with the Braves, and this is what Martinez saw: Sánchez easing into his small rocker step, his right foot pivoting against the rubber, his glove glued to his hip as they turned together, the ball hiding—and hiding some more—until it appeared from behind his right ear. Then that windup again. Then again. Then his vision blurring, as if Sánchez were throwing underwater, before Martinez felt a sharp pain in his chest.

He figured it would pass in a second or two. It felt like a cramp, and he stretched his right arm like a windmill, but soon lost feeling from his shoulder to fingers. Next his left thigh went numb. He had trouble catching his breath. He called for Paul Lessard, the Nationals' head athletic trainer, and Lessard made a quick decision.

Martinez had to go to the emergency room. He had to go right now. He tried to protest, saying the game was almost finished, but Lessard didn't budge. They walked Martinez through the clubhouse, making no announcement to the team, and an ambulance was waiting inside the stadium. He was strapped into a gurney and wheeled into the back. He was immediately hooked up to a heart-rate monitor. The technicians pumped fluids into his body in case of dehydration.

Once they rolled into a bright afternoon, bound for Washington Adventist Hospital, Martinez's mind raced. He thought this couldn't be a heart attack, that he was healthy, worked out every day, tried to limit the steak, wine, and late-night meals. But if it was, and he was in danger, then what? What about his kids? What about his girlfriend, his parents, his brothers and extended family? What about his players, the ones scratching through the heat of a pennant race, who all counted on him being there, the same old Davey, with a smile every day?

What happened if this, whatever this was, took him away from them? What if the consequences were much worse? A machine kept beeping behind him, suspending his inner monologue, steering his attention to the high-pitched noise. He clung to the beeps, letting them trick him into a rhythm, figuring each inched him closer to help. But that didn't stop what ran through his head, over and over, until he was repeating words only he could hear.

I'm going to let so many people down.

When Martinez arrived in a hospital room, was hooked up to new machines, stabilized, and rested from a long nap, the first questions were about stress. He managed a major league baseball team. He was turning fifty-five in two weeks. The season had been filled with tension—enough to warrant a stress test without the pain—and Saturday, the afternoon before his chest tightened, was no different.

The Nationals were crushed by the Braves, 10–1, to fall 9½ back of first place in the division. They were bound for the wild-card game, a single-elimination contest to start the playoffs. Boiling a six-month season into nine innings was a chilling prospect, as if the result could be decided by a coin flip. Earlier in September, when the Braves were pulling away with the NL East, Patrick Corbin summed that up with a made-for-radio quote: "That's why I think winning your division is so important. If you got one game, anything can happen."

But that's not what left Martinez shaking in frustration by Saturday's end, the night before he was rushed to the hospital. Runners were on first and second with no outs in the seventh, Fernando Rodney was on the mound for Washington, and Charlie Culberson was up for Atlanta. The score was tied, 1–1, and Culberson squared to bunt. Rodney challenged him with a high-and-tight fastball, seeing if he could get a pop-up, but the ball kept tailing, and tailing, until it was tailing straight into Culberson's face. His attempt to dodge it was a millisecond too late.

Culberson writhed in pain by home plate, lying with his back on the dirt, and medical staff sprinted to him. A towel was pressed against his face to stop a rush of blood. Rodney took a few steps toward Culberson, his arms hanging at his sides, and had flashbacks to 2008, when he hit Tampa Bay catcher Shawn Riggans in the chest with a fastball. This was worse. Culberson soon left the field on a medical cart and went straight to the emregency room. Tests revealed "multiple facial fractures," and he was finished playing for the season.

But before that was determined, and even before the game resumed, Martinez was put under a hot microscope. While Culberson was still down, Martinez stepped out of the dugout for a conversation with the home-plate umpire, Tim Timmons, who ruled that Culberson had offered at the pitch. Culberson's replacement was not granted first base. He would instead face Rodney in a 0-1 count. Braves manager Brian Snitker steamed out to defend Culberson and was ejected. Social media lit up with criticisms of Martinez, saying he had no respect for Culberson in a life-threatening situation. So, in turn, Martinez's life was threatened from behind computer screens.

That left Martinez to explain himself on two fronts. His hand shook on the table while he stumbled through a postgame press conference. He stuck with Rodney, who was visibly affected by the incident, and never went to check on the veteran. He had Rodney face eight more batters after he hit Culberson, the bullpen allowed 9 runs in all, and the Nationals suffered their 8th loss in 12 games.

Martinez only offered that Rodney "seemed okay" and "kind of made little gestures to him back and forth" to signal he was fine to stay in. That's why Martinez didn't feel a mound visit was necessary. He added, on behalf of Rodney, that he knew the pitcher felt awful about what happened with Culberson. Rodney left the clubhouse before speaking with the press. Snitker was down the hall saying that, thankfully, the pitch missed Culberson's eye socket and he was awake. Then came the issue of who initiated the conversation between Martinez and Timmons.

The umpire told a pool reporter that Martinez called him over and specifically asked for an appeal on whether Culberson had swung. Timmons added that he was fully focused on Culberson's health until Martinez made the request. Timmons finished by expressing a need to make a call regardless of the circumstances: "We're always sympathetic to a guy hit in the eye. But the rules are the rules."

It all made it seem as if Martinez had little sympathy for Culberson. While addressing media after the game, Martinez didn't know about Timmons's public account. Martinez heard it later, once he was back in his office, and was enraged by how Timmons laid out the events. Martinez had trouble sleeping that night and, by the next morning, wanted to tell some of his side.

Snitker had lightened his stance and accepted that Martinez did what any manager would. But everyone still wanted answers from Martinez himself. He seemed on the verge of tears when he waded into explanations about Timmons's interview, Culberson's status, and why he didn't hook Rodney when that seemed like an obvious choice. He described the aftermath as "not the way it was portrayed to be" by Timmons. Then Martinez declined to go any further, maybe to his own detriment, leaving the rest up to ridicule and interpretation.

"The last thing I wanted to do was be a jackass," he said, a line ripe for quick counterarguments all over the internet. "They understood. It's part of the game. We're in a one-to-one game. I would think that everybody would understand. It's unfortunate. It stunk."

And that was it. An unfortunate instance that stunk and was now behind them. Martinez called Snitker to touch base and check on Culberson. The infielder was headed back to Atlanta for more tests. There was confidence he'd be okay, at least with time, and both teams readied for a series finale that was normal, just another mundane game, until Martinez disappeared in the sixth.

"I asked myself, 'Is this game really stressing me out that much?' " Martinez recalled later in September. "We had been in really tight games and the race, what happened with Culberson was unfortunate, and I just worried that it had maybe become too much. I requested that they do a stress test just to see. It seemed to make the most sense."

But the examination revealed nothing to worry about. The doctors even told Martinez that, based on the feedback, he was "as calm and normal as anybody we've seen." They scheduled a cardiac catheterization for Monday morning, to explore Martinez's chest and heart, and see what could have caused the pain. Those results were also positive—or negative, in medical speak—showing no additional issues or long-term concern.

Martinez just had to rest and recover, giving him no chance to join the Nationals in St. Louis for a midweek series against the Cardinals. Bench coach Chip Hale would manage in his absence.

Martinez protested that, too, pleading that he was fine to travel and had to get back. But, like Lessard, the doctors were not hearing it. He couldn't fly for three or four days, at a minimum, and had a new list of dietary restrictions.

Caffeine was off-limits now. So was wine, for the foreseeable future, and he was forced to substitute vegetables for red meat. For the first Cardinals game, he texted Hale a lineup from his hospital bed. He called Mike Rizzo and told the general manager he'd be back soon, even if that wasn't up to him. Martinez then watched his club lose again, continuing its subpar September, putting its playoff position in an ounce of jeopardy.

The bullpen lapsed in the seventh. This time it was Hunter Strickland, one of the deadline additions, issuing the game-winning double. He slumped by his locker in the aftermath, staring straight into it, while teammates cycled by to pat him on the back. Martinez rewound to the seventh, dissecting Strickland's decisive pitch to Marcell Ozuna, before a nurse suggested sleep.

Hale pressed the right buttons and they didn't work. Martinez knew that feeling all too well, of standing in the dugout while relievers failed, and failed, until there was nothing to do but explain why they'd entered in the first place. That was a helpless spot for a manager. And it was even worse from eight hundred miles away.

Martinez was released from the hospital on September 17, a day after the catheterization procedure, and was ordered to do nothing but rest. He had no clue how to fill all his free time. There were no scouting meetings, no pregame press conferences, no batting practice cages to stand by while his players sprayed hits into the field. There was no game, at least not for him to manage, aside from texting Hale another lineup in the early afternoon. He wanted to break out of his Navy Yard apartment, feel the fresh air, and start sprinting toward St. Louis if he had to.

But that wasn't going to happen. Instead, as a last-ditch option, Martinez turned on his iPad and clicked around. Much of his job is filled with statistics and analytical breakdowns. He could recite Howie Kendrick's splits against every reliever in the Braves' bullpen. He could, with little warning, give Doolittle's numbers against the Mets' order or explain why Wander Suero's cutter worked against certain left-handed hitters.

Martinez's brain had large filing cabinets for such information. They included a mix of data the public could access—from Baseball-Reference.com, or FanGraphs—and data from the Nationals' internal algorithms. Martinez regularly chatted with Sam Mondry-Cohen, the club's assistant GM in charge of analytics, to learn more about his work. Rizzo had promoted Mondry-Cohen and Mike DeBartolo, both analytically minded, to assistant general manager before the season. That gave them greater say in day-to-day operations, and Martinez factored their advice into each of his decisions.

The front office was old-school, constructed in Rizzo's image, but still searched for any edge in numbers. One of Martinez's defining skills was relaying the analysts' findings to players, who are often skeptical of computers and calculators. It was Jayson Werth, a longtime outfielder in Washington, who had suggested that nerds are ruining baseball. The advent of *Moneyball*, the 2003 book written by Michael Lewis about the Oakland Athletics, gave a window into how Billy Beane, the Athletics' GM, used sabermetrics to do a lot with little. The Athletics didn't spend money. They did, however, use algorithms to maximize the cheap talent on their roster.

Moneyball turned MLB into a copycat league, with everyone trying to mimic Beane's commitment to advanced analytics. But while some have embraced this, and seen it as a path to improvement, others view sabermetrics as a way to devalue talent. Why sign a proven veteran when a twenty-four-year-old fits right into a formula? Why sign an experienced reliever if, based on numbers, three low-cost ones can handle the job, and maybe even do it better? Why offer long-term deals if they've long proven to be a trap?

That battle has waged beneath baseball's surface for more than a decade now. The labor implications are significant. There are fractures between executives and players, who can feel they are being molded into machines. The modern manager has to understand the players' worries, weed them out with kid gloves, then bridge the gap between new age thinking and how the game operates on the ground level. They have to constantly weigh logic with feel. That's what most of Martinez's interactions with numbers centered on.

Yet that left little opportunity to take a basic, bird's-eye view of his team. He knew the Nationals buried a 19-31 start with the best 70-game stretch in club history. But he wanted to get inside of that surge up the standings. Now, with nothing but time to kill, was his chance to do that. Martinez stared at his iPad and wondered where to start. He began clicking through Baseball-Reference, an internet hub of statistics, and went through each of his players' pages. Then he tumbled down a tunnel of information.

A week and a half was left before the playoffs, so Martinez had about a full year's worth of data to digest. Take his twenty-year-old left fielder, Juan Soto, who was coming off one of the best teenage seasons in history. Soto had somehow improved at the plate and would soon finish with 34 homers, 110 RBI, 108 walks, and a .949 on-base-plus-slugging percentage in 150 games. He was already a superstar.

Or take Kendrick, his thirty-six-year-old utility player, who was having the best run of his career. Kendrick would end up with a .344 average, 17 homers, and 115 hits in only 370 plate appearances, all coming in scattered starts or as a pinch hitter.

They found a workload that kept Kendrick healthy *and* in a rhythm. Then take Trea Turner, his leadoff batter, who excelled at the plate, had an improving on-base percentage, but could have attempted a few more steals. Take Rendon, an MVP candidate, and Martinez marveled at his enduring ability to walk and strike out at a near-identical rate. Take the Nationals' two catchers, Yan Gomes and Kurt Suzuki, and Martinez checked if a platoon had produced the desired results.

Take Max Scherzer, Stephen Strasburg, and Patrick Corbin, scan the numbers next to their names, and Martinez had the best rotation in baseball. They ended the year ranked second, third, and fourth in strikeouts in the National League. Strasburg had 251, Scherzer had 243, and Corbin notched 238, keeping pace with his knee-buckling slider. That led Martinez to check out his bullpen, and the promising progress from Sean Doolittle, and that's what led the manager's mind elsewhere.

What Doolittle could and couldn't handle had nagged Martinez all season. He knew he'd taxed the closer early on. He also knew, as he'd explain to Doolittle, the media, or anyone who pressed him on the strategy, that it was a necessary survival tactic. And this was just one element of Martinez's delicate balancing act.

With the league's oldest roster, he had to temper aggression with heavy doses of restraint. Rizzo ran counter to recent trends by emphasizing experience and reliability over expandability and youth. The Nationals believed this was why they'd rebounded from such a bad start. Their clubhouse had lived through every up, every down, and every challenge the sport could offer.

Fernando Rodney debuted in 2002, when Soto was three years old, and now took reliever Wander Suero under his wing. Gerardo Parra, Brian Dozier, and Aníbal Sánchez had been rowdy since the early 2000s. Zimmerman was a model of measured perspective. Eaton and Scherzer were the fiery leaders, loud and chatty, while

Strasburg, Rendon, and Zimmerman were more like quiet metronomes. Martinez's challenge was to avoid injuries and burnout.

"Most teams would rather take a chance on a rotating door of young players that they can pay $550,000, and if it doesn't work out, you can option them down and try someone else out," Zimmerman explained in July. "I get that as a strategy. But I think with veterans you often know what you're going to get. And it's hard to analyze or put into an equation what their perspective can bring, helping young guys, knowing how the season goes, all of that."

When asked, right then, if a team built with older players had any drawbacks, Zimmerman rubbed his chin and squinted. He had used a twenty-minute interview to detail every benefit of Rizzo's approach, and how the Nationals were better off for it. But he could admit to a few complicating factors.

"I'm sure he would like to play a lot of these guys every day, keep pushing the starters, go all in for the win every night," Zimmerman said of Martinez. "What manager wouldn't want to play his best guys as much as possible? He's only human. His job is based on results. But a lot of us need the rest, need to be handled pretty carefully, and I know he puts a lot of thought into it. It's easy to ridicule bullpen decisions or who's in the lineup every day, but there's a lot to consider behind the scenes. I'm not envious that he's the one who has to figure that stuff out."

So there Martinez was in mid-September, trapped inside, thinking about it some more. Soto, Rendon, and Turner had yet to sit since returning from the injured list in the spring, but could handle those physical demands. Kendrick, Zimmerman, Suzuki, Cabrera, and Eaton were trickier. The pitching staff, from Scherzer to Doolittle, was an even bigger conundrum.

Martinez wanted to play Kendrick as much as possible, but Kendrick was only a year removed from a right Achilles tear, and months removed from a hamstring strain. Zimmerman's foot issues could return at any second. Suzuki, though much better at the plate than Gomes, was thirty-five and playing the sport's toughest position. Eaton never wanted to rest and was grumpiest when forced to, but Martinez felt the need to give him a breather every once in a while.

He frequently had his starters top 100 pitches to minimize the bullpen's influence on games. This was another old-school tactic. Strasburg's 209 innings would be his most since 2014. Scherzer, despite missing six weeks in the summer, averaged 6⅓ innings per start. Corbin would make 33 appearances, tying a career high, and average 103 pitches an outing. The reliable arms in the bullpen, Doolittle and Daniel Hudson, then Tanner Rainey to a lesser extent, were pitching much more than Martinez would have liked. This all made him worry about how fresh the staff, and the team, would be going into the playoffs. They were close to clinching a wild-card spot despite the Cardinals and Brewers closing in. That's why October had crept into Martinez's head.

And that's when Martinez realized he'd been thinking way too much. In some ways, the Nationals were built for the playoffs. Even if bullpens were rising in prominence, and starters had lost some postseason influence, maybe Scherzer, Strasburg, Corbin, and Sánchez could transcend that trend. Even if the best offenses were crushing homers, and trusting boom-or-bust theories, the Nationals could score in other ways.

The previous fall, eight of the ten playoff teams ranked in the top ten in total home runs, and each hit more than 200. The Nationals finished thirteenth, with 191, and missed the postseason altogether. The correlation between home runs and success was clear. This fit what traditionalists bemoaned as the rise of "three true-outcome baseball," with an alarming percentage of at bats ending with a walk, strikeout, or home run.

A prevailing theory was that a "juiced" baseball would lead to a record 6,776 homers this season, shattering the mark of 6,104 set in 2017. During All-Star festivities in July, Astros pitcher Justin Verlander, a leading Cy Young candidate, told reporters that the ball was "one hundred percent juiced" and called it a "joke." It seemed prudent to sell out on hitting as many home runs as possible. Teams could emphasize power or risk slipping behind. Any gray area had disappeared.

But while the Nationals would again finish thirteenth in total homers, this time with 231, their overall numbers improved. That showed in the advanced analytics, of all places, once months of statistics were added up. The Nationals excelled with patience, plate discipline, and contact. They got on base more than any club in the NL, only trailing the Houston Astros in that category. They made contact more than any other club in the NL, only behind the Astros in that category, too. Just one NL team, the Dodgers, swung at fewer pitches outside the strike zone. Just five teams in baseball were better at making contact at those pitches when they did swing.

It was different, in 2019, for a contending club to play this way. But maybe, Martinez figured, it was different enough to work. His internet dive went from a reflective year in review, to dissecting his entire approach, to convincing himself that, yeah, this could be the team that broke through.

The reasons were there in the second game against the Cardinals, when Corbin struck out 11, five hitters notched an RBI, and Hudson recorded the final 6 outs of a 6–2 win. Then they disappeared the next day, Martinez's third away from the team, when Washington lost and the wild-card race kept tightening.

The Cubs and Brewers were each 1½ games behind the Nationals, who dropped the series finale in St. Louis after another wacky seventh. Scars from a tough stretch showed in the clubhouse after the game. Since it was the final road trip of the season, and swinging to Miami, the rookies were required to dress up for the flight.

This year's theme was mermaids, meaning Robles, Raudy Read, Tres Barrera, Austin Voth, and Andrew Stevenson each pulled on green-sequined pants and a purple top.

Read tried to lighten the mood by strutting from the bathroom to his locker. Robles did the same and offered to take selfies with whoever liked his costume. But no one wanted to indulge. Not right now. Not after dropping two of three in St. Louis, making far too many mistakes, and, if that weren't enough, missing their manager for a whole series.

Scherzer was agitated during a short session with reporters. He lingered after it, as if he had something to say, but instead shook his head and headed for the showers. The Nationals were 83-68 and had their wild-card lead slimmed to two games. At about the same time, from a couch that needed a break, Martinez was finalizing his plans to meet them in Miami.

He didn't care that the doctors had not yet cleared him to travel. He was antsy and full of fresh ideas. He had to get back.

"Uh-oh! Uh-oh!" Gerardo Parra yelled inside the visitors' clubhouse at Marlins Park on September 20. "The man! There's the man!"

Martinez had just ducked into the room for the first time. His graying five-o'clock shadow made him look worn down. He carried a cup of hot soup to combat an oncoming cold. As players trickled into the clubhouse that Friday, turning around two corners on the way to their lockers, they could hear Martinez's voice. But they waited for him to emerge, after his catch-up meetings and the usual game-day business, before welcoming him back.

Parra's voice blended into a round of jokes from a half dozen players. Martinez leaned into a group hug, telling them he was all right. He put down his soup, freeing his hands, and pretended to throw a flurry of punches at Wander Suero. The reliever danced away and let out a high-pitched cackle. Martinez chased him for a step, springing into motion, then laughed while walking back to his office.

"Skip!" barked Scherzer, stopping Martinez midstride. The manager turned toward his ace, and they embraced in a bear hug, slapping each other's back and holding on. Between the Nationals' last game, that loss to the Cardinals, and their next one, against the Marlins that night, the Cubs suffered three losses in fifty-two hours. The Nationals were back in a comfortable playoff position. There were many reasons for relief.

"You okay?" Scherzer asked quietly. "Just a little scare?"

"No, no, no. Big scare. Big fucking scare."

"Shit, man. It's great to have you back."

"Yeah, it's good to be here." Martinez then narrowed his eyes and looked right into Scherzer's. His grip tightened on the pitcher's shoulder, and he lowered his voice to a near whisper. "Scherz . . . let's fucking go."

12

162+

September 24, 2019

When a storm didn't stop on June 17, 2019, drenching Washington for hours, September 24 became a compelling day on the schedule. A weather postponement in June for the Nationals and the Phillies led to a split doubleheader in the final week of the season. When that was decided, about three months ahead of time, it was hard to know what could be on the line. It could have been the Nationals' last shot to catch the Phillies in the playoff race. Or, if the Nationals' turnaround was a mirage, the Phillies could have used it as a final tune-up for the postseason. Or maybe both clubs would be ready to fold.

In mid-June, when the Nationals were just beginning to click, the Braves led the division, the Phillies were right behind them, and Washington was still finding itself. But by mid-September, once they arrived home from Miami for their last home stand, the Braves had won the NL East, the Nationals were close to a wild-card berth, and the Phillies were nearly eliminated.

The Phillies were supposed to be the class of a competitive division, with Bryce Harper and a list of marquee additions. But that never materialized. The end of the year was here, the Nationals and the Phillies had five games in four days, but the biggest uncertainty—

if it could even be called that—was how long it would take the Nationals to clinch. The Cubs had lost five in a row. The Brewers and the Cardinals were battling in the NL Central, with the Cardinals a bit ahead, and one of them would meet the Nationals in the wild-card game. The Nationals just had to officially get there.

When the players showed up Monday afternoon, something was off in the clubhouse. The furniture hadn't moved. The TVs showed what they always did, MLB Network and the Golf Channel, and a vanilla scent wafted off a candle in Martinez's office. That was all normal. So what was the difference? And what, players started asking each other, was with the plastic above each locker?

The staff had fastened rolls of plastic there, tying them together with twine, in anticipation of a party. They'd be undone to protect the lockers from champagne spray once the Nationals were headed to the postseason. Their magic number was down to four. They just needed a combination of their wins and Cubs losses to total that. But since that hadn't yet happened, and they could still technically lose out and miss the playoffs, the plastic wasn't welcome.

Once the Nationals beat the Phillies later on, 7–2, the magic number was slimmed to three. The Cubs were trailing in Pittsburgh. Philadelphia had nothing left. Yet Adam Eaton couldn't stop thinking about the plastic.

It had been hanging in the clubhouse, still undone, when Drew Storen addressed the media after the final loss of the Nationals' 2012 season. Storen was one out away from a save when he gave up that 2-run single to Pete Kozma to lose the NLDS. That night, carts of alcohol had to be rushed down the hallway and away from the Nationals, who were supposed to crack into it. The Cardinals did instead, soaking the visitors' clubhouse at Nationals Park, and showing why baseball players are allergic to assumption.

"I'm not happy with that. It's a distraction in my book and shouldn't have happened," Eaton told a few reporters while the room emptied out. He quipped that he wanted to "do a Chris Sale and rip every single one" of the plastic sheets down. Eaton was teammates with Sale on the White Sox when Sale used scissors to cut up a throwback jersey in the clubhouse. Sale's reasoning was that he didn't want to pitch in it, and he was sent home for his behavior. Now Eaton appeared ready to risk the same.

But it was clear the plastic wouldn't hang much longer. The September 24 doubleheader was the first opportunity to ensure that. If the Nationals swept the Phillies and the Cubs lost, the Nationals were in the wild-card game. The first step of that process went as planned, with Washington edging Philadelphia, 4–1, in the afternoon. Now one more win, and a little help from the Pirates, would do it.

The Nationals had Max Scherzer going against Aaron Nola in the nightcap. Brad Miller tagged Scherzer with a 3-run homer in the first, and a solo homer in the fourth, and it seemed as if the Nationals, down 4–1, struggling with Nola, might have to keep the Campo Viejo and Bud Light on ice.

But catcher Yan Gomes nudged the offense into gear. With Kurt Suzuki dealing with right-elbow inflammation, Gomes had started in 14 of the last 16 games. He was coming off an All-Star season with the Indians when Washington traded for him the previous November. Yet for most of the year, before Suzuki was sidelined, Gomes disappointed at the plate.

His average sagged to .198 in July. His bat looked afraid of contact. He couldn't find a rhythm without playing every day and only did, unsurprisingly, when his plate appearances increased in September. Now he ripped a solo shot off Nola in the third, his 6th homer of the month, and followed with a sacrifice fly in the next frame. That brought the Nationals within two runs. Then Trea Turner took care of the rest.

Turner was still swinging with nine fingers as the year wound down. His right index finger wouldn't totally straighten until off-season surgery. The side effects showed every once in a while. Sometimes his throws sailed high of first base. Sometimes the bat slipped out of his hand and floated into the protective netting behind home. But other than that, and the lingering pain, Turner was his usual self.

The twenty-six-year-old was a catalyst atop the Nationals' order, one of the league's best base stealers, and came up in the sixth with the bases juiced. The Phillies had two outs. They had just swapped out Nola for reliever Jared Hughes, and Turner took a first-pitch strike at the bottom of the zone. But Hughes went low again, putting a sinker on the inside edge of the plate, and Turner rocked it straight into the Phillies' bullpen.

He watched the ball for a second, maybe two, and calculated the stakes in his head. Everyone in the ballpark joined him. With 4 runs coming in, and a 2-run lead ticking onto the scoreboard, the hit could blast the Nationals, once 19-31, once left for dead, into one of ten playoff spots. Turner shot his arms out, as if he were a human airplane, and screamed. He gave a swinging high five to first-base coach Tim Bogar. Turner kept yelling—"Woo! . . . Come on! . . . Let's go!"—and the stadium matched his energy.

Matt Adams knelt on the dugout steps and slapped the dirt with two open palms, over and over, while his face turned red. Asdrúbal Cabrera, Victor Robles, and Howie Kendrick, who'd reached and scored in front of Turner, waited to embrace the shortstop. Turner then ducked out of sight and into Martinez's open arms. They wrapped each other in a bear hug, sharing that second, before Turner led teammates in a dance out of the *Remember the Titans* movie.

Dancing was the cap of home-run celebrations. But the crowd was getting louder, and louder still, until Turner emerged for a curtain call. He waved his right hand through the air, demanding more noise, and some twenty-two thousand people listened. Then they began a countdown of the final nine outs.

The first three were recorded by Hunter Strickland, who yielded a second-deck homer to Bryce Harper, his old nemesis, but allowed nothing more. The next three were handled by Javy Guerra, who was designated for assignment on July 31, was brought back a few days later, and stuck on for the entire pennant race. And the last three belonged to Hudson, the savvy deadline addition, who got a lineout, groundout, and, finally, Maikel Franco to belt one into left-center.

It looked bound for grass, like a sure double, a small hitch for the Nationals before Hudson closed it out. But Robles sprinted eighty-six feet to make the catch. His defense had often lifted Washington, especially after Harper stumbled in center throughout 2018, making this an apt exclamation point. A gold chain jangled against Robles's chest while he scaled the wall. Hudson tracked the ball to Robles's glove and, once it was secured, smacked his own mitt and started toward Gomes. The Nationals could rejoice in a win, and in taking both ends of a doubleheader, but now they had to wait.

The big screen in right field immediately flipped to the Cubs-Pirates game. Fans stayed in their seats to watch. The Nationals stayed on the field, gathering around the mound, fixing their eyes on what unfolded in Pittsburgh. The Pirates were polishing off a 9–2 win. They just needed two more outs, then one, then the Nationals were able to celebrate at last, by raising their arms and using the grass as a trampoline.

The plastic was pulled down. Buckets of alcohol were waiting inside. The players scattered in all directions, unbuttoning their jerseys, and were pulled into television and radio interviews. Martinez was called over by Alex Chappell, the team's sideline reporter with the Mid-Atlantic Sports Network. The audio of their conversation blared through a stadium that had yet to clear out.

"This team started nineteen and thirty-one," Chappell said to a rush of cheers. "What you just did was historical. How do you put these emotions into words?"

"Well, I can't put my emotions into words, I can tell you that right now, but what these guys went through all year . . ." Martinez paused and shook his head. His voice was already cracking. Tears weren't far behind.

In June, when there was still just the faint hope of a comeback, Martinez called Mark Campbell in for a meeting. Campbell, the team's director of mental conditioning, had been a full-time employee, and full-time member of Washington's traveling party, since 2017. He is available to discuss anxiety, coping mechanisms, and, through open communication, eliminate the stigma surrounding mental health issues. Martinez felt Campbell was close to the players, knew how much the bad start had weighed on them, and might have an idea of how the staff could help.

What Martinez really wanted was a slogan the club could rally around. He and Campbell put some thought into it, throwing words against the wall, and settled on "Stay in the Fight." They soon printed black T-shirts with the saying on it. The reverse side, right under the back neckline, had *162+* written in small red print. The number was for how many games the Nationals had to reverse course. The + was for right now, the night of September 24, when they had earned the sacred right to play on.

The guys wore their shirts all the time, in warm-ups, weight-room sessions, even beneath their uniforms during games. Martinez saw the phrase—*Stay in the Fight*—wherever he looked and began slipping it into press conferences. And it was all he could think of with Chappell's microphone by his chin.

". . . I'm proud of every one of them," Martinez continued, a smile growing with each word. "This is not over. We're not over. . . ."

". . . Hey! . . ."

"We're going to stay in it. We're going to stay in the fight."

Martinez took a few slow steps away. He was needed in the clubhouse. He had to think of a toast, some way to sum this all up, deliver his feelings again, this time to his players and staff, and kick-start a banger. But first he leaned back to make his promise once more.

"We're going to stay in the fight!"

The next six or so hours were a blur. A conga line was led by a whistle-blowing Aníbal Sánchez, much like the one in Chicago, except champagne leaked from front to back. A playlist jumped through Dominican rap, reggaeton, and twanging country, then continued its trip around the world. "Baby Shark" blared and Gerardo Parra led his teammates in a mega-shark-clap. Brian Dozier went viral for losing his shirt and singing every word to Pedro Capó's "Calma," a summer hit by the Puerto Rican pop star. His Latin American teammates danced around him, lost in the chorus of "Calma," vowing to hit the beach and cure their souls.

But for now, for as long as this lasted, the alcohol would have to do. There was enough beer to fill a fraternity house, or four. There was enough champagne for a wedding, or six. The floor felt like a sponge, sopping and slick, and players guided across it as if they'd gone from the bar to an ice-skating rink. They danced through puddles, danced along the plastic-lined floor, danced past 11:00 p.m., then midnight, once their wives and friends were invited in.

Scherzer pulled in Kurt Suzuki, gripped the catcher's beer-soaked neck, told him he loved him, then told him again, and promised the Nationals would play deep into October. Scherzer looked at the room, at the team he had so often lifted across four seasons, and smiled, sipping champagne, before offering an even grander prediction.

"We did it. We did it in a fucking doubleheader!" Scherzer roared into Suzuki's ear. "That means we can do anything!"

"I hear you, brother. I hear you," Suzuki said, chill amid the madness, moving his head to avoid the flying foam.

"Do you, Zuk?" Scherzer asked, even louder now, before letting out a big laugh. "We clinched, baby! Anything!"

Their minds, however foggy, were tuned to the past and the future. Rizzo praised the team for sticking together, for never resorting to anonymous quotes or selling each other out. Martinez did the same, though a little less aggressively, and kept reaching for his favorite date.

May 24 came up a lot that night. They were the ninth team to go from 12 games under .500 to the postseason. They did it because on May 24, after that four-game sweep in New York, their manager was calm enough, or crazy enough, to keep saying they could. It all circled back to that, May 24, when they were 19-31 and staring down death. Yet here they were.

"I thought we hit the bottom then," Martinez yelled over the music. Rizzo came from behind him and poured something down his neck. Martinez scrunched his shoulders and shrieked: "Is that the juice? It better be the juice!" He was drinking Welch's grape-juice cocktail because of his doctor's orders. No alcohol this close to the procedure. No questions asked. So Martinez left it to his players, his coaches, the front-office staff, scouts, ownership, analytics and the video team—anyone who had a hand, however big or small, in making this possible.

The players told Martinez it was for him, for his heart, for what he went through in September to get back to the field. Fuck that, he shot back. It was for all of them, and they were all needed if the Nationals planned to celebrate like this again.

The next afternoon, with the hangovers still fresh, Martinez lounged in his office with a few members of his staff. The beer scent still lingered in the clubhouse. There was another game to play, against the Phillies at 7:05 p.m., and Martinez had to plan. But first he was interested in some light reflection.

Martinez pushed himself off a leather couch and began digging through a desk drawer. He kept a stack of each lineup card from the entire season, commemorating the wins and losses, the wild games, the days that would otherwise be forgotten. The one he was looking for was deep in the pile. He soon fished it out, after some heavy lifting, and started reading the Nationals' batting order from a May 5 game in Philadelphia.

"Leading off, Victor Robles . . . batting second, Wilmer Difo . . . batting third, Adam Eaton . . . fourth, Kurt Suzuki . . . fifth, Brian Dozier . . ." The room buzzed with laughter. That was one of the lowest points of the Nationals' bad beginning. They were without Turner, Rendon, Soto, and Zimmerman due to injures. Rookie Jake Noll started at first, fresh off a red-eye flight from Fresno, and made an error on the first ball hit to him. It was embarrassing then, to field such a sorry team, to be scrambling so early in the year. But now it was a look at how far the Nationals had come, and all that had changed.

They were healthy by the start of June. Their rotation deepened to four solid starters once Sánchez hit a stride. The bullpen went from historically awful, to a normal level of awful, to even resembling average a few nights a week.

The Nationals finished the season on an 8-game winning streak, sweeping the Phillies through 5 games, then sweeping a 3-game series with the Indians. They knocked both clubs out of playoff contention. Martinez rested Rendon, Soto, and Turner for the first time in four months. He lined up Max Scherzer to start the wild-card game, and the streak ensured the Nationals would host it, and it was soon set that the Milwaukee Brewers were coming to town.

When the Nationals got back to the clubhouse that Sunday, after beating the Indians, Martinez walked in carrying a scuffed-up baseball. He always kept one used ball, put it in his back pocket, then had the player of the game sign it. Then he put it in a hard plastic case, wrote the date on the case in black Sharpie, and placed it on a wooden shelf next to all the others, one from each of the Nationals' victories. He went up to Joe Ross and handed it to him. A few guys patted Ross on the back and joked, "What did he do?" Ross threw 6 innings, holding the Indians to 1 run, and struck out 8. So he scribbled his name—a low-slung *J* that looks like a fishbowl, a big, crooked *R*, then squiggly cursive to finish it out—and thanked Martinez for the nod.

The manager brought it to the hallway between his office and the trainer's room, snapped the ball into its case, and set it down in order. Players often looked at the display in passing, counting how many balls were theirs, remembering that night in July, or this night in August, or when *that* happened, so long ago. Now there were 93, representing 93 regular-season wins.

They needed one more, over the Brewers in the wild-card game, and just eleven after that.

13

Juan Soto Things

October 1, 2019

While Martinez prepared for the Brewers, running every scenario through his head, reading scouting reports until his eyes hurt, he heard a knock on the frame of his office door. It was Jack McKeon, an unlit cigar dangling from his lips, with a voice Martinez would have recognized in a packed train station. Martinez had asked to see him. McKeon was used to being the one who called people in.

He waddled along the carpet and took a seat in a chair across from Martinez's desk. McKeon was eighty-eight years old, his white hair was fraying, but he was witty and whip smart as ever. That's why Rizzo had hired him as a special front-office adviser before the season. It couldn't hurt to have McKeon's sixty-plus years of experience to pick through, including his 2,042 games as a manager, 1,051 of them wins, and a World Series title with the Marlins in 2003. Plus Rizzo liked collecting drinking buddies, and McKeon always had a few cigars in the breast pocket of his short-sleeved button-down shirts.

McKeon just wasn't allowed to light them anymore. His doctor ruled against it, with his aging lungs and all, but he often chewed one to enjoy the taste. There were some things he couldn't give up.

Baseball was another. So once Martinez cued him, McKeon jumped back to October 4, 1999, to a game between the Mets and Reds at Cinergy Field in Cincinnati. McKeon was the Reds' manager. The teams finished with the same regular-season record, 96-66, and wound up tied in the wild-card standings.

That forced them into one matchup for a spot in the post-season. There wasn't a wild-card game then, since the wild-card leader advanced right to the divisional round, but this was the same concept. McKeon's club had nine innings to keep its season alive.

The difference twenty years ago is that he didn't get to reset his roster for the one-game playoff. Martinez could, with forty guys to choose from, and McKeon's advice was to prepare for any possible situation. Carry a couple pinch runners. Carry a second starter to come out of the bullpen, and a third starter in case Max Scherzer was chased early, and a fourth in case the contest went to extra innings. Maybe carry a third catcher to use in an emergency.

The end of McKeon's story was that the Reds lost, 5–0, once Al Leiter threw a complete-game shutout for the Mets. It sapped the game of much strategy or intrigue. McKeon parted with a joke, as he was known to, and told Martinez he would be just fine.

"He could have thrown his glove up there and we wouldn't have been able to hit it," McKeon said, remembering Leiter's gem, before heading to bend another ear. Martinez was way ahead of McKeon in one regard. He had pinned Scherzer as his starter a few weeks back. But he regularly described it as "all hands on deck" with his pitching staff, and hinted that Stephen Strasburg, Patrick Corbin, and Aníbal Sánchez could be available in relief against the Brewers. If the Nationals beat the Brewers and needed a starter two days later, to face the Dodgers in Game 1 of the NLDS, they would take that conundrum in stride. Their entire focus was on getting there.

The Nationals' regular-season bullpen ERA, 5.66, was the worst ever for a playoff team. That's why Martinez was ready to plug in Strasburg, Corbin, or Sánchez if an out was needed. The hope was that Scherzer would go seven strong, maybe even eight, and get the ball directly to Sean Doolittle and Daniel Hudson. But there needed to be a contingency plan—or five—should Scherzer's outing be any shorter. If he met trouble, and let the Brewers build an early lead, Washington had larger issues.

Milwaukee's bullpen was better than the 17th-best ERA in baseball. The Brewers had acquired Drew Pomeranz, the lefty Rizzo wanted at the trade deadline, and Pomeranz was lights-out during their sprint up the standings. Brent Suter came up in September and posted a 0.49 ERA in 9 appearances. Josh Hader was one of the game's best relievers, even if his 2019 numbers were a little closer to human. He still struck out 16.4 batters per 9 innings and had 37 saves. The Brewers lost MVP candidate Christian Yelich to a fractured right kneecap on September 11, yet won 12 of their last 17 games to claim the second wild-card spot. And their deep pitching staff was a main reason why.

"You know, the rosters aren't put together the same way for every team. That's what makes this fun, right?" remarked Brewers manager Craig Counsell before the wild-card game. He was asked about the contrasting approaches, how the Nationals bullpen was something they avoided, while his was a defining strength. Counsell's starter, Brandon Woodruff, had not thrown more than three innings since July 16. Scherzer was expected to do that before he was fully warmed up. "We've got different styles and different ways to attack games and to win games, and I think this game is a great example of it."

But once the wild-card game began, and both teams carried those strategies onto the field, it took seven pitches for the Nationals to hiccup. Scherzer toed the rubber to thundering cheers, his mouth fixed in a scowl, his trademark song—"Still D.R.E." by Dr. Dre—blaring over the stadium speakers. It was a reminder that, despite the list of injuries, and despite his turning thirty-five in late July, Scherzer was still capable of dominance. Yet he had only flashed that since coming off the IL in August.

Scherzer had a 4.74 ERA in his seven starts to close the regular season. He allowed three or more earned runs in four of the outings. His fastball velocity was there, hovering between the mid and high 90s, but its usual zip and tail were missing. His breaking pitches weren't as crisp. He lamented the slow process, saying he knew it was coming, but that foresight didn't make it any easier.

There were calls for Martinez to start Strasburg against the Brewers, and effectively name a new ace for the postseason. Strasburg closed the year with a 2.40 ERA in September. Yet Martinez stuck with Scherzer, citing his performance beyond the last five weeks of the year, and the trust looked misplaced once Milwaukee came to bat. Leadoff hitter Trent Grisham watched Scherzer's first two pitches sail way wide of the strike zone. Scherzer was jacked up, maybe a little too much, and his last offering of the at bat, a 99.2 mph fastball, put Grisham on with a walk.

The sellout crowd rustled with nerves. Then it went flat, like a popped balloon, once Scherzer reared back and challenged Yasmani Grandal. The Brewers' switch-hitting catcher had 17 homers off righties during the regular season. Now he had another, stalking a first-pitch fastball, sending it over right fielder Adam Eaton and off a metal bench in the Nationals' bullpen.

Grandal circled the bases with a brisk jog. Scherzer circled the mound with a shaking head. He found a slight footing after that, retiring the next three batters, but was tagged again in the top of the second. Eric Thames, another powerful lefty, lofted a curveball into the right-field seats. Scherzer watched it soar, his shoulders slumped, before straightening and asking for a new ball. He had recorded 3 outs and allowed 3 runs. The loudest part of the ballpark was behind the visitors' dugout, where a section of Brewers fans shouted against boos. The rest of the building was shocked.

Counsell began plotting his next moves. Woodruff worked a scoreless first, and a scoreless second, and got the first two hitters of the third before Trea Turner jolted Washington awake, ripping a solo shot out to left-center. A 3–0 hole felt like a moon-size crater. But a 3–1 deficit, and a morsel of momentum, was something the Nationals could work with.

Suter started stretching in the Brewers' bullpen. And while no Nationals reliever threw yet, even as Scherzer wobbled, a plan was set into motion. Erick Fedde wasn't on Washington's wild-card-game roster. But the twenty-six-year-old pitcher still sat in the bullpen, as he had for parts of the season, and chatted with the active and inactive relievers. A group of them sat up in the tunnel, in a row of folding chairs, because that's where the television is propped to a concrete wall. Fedde had been a starter for most of his career, but recent stints as a reliever, scattered throughout 2019, had taught him to track games in a different way.

Long relievers, the role Fedde had filled, have to always be ready. They have to prepare as if a starter will get hooked early, sometimes as early as the second or third inning, when the reliever will be told to warm up fast and rush to the mound. So when the top of the fifth began, and Scherzer gave up a one-out double to Thames, and it was clear Scherzer couldn't go much longer, Fedde's senses tingled. He checked when Scherzer would hit, and the righty was due up fourth in the next half. If the Nationals got a runner on, Martinez would lift Scherzer for a pinch hitter. Fedde was sure of that.

Except this was useless information to him. He was never going to pitch. But who *could* enter, and might not have calculated the situation quite yet, was Strasburg. Fedde went and told Strasburg to maybe get loose, *I mean, if you want to*, knowing Strasburg has a routine and might bristle at suggestions. But Strasburg later admitted he wasn't considering it until Fedde came over.

The Nationals did put a runner on in the bottom of the fifth, once Victor Robles singled with two outs, and Martinez did pinch-hit for Scherzer with Brian Dozier. Scherzer was finished at 77 pitches. Fedde's intuition was spot-on. Strasburg, by that point, was loosening up his arm, and entered after Washington stranded two runners on base.

Strasburg had pitched 1,457⅔ major league innings, across the regular season and playoffs, and zero began with him jogging through right field, the game already in full swing. He had not come out of the bullpen since his freshman year at San Diego State in 2007. He was often pegged as the Orchid, his toughness questioned, the narrative being that he wilted when it was hot, or he didn't get all the calls, or when anything about his rituals, down to the temperature in the cold tub, was off.

But the organization had seen a change in him this season. It wasn't just that he was healthy from start to start. He was calmer. He smiled more. He talked more in the dugout, offering advice to younger pitchers and even dancing when he hit a homer in July. Martinez only asked him to relieve because he thought Strasburg, this thirty-one-year-old version of him, could handle it. And now the manager needed Strasburg's absolute best.

The ideal spot for him, at the start of the night, was protecting a lead, whether he was bridging the gap between Scherzer and the back-end relievers, or finishing off a win himself. The spot he wound up in, by the top of the sixth, was making sure a slim deficit didn't grow.

Strasburg did that in the sixth when he yielded a leadoff single, induced a double play, and struck out Lorenzo Cain to end the frame. But the Nationals were blanked in the bottom half by the left-handed Pomeranz. Strasburg then did it again in the sev-

1

The Nationals officially introduce starter Patrick Corbin on December 7, 2018, showing they have all but moved on from free agent outfielder Bryce Harper.

2

Trea Turner breaks his right index finger after getting hit by a pitch in the Nationals' fourth game of the season. It was the first of many injuries the team dealt with in April and May.

3

Dave Martinez spent a little more than three seasons of his sixteen-year career playing for the Montreal Expos, which relocated in 2005 to become the Washington Nationals.

4

Dave Martinez looks on during a game against the Marlins on May 24, 2019, when the Nationals were 19-31 and near the bottom of the standings.

5

Max Scherzer pitches with a broken nose on June 19, 2019, throwing six scoreless innings against the Phillies at Nationals Park.

6

Gerardo Parra brings a new spirit to the Nationals with rose-tinted sunglasses and a shark bandana, an ode to his using the children's song "Baby Shark" as his walk-up music.

7 

Anthony Rendon speaks with the local media in August 2011, two months after the Nationals selected him, an infielder from Rice University, in the first round of the MLB Draft.

8

Anthony Rendon crushes a home run during the Nationals' three-game sweep of the Cubs at Wrigley Field in late August 2019. Those three wins gave Washington control atop the wild-card standings.

9

Kurt Suzuki gets a celebratory Gatorade bath from Trea Turner after hitting a walk-off three-run homer against the Mets on September 3. The Nationals completed a miracle six-run comeback to steal the win.

10

Trea Turner stares down a grand slam that helps the Nationals secure a doubleheader sweep of the Phillies on September 24 and clinch a postseason spot.

11

Juan Soto celebrates between second and third base after slapping a go-ahead single off Josh Hader in the eighth inning of the National League Wild Card Game.

12

Juan Soto is hugged and kissed by his father, Juan Jose Soto, after the Nationals beat the Brewers, 4–3, in the wild-card game. Soto's eighth-inning single stood as the winning hit.

13

Stephen Strasburg poses for a portrait after the Nationals drafted him, a starter from San Diego State University, with the first overall pick in the 2009 draft.

14

Stephen Strasburg readies for his next pitch in Game 2 of the National League Division Series (NLDS), one of the five contests he won during the postseason.

15

Max Scherzer after escaping a bases-loaded jam against the Dodgers in Game 4 of the NLDS.

16

Howie Kendrick's tenth-inning grand slam gives the Nationals a 7–3 lead over the Dodgers in Game 5 of the NLDS.

17

Aníbal Sánchez salutes Cardinals' hitter José Martínez, whose eighth-inning single spoiled Sánchez's no-hitter in Game 1 of the National League Championship Series (NLCS).

18

Mark Lerner, the club's managing principal owner, hangs by the batting cages during the NLCS. Lerner was traveling with the team for the first time since he had his left leg amputated in 2017.

19

Ryan Zimmerman directs a small "Baby Shark" clap to the dugout during Game 4 of the NLCS, while the Nationals were in the process of sweeping the Cardinals in dominant fashion.

20

Ryan Zimmerman, the first draft pick in Nationals' history, raises a fist after hitting a walk-off homer in the first game at Nationals Park in March 2008.

21

Nationals’ closer Sean Doolittle wields his blue lightsaber while the team celebrates its NLCS victory in the home clubhouse at Nationals Park.

22

Juan Soto exhibits the “Soto Shuffle” during an at bat against Astros’ starter Justin Verlander in Game 2 of the World Series.

23

Victor Robles jumps in frustration at a questionable seventh-inning strikeout call in Game 5 of the World Series. That frustration was team-wide as the Nationals squandered their series lead by losing all three home games.

24

Juan Soto carries his bat all the way to first base after homering off Justin Verlander in the fifth inning of Game 6. It was an imitation of how Houston's Alex Bregman celebrated a home run earlier that night.

25

Trea Turner lunges to touch first base while a throw passes Houston's Yuli Gurriel in the seventh inning of Game 6. Turner was called out by home-plate umpire Sam Holbrook for running too far inside the base path.

26

Dave Martinez is irate with Sam Holbrook while arguing the runner's interference call against Trea Turner in Game 6. Martinez was ejected by Holbrook, and it took three of his coaches to get him off the field.

27

Houston's George Springer looks up at the right-field foul pole after Howie Kendrick hits it with a two-run homer in the seventh inning of Game 7. The blast gave the Nationals a 3–2 lead.

28

Howie Kendrick and Adam Eaton cap Kendrick's go-ahead homer by pretending to race cars in the dugout, one of the Nationals' many celebration rituals.

 29

Daniel Hudson opens his arms to embrace Yan Gomes after striking out Houston's Michael Brantley to give the Nationals' their first World Series title—the city's first in ninety-five years.

30

Stephen Strasburg, the World Series MVP, chugs beer as it funnels through the World Series trophy.

31

Red confetti covers Constitution Avenue during the Nationals' victory parade on November 2.

32

Mike Rizzo addresses a sea of fans toward the conclusion of the parade ceremonies, with the trophy, team, and Capitol Building in the backdrop.

enth, setting Milwaukee down in order, punctuating that inning with back-to-back strikeouts. But the Nationals were again blanked in the bottom half, falling one-two-three against Pomeranz, and Counsell was about to make his final move.

Hader was up in the bullpen, his long blond hair flopped against the back of his neck. Strasburg did his part in the eighth, handling the Brewers one more time, and that was it for him. He'd thrown 34 pitches and his spot was due up second. Milwaukee couldn't touch him, his fastball or changeup, his slider or curve, but still couldn't have dreamt a better circumstance.

They were six outs from advancing, and handing Washington another playoff nightmare, with Hader on the mound. When he struck out Robles swinging, dialing a high fastball up to 98 mph, their countdown was down to five. The stadium was blanketed by a feeling of here . . . we . . . go . . . again. Then Michael A. Taylor knocked a weight off his bat, leaving it resting by the on-deck circle, and started toward the plate.

A minuscule sample size suggested using Taylor against Hader. They had matched up twice in two seasons, and Taylor had a walk and home run. But Taylor had also spent most of the summer in the minors, searching for his swing, after the Nationals sent him down to make room for a healthy Zimmerman in late June. Taylor watched the bulk of their run from a bare apartment in Harrisburg, Pennsylvania. He was back up in early September, once rosters expanded, but had fallen well out of favor.

Taylor, once a contender to start in center, was relegated to deep bench for a second straight season. It didn't matter how well he defended, or if his bat had some pop, because Soto, Robles, and Eaton were in his way. Martinez had Taylor and Andrew Stevenson as pinch runners for the wild-card game—just as McKeon had suggested—but it was hard to imagine either of them hitting. Yet here Taylor was, stepping in against Hader, tasked with brewing a rally from scratch. He took two balls to get ahead. Hader fought back, getting Taylor to miss a fastball and foul off another, before an errant slider ran the count full.

The next pitch rode high and tight, right on Taylor's hands, and Taylor reacted as if it had hit him. Home-plate umpire Mike Everitt signaled for him to take first base. Hader, figuring it was the correct call, leaned back in frustration and turned his focus to Turner. But Counsell told Everitt to wait a second. Replays showed that the pitch may have struck Taylor's bat handle, not his hand, meaning it was a foul ball and the at bat should continue.

Counsell asked for a replay review and the umpires put headsets on. A team at the league offices in New York watched the play over and over. They set the tape to slow motion. They checked every available angle. The cleanest look, shot with a camera from the first-base dugout, appeared to prove Counsell right. The bat knob rattled as if the ball hit it before anything else. The impact didn't seem softened by contact with Taylor's hand. But the call stood, triggering a wave of cheers, and Taylor stayed put on first.

That's when Soto began lingering by hitting coach Kevin Long. Three batters were still ahead of Soto—Turner; Ryan Zimmerman, who pinch-hit for Adam Eaton; and Anthony Rendon—but Soto wanted to pick Long's brain. Soto did this before at bats, in big moments or small, to plug bits of Long's knowledge into his approach. They discussed what pitchers were throwing in certain counts, what they weren't, and how certain situations, such as the numbers of outs, or runners on base, might dictate what Soto would see.

Soto had expected to face Hader before game's end. The lefty-lefty matchup, and Hader's habit of winning them, made too much sense for the Brewers. Soto had asked Jonathan Tosches, the club's direct of advance scouting, for a detailed report on Hader that afternoon. Tosches's job was digging for details, tailoring the data to each player's liking, taking video and numbers, mashing them together, and landing on sound advice. But he only had a simple direction for Soto: look for a high fastball from Hader, and don't miss it.

Now, about six hours later, Long was saying the same. Hader threw his slider about 15 percent of the time during the regular season. That number would skew for Soto, who wanted to hit heat, but he would likely see one fastball, and only one, in the upper half of the zone.

He kept chatting with Long while Turner struck out, giving Hader two outs in the inning, before Zimmerman extended it with a broken-bat single. Next Anthony Rendon walked, when it was clear Hader wanted no part of him, and it all came down to this.

The bases were loaded. Four outs separated the Nationals from one fate, the Brewers from a far better one, and, for Soto, this is all baseball ever was: a bat in his hands. A pitcher on the mound. A chance to hit, to feel the vibration through his wrists, to watch his work find grass, or kiss the sky, while he shut the rest out.

If Soto was one last hope, the last breathing reason to believe, he didn't see it that way. The packed stands could have been empty. The field could have cleared, too. The biggest at bat of his twenty-year-old life could have been anywhere, at any time, and nothing would have changed. It could have been in a minor league ballpark in Harrisburg, Pennsylvania, or Hagerstown, Maryland, or on a small field in some small Florida town. It could have been on a dusty diamond in the Dominican Republic, off a side street in Santo Domingo, with the other kids telling him to swing like Robinson Canó, like Manny Ramírez, like any of their heroes who felt so far away.

Or it could have been here, with everything on the line, with the line bending beneath the weight of history, and Soto would have still smiled, licked his lips, and shrugged. He had Josh Hader right where he wanted him.

What Juan José Soto could count on, no matter the weather, no matter what was going on, was that his son wouldn't want to go home. By day, Juan José was a salesman. But by night, when schools emptied and the neighborhood chirped with activity, he was a catcher in one of Santo Domingo's many men's baseball leagues. And he always brought little Juan along.

Juan was glued to the chain-link fence, a pint-size bat in his grasp, begging for the games to end. It's not that he didn't want to watch. He loved seeing his dad swing, squat behind the plate and sling jokes with his teammates by the bench. Juan just badly wanted to be out on the field himself. So once the final outs were tallied, and the small crowds melted into the warm Dominican evenings, Juan went to the plate, his dad went to the mound, and the five-year-old tapped hits all over the dirt. They did this until Juan José's arm tired or daylight disappeared, whatever came first, and picked up the routine at home.

The pint-size bat was replaced by a glass soda bottle. The balls were replaced by bottle caps, screwed off by Juan's tiny thumbs, and his dad lobbed them his way in the living room. Then Juan swung the bottle and sent those caps pinging off the floor and walls. His hand-eye coordination was evident, even at such a young age, and soon Juan spent every afternoon at the local park.

His idol was Canó, a Dominican native, whose left-handed swing was easy to mimic. Soto would stand upright, his knees slightly bent, and load his hands by his back ear. He then lifted his front foot a bit, same as Canó, and unleashed an upper-cut swing that made a *whooshing* sound. He sometimes did it so hard that he lost his balance. If the adults called him little Juan, his friends called him little Robbie, having seen him spend hours in that stance. Juan was imagining the homers rocketing off his bat, making that noise he heard in YouTube videos, before landing in the second deck at Yankee Stadium. Juan had no clue where that was. He just knew he wanted to play baseball in America.

But as he got older, and baby fat still hung on his frame, that felt like a too-distant dream. He wasn't tall and thin like the other teenagers. He was pudgy and average height, and had trouble standing out at a youth academy in Villa Miella, a village just north of where he grew up. So he woke up before the other fifteen-year-olds, before the beating sun, to sprint up steep hills. He drenched himself in sweat, dunking his face in any water he could find, and, once back at the fields, stayed committed to being the best hitter of the bunch.

Yet that's not what initially brought Modest Ulloa to see Soto play. Ulloa, a longtime Dominican-area scout for the Nationals, got a tip from a reliable source. There was a left-handed pitcher he had to see. The kid's fastball was in the low 80s, topping out at 82, a promising arm. The game was on a Sunday in 2014. Ulloa didn't usually work Sunday. But if there was a chance he'd find something, he showed up. That was his personal rule.

The left-handed pitcher was Soto, and he did enough to pique Ulloa's interest. Ulloa worked for Johnny DiPuglia, who had restored the Nationals' presence in the Dominican Republic, and texted his boss. Ulloa knew Soto wouldn't pitch in the second game of the afternoon. But Ulloa stayed, figuring he was already there, and was taken by a smooth center fielder. *This* kid read a line drive off the bat, glided into the gap, and caught it without the slightest hitch. Ulloa asked around the stands for the center fielder's name. That was Juan Soto, too, he was told, and the same people suggested he wait until Soto got into the batter's box.

Three hits later, across three at bats, and Soto became Ulloa's top priority. The Nationals would sign him to a $1.5 million bonus, their largest ever to an international player, and he soon moved north to West Palm Beach, Florida, leaving the Dominican Republic and his family for the first time. He was only sixteen years old. He spoke bits of English, from the lessons his mother made him take as a kid, and practiced by ordering off the menu at a nearby McDonald's. Two injuries, a fractured ankle and right-hand surgery, limited him to just 32 games in 2017. That was supposed to be his first full minor league season. He instead spent it on the bench, longing to play, and launched himself into another initiative.

The Nationals required Latin American players to study English for one hour a day, five days a week. They were each given a log-in for Rosetta Stone. A couple years back, when Soto was new at the Dominican Academy, he decided to rip through the program, staying up late to double the daily requirement. He told bilingual coaches to use only English around him. And now, since he couldn't play and had hours to kill outside his rehab, he expanded his vocabulary.

Soto's plate discipline was well beyond that expected for his age. His ability to tweak his mechanics, from one rep to another, was equally impressive. But his commitment to a second language, and aptitude to learn it, drew even more attention from the organization. He was near-fluent when he showed up for 2018, his injuries healed, and was the star of Washington's minor league camp.

Matthew LeCroy, the manager of the AA Harrisburg Senators, wondered how long Soto could last below the majors. His batting practice bordered on spectacle. His strength was ready for the show. When the Nationals needed a few extra players for an exhibition game that spring, Soto's name was on the list. His first at bat was against a left-handed pitcher and he appeared overmatched. He swung at a slider in the dirt and missed it by a foot. But when the pitcher tried it again, dialing into the same spot, Soto watched it go by. He looked at Dave Martinez in the dugout and nodded to the Nationals' manager. Martinez thought Soto would strike out, that any nineteen-year-old would, that these sliders would twist him into knots. Then that take taught him something about Soto. Then the pitcher tried another slider, this one a little higher, and the kid crushed a double off the left-center wall.

Martinez made sure to remember the name, and it wasn't long before he sat in his office, inside National Park, and heard it over the phone. Soto started that season with the low-A Hagerstown Suns. Patrick Anderson, the Suns' manager, once watched Soto face a rickety, erratic pitching machine and still have an idea of where each pitch was going. Soto hit .373, drove in 24 runs, and, after 16 games, was promoted to the high-A Potomac Nationals.

Tripp Keister, Potomac's manager, noticed his entire lineup grow more patient once Soto joined the team. But they would have to keep it going without the budding slugger. Soto hit 7 home runs in 62 at bats, and, after 15 games, he was promoted to play for LeCroy and the Senators. His batting practices in Harrisburg were like a replay of spring. LeCroy saw that Soto had a purpose with each swing, that he didn't only spray hits to left, right, and center, but through the gaps and down the lines, too.

In Washington, while Soto was finding his groove with the Senators, the Nationals lost outfielder after outfielder to the injured list. Victor Robles, their top prospect going into the year, was out with a hyperextended left elbow. Adam Eaton went down in April of 2018 with an ankle injury. Brian Goodwin and Rafael Bautista were banged up. Then Howie Kendrick ruptured his right Achilles on May 19, sidelining him for the season, and DiPuglia called Mike Rizzo.

"What's up with Howie?" DiPuglia, the club's director of international operations, asked the general manager.

"He tore his Achilles, he'll be done for the year," Rizzo answered. "What do you think we should do?"

DiPuglia had an idea. Soto had played just 8 games above high-A, a minuscule amount, but DiPuglia thought he was ready. No, he knew Soto was ready. DiPuglia held his thought, letting a few beats of silence pass, because he didn't want to sound crazy. Bryce Harper, once a far-bigger prospect, played 37 games for the Senators and 21 more AAA before he was called up at nineteen. Ken Griffey Jr., considered one of the brightest teenage talents in history, played 17 games in AA before debuting in 1989.

Promoting Soto would have been unprecedented. But Rizzo reached the decision on his own.

"We're going to bring up Juan Soto," he told DiPuglia, and that was quickly relayed to Martinez in Washington, then LeCroy during a doubleheader in Richmond, Virginia. The Senators were facing the Richmond Flying Squirrels. LeCroy got word between games and, with no time to call Soto into his office, went into the cramped visitors' clubhouse.

The manager had played eight major league seasons with the Minnesota Twins and Nationals. He would never forget his first call-up, back in 2000, and wanted Soto to remember this moment. He interrupted a paper-plate meal and told everyone to quiet down. Then he just blurted it out.

"Mr. Soto is going to the show!" LeCroy yelled, and before Soto knew what was happening, before he had a second to think, his teammates were mobbing him by his locker. He couldn't stop smiling. No one else could, either. Soto had to pack fast, throwing his cleats and gloves into a duffel bag, and was in a car headed to Washington before the second game began.

"And I knew something right then," LeCroy recalled a few months later. "Juan Soto wasn't coming back to the minor leagues."

It took 494 plate appearances for Soto to become of the best teenage hitters ever. His final statistics of 2018, at nineteen years old, were a bright spot of the Nationals' playoff-less year: 77 runs scored, 121 hits, 22 homers, 70 RBI, 79 walks against 99 strikeouts, a .292 average, and .406 on-base percentage. His 22 home runs tied Harper's total when he was nineteen and fell two short of the teenage record set by Tony Conigliaro in 1964.

Soto walked more than any other teenager in history. His three multi-homer games, including one at Yankee Stadium, were the most ever by a teenager. He became the youngest player to finish a game with three steals. There seemed to be a new milestone every day, and more reasons to list him with Hall of Famers such as Mel Ott and Ken Griffey Jr., or established stars such as Harper and Mike Trout.

In September of his rookie year, after he had slipped into a slump and shaken it off, he was asked to explain. Soto did his interviews alongside Octavio Martinez, the club's interpreter, but always answered in English. Martinez was only there if Soto needed a confusing question translated to Spanish. Soto smiled a bit at this one, thinking of how to describe his approach, and chose four words that soon splattered across the internet.

"Just Juan Soto things," he said with a grin, and a half dozen reporters rushed to punch the quote onto their Twitter feeds. It immediately went viral and was on T-shirts by the next morning. That was a Juan Soto thing in itself, a snapshot of his climbing influence, and that's what it took to get buzzed by Canó that next offseason.

He was sitting at home in Santo Domingo, wasting time, when his iPhone vibrated on his lap. Soto didn't recognize the number. He was a bit weirded out that they, whoever they were, wanted to FaceTime. But he decided to answer, anyway, swiping his thumb left, and his screen filled with Canó's smiling face.

Soto didn't know what to say. The two had never met before. The voice saying "Heeeeey, Juan!" was familiar from interviews Soto studied as a kid. Now he had so many questions to ask. The first was why Robinson Canó, a Dominican legend, was calling him, Juan Soto, who had fewer than 500 plate appearances to his name?

A friend of Canó's and Soto's had reached out to Canó for a

book she was writing on Dominican baseball. She mentioned to Canó that he was Soto's favorite player as a kid. So Canó asked for Soto's number, dialed it on that quiet January afternoon, and did most of the talking. Canó had just been traded from Seattle to the Mets, and told Soto to reach out if he ever needed anything. Canó told him they would catch up more on Opening Day. Canó told him it would get harder, that pitchers would form a plan, that he was on everyone's radar after what he did as a rookie.

Then Canó told Soto to keep being himself. There might be people who would try to temper his enthusiasm. They might object to his routine at the plate, the way he kicked around dirt and wagged his hips between pitches, a small bit of theater that Dave Martinez coined "the Soto shuffle." They might try to strip him of his swagger, of his Dominican flair, because baseball doesn't like it when young Latin players step out of line. But you have to shut them out, Canó explained, and stick to what got you here. Or else you wouldn't be Juan Soto anymore.

"*Get the high fastball. Don't miss it. Get the high fastball. Don't miss it. Get the . . .*"

Then he got it and missed it. Hader went straight at Soto's sweet spot, with a hands-high fastball in the middle of the plate, but Soto fouled it straight back into the screen behind home. He grimaced. That was the pitch he had to crush.

But that's when Canó's advice kicked in. When Hader next came with a slider, and it was maybe two feet outside, Soto sprang into the most theatrical "Soto shuffle" of his young career. He did two sweeps with his feet, pushing the dirt around, staring at Hader with a look of mock surprise. Soto's eyebrows were raised. His shoulders were, too. He used his right hand to grab his crotch, grinned while doing so, and kept his gaze fixed on Hader. Then Soto wiggled his shoulders, one after the other, and settle back into the box.

Hader's slider was all over the place. Soto knew then, that with no option to walk him, he would see more fastballs in the strike zone. He just didn't think Hader would go back to the same as his first pitch. But he did, and Soto roped a line drive into right, and it found grass, in front of a charging Grisham, to start a carousel around the bases.

Dave Jageler, calling the game for the Nationals' radio network, had never heard such a crowd roar inside his headset. But it was quickly followed by another, an even louder one, sounding as if his ears were inside a crashing wave. The first was for the hit, a line-drive single, when it was clear that both Taylor and Stevenson would score and tie the game. The second, though, came after the ball skipped off the field, shot in the opposite direction from where Grisham was moving, nicked his glove, and rolled toward the wall.

Washington had seen a few bounces like this. The first was in 1924, in the twelfth inning of the World Series, when Earl McNeely's chopper hit a rock, leaped over the head of Giants third baseman Freddie Lindstrom, and the Washington Senators won it all. But then baseball left town, the summers went quiet, and fate changed. The final bounce in 2012, after Drew Storen had allowed 4 ninth-inning runs to the Cardinals, was Pete Kozma's go-ahead single finding room in front of Jayson Werth. The critical bounce of 2016 was a slider splitting catcher Matt Wieters's legs and going all the way to the backstop, prolonging a Cubs rally that did Washington in. Javier Báez's swing hit Wieters in the mask, and by rule, Báez should have been out to end the inning. But home-plate umpire Jerry Layne missed the call, Wieters soon bounced a pickoff attempt into right, and the Nationals never recovered.

Bounces were everywhere. They just never went Washington's way.

Now tell that to Grisham, who had that ball dart away from him, as if some baseball god, maybe tired of watching Washington wail, stuck a finger out of the ground and flicked it into forever. Tell that to Hader, who jogged off the mound, the loneliest place in an exploding ballpark, and watched Taylor score, then Stevenson score, then Rendon get waved around third toward home. Then tell that to Soto, who passed second, got caught in a rundown along the well-traveled dirt, and was celebrating before Mike Moustakas tagged him out.

Soto ripped off his helmet, hopped from the dirt to infield grass, and smacked his chest. He screamed, "Let's go!" while the field cleared and he was the only player left on it. Fans hugged, howled, and heaved beers into the air, dotting the night with small clouds of foam. Soto caught his breath and was handed his hat and glove. The Nationals led, 4–3, and needed three outs to advance.

The bullpen, meanwhile, was frantic with activity. Because Soto was out on the play, there were no at bats between the go-ahead hit and top of the ninth. Doolittle was prepared to enter from the third inning on. But he was glued to Soto's single, watching it from that metal bench, untill Javy Guerra shook his shoulders and yelled, "Dude! Warm up!" The call was already in for Hudson, who, upon hearing the Nationals were ahead, tossed a ball over his shoulder and stomped toward the bullpen door. There was no time for his usual amount of warm-up pitches.

Hudson struck out Thames swinging. Lorenzo Cain then singled, putting the tying run on base, and forced the crowd to consider disaster. But Orlando Arcia popped out to catcher Kurt Suzuki, keeping Cain where he was, and Ben Gamel took one pitch before driving a high fastball to center. It sent Robles backward, and Hudson's eyes widened. Yet Robles had a beat on the liner, settled under it a few steps from the fence, and a win—the Nationals' first ever in an elimination game—nestled into the webbing of his leather mitt.

Soto sprinted in from left, screaming again, but stopped short of the dirt. He knelt down to the field, the one that had finally cooperated, and pounded his chest before joining a mosh pit by the mound. Once he'd slipped on a wild-card-champions T-shirt, and embraced teammate after teammate, Soto found his mother, Belkis Pacheco, and wrapped her in a hug. They rocked back and forth, tangled in the madness, until Juan José Soto sneaked behind his son.

He took his son's shoulders and pulled him backward. They tumbled onto the grass, as if they were wrestling on the living-room carpet, and Soto couldn't stop laughing. His younger brother, Eilan, joined them and cameras rushed around, snapping photos of the proud father and his prodigal son.

It was a week since their last celebration, and the Nationals brought it up a notch. The music felt louder. The alcohol reached every crevice of the room. Sean Doolittle, a noted *Star Wars* fan, walked around holding a blue lightsaber. Turner put on an old-school NC State football helmet and filled his face with a pair of ski goggles. He sipped tequila straight out of the bottle. When he went to the interview room, and sat down next to Soto, the moderator cracked, "I think that's Trea Turner on the right." Turner deadpanned, his face stiff, "You don't know that."

"I mean, most of the guys, we know he likes to throw high heaters, and not much sliders," Soto explained when pressed on his approach to facing Hader. "He just throws a lot of heaters. We try to make him throw strikes. We just make sure he throws strikes. And then when they come up, like I say, I know he's going to try to attack me."

The drinks kept flowing in the clubhouse. Doolittle pulled Scherzer close and, with reggaeton thumping, yelled, "We fucking did it again!" Strasburg fished a handful of Bud Lights from a bucket and passed them out. Dozier sang "Calma" again, and his shirt was off, and Yan Gomes joined him to make it a clothing-optional party. Soto stood on the edges, a smile planted between his cheeks, and went digging through a recycling bin. His teammates were calling him over to dance. He didn't want to be empty-handed and seem out of place, so he found an empty Campo Viejo champagne bottle and carried it into the mix.

Call it a Juan Soto thing. His twenty-first birthday was still twenty-four days away.

14

Questionable Decisions

October 3, 2019

The music was a bit quieter, the evening air a bit cooled, and the Nationals had a chance, finally, to take a few long breaths and look around. They'd clinched a spot in the National League Division Series. They'd drank as if they were at a bachelor party. They'd slept for a few hours, if that, before boarding a cross-country flight to Los Angeles. Then they'd landed in the late afternoon, dropped their stuff at the team hotel in Pasadena, and drove west on the 110 for a workout at Dodger Stadium.

It was easy, in the moments after the wild-card victory, then in the daze of restless travel, to wonder if it had all been a dream. But the Nationals were really here. The ballpark was empty aside from them, a growing pack of reporters, and staff readying for Game 1 of the NLDS on Thursday night. The bright lights were flicked on, shading the rolling hills beyond center into the backdrop. Washington took batting practice at half-speed, knocking hits off the dirt and grass, while a member of its front office watched from the dugout.

"What happened the other night, Soto, Hader, it was awesome. Really awesome. But I feel like the narrative's a bit off," he explained. "I've seen words like *exorcism* and *redemption* thrown around because it seems like we can never win that big game. But now we're back to where we've always gotten to. We need to win this series to act like we've gotten over the hump."

In their way was only the NL's best team, and one of the league's model franchises. The Dodgers went 106-56 in the regular season and wrapped up their division on September 10. September was their best month of the year, with a .750 winning percentage, and they now aimed to roll into a third consecutive World Series appearance. Except this time they planned to win their first title since 1988, and saw Washington as a small speed bump in their path.

The Dodgers' lineup was loaded, from MVP candidate Cody Bellinger, to the versatile Justin Turner, to a cast of dangerous lefties in Max Muncy, Joc Pederson, Corey Seager, and rookie Gavin Lux. Their bullpen, though a bit shaky throughout the year, had closer Kenley Jansen and two reliable setup men in Pedro Báez and Kenta Maeda. They turned promising young starters into additional relief options for the postseason. And their rotation was stacked with Clayton Kershaw, Walker Buehler, and Hyun-Jin Ryu, putting starting pitching at the center of the series.

By October, Kershaw, Buehler, and Ryu had shown some cracks. Ryu was once on a Cy Young Award pace, with a 1.64 ERA in mid-August, but then gave up 7 earned runs in back-to-back outings. Buehler, a budding star at twenty-five, was still searching for consistency. Then there was Kershaw, once the most dominant pitcher of this generation, who no longer had the velocity or curveball of his prime.

But even if they had slipped a bit, it was a rare rotation that could match up with Scherzer, Strasburg, and Patrick Corbin. And with the league de-emphasizing starting pitching, especially in the postseason, each club carried tints of the past.

The Red Sox had edged the Dodgers in the previous World Series by utilizing starters out of the bullpen. The Yankees and Rays, two

AL playoff teams, were often using multi-inning relievers in place of starters. Pitching roles were fluid as ever. Yet the Nationals and the Dodgers believed, down to their cores, that success was built on a strong rotation.

The Game 1 matchup was Buehler against Corbin, since both Scherzer and Strasburg had been used to beat the Brewers. Buehler, despite his age, already had four postseason starts. That included blanking the Red Sox for 7 innings, allowing 2 hits and striking out 7, in Game 3 of the 2018 World Series. Dodgers manager Dave Roberts had his pick of Buehler, Kershaw, and Ryu for the series opener, and went with Buehler so he could be ready for a potential do-or-die Game 5.

Yet Corbin had little to no experience in high-pressure games. When asked for the biggest start of his life before this one, his flat response—"I don't know, I've never pitched in the playoffs"—was telling. Corbin had never lost in a two-year high school career, going 14-0, but Cicero–North Syracuse couldn't solve the section playoffs. When Corbin was a junior, he was saved for what was expected to be a tough semifinals opponent. But the team was upset in the quarters and he didn't get to pitch. The next year, Corbin's last shot at a state championship, they used him in the quarters to ensure a spot in the semis. He won, the Northstars lost in the next round, and he still never got to pitch for a title.

"It was never his fault," recalled Jim Ilardi, one of Corbin's high school coaches. "He just would be ready to pitch in the next game and we'd lose. We'd wind up having our best guy on the bench. It's funny how it seemed to always work out that way."

Then in 2017, when Corbin was with the Diamondbacks, he was slated to face the Dodgers in Game 4 of the NLDS. But the Dodgers swept Arizona and he was left watching three losses from the dugout. He was, in theory, able to handle heightened stakes.

He was maybe even primed to ignore them. Coaches often describe him as having "no pulse," meaning his energy and nerves stay steady in all situations. He just didn't have a chance to prove it until now.

But his first attempt did not go well. Corbin started the game by walking leadoff batter A. J. Pollock on six pitches, none of which were his top-rate slider. He struck out the next two hitters, seeming to find a rhythm, but walked the next three to bring in a run. Corbin tried to bait the Dodgers with sliders below the zone. Yet most of them were so far outside, or so far in front of the plate, that it was easy to let them pass.

Corbin wiggled out of the first inning at 31 pitches. He settled in from there, even if his pitch count kept climbing, but the offense couldn't touch Buehler. The Nationals left the bases loaded in the fourth when Asdrúbal Cabrera hit a weak grounder in front of the mound. Buehler otherwise carved through Washington with his high-90s fastball and roller-coaster curve. He struck out 8 batters in 6 scoreless innings. When he exited, the Dodgers had a 2–0 lead after Howie Kendrick's second error led to a run.

Despite Corbin's shakiness, and a total offensive lapse, the Dodgers had only scored on blatant mistakes. That was a slight cause for comfort as the late innings arrived. Washington was in striking distance and had gotten to the Dodgers' bullpen. The problem, though, was that Martinez was forced to roll out his.

The Nationals put seven relievers on their NLDS roster: Sean Doolittle, Daniel Hudson, Tanner Rainey, Wander Suero, Fernando Rodney, Hunter Strickland, and Austin Voth. Only two of them, Doolittle and Hudson, had shown even a semblance of reliability during the regular season. With Doolittle being the only lefty and needed for high-leverage spots, the Dodgers' left-handed hitters presented a real challenge for the middle and late innings. Roenis Elías had reinjured his hamstring in September and wasn't ready to be activated. This was the reality of bringing a bad bullpen into the postseason.

And even with such thin personnel, Martinez's bullpen management was viewed as a disadvantage heading into the series. The consensus was that Dave Roberts, known as one of the league's more cerebral managers, gave Los Angeles an edge in the dugout. Martinez's first moves of the NLDS did little to shift that opinion.

He turned to Tanner Rainey in the seventh, and Rainey got one out before yielding a walk and single. That led Martinez to insert Rodney, the league's oldest player, who struck out Bellinger, walked Chris Taylor, then gave up an RBI single to Muncy. That stretched the Dodgers' lead to three, and it stretched even further when Strickland gave up two homers in the eighth.

Lux hit the first. Pederson wacked the second. All three of the Dodgers' run-scoring hits were by left-handed batters against right-handed pitchers. The Nationals' lack of a second lefty reliever was both apparent and costly. They soon limped out of a lopsided loss, 6–0, and Martinez was grilled for punting away a close game. Why didn't he turn to Hudson or Doolittle when Washington trailed by only two runs in the seventh? Why didn't he give his offense an opportunity to come back? Wasn't it exactly that, charging from behind, that got his club here in the first place?

"I liked the matchup with Rodney, with the changeups on Bellinger, he got him out," Martinez reasoned, half-heartedly, in his postgame press conference. "The big at bat was Taylor. He had him 0-2, went 0-2, 4-2, and then walked him. And then again I liked the matchup with the changeups on the lefties at that particular moment. He had two outs."

Rodney just couldn't get a third without permitting damage. That's what Martinez couldn't hide from. The Nationals looked entirely overmatched, and the bullpen was jolted around like a rag doll, and the shine of the wild-card victory had worn all the way off. But it was that game, the win against the Brewers, that lent important context to Martinez's questionable decisions.

He had already dropped a few clues of how he might deploy his staff in this series. That Wednesday, before the Nationals were shoved into a hole, Martinez slipped this into an answer on possibly using starters as relievers: "These are all one-game playoffs. They all are. It's important if we're winning, to win. To get ahead, stay ahead. So we're going to use all options necessary to win."

All options necessary hinted at what the Nationals had discussed for the last month. They had a plan, a way to mask their glaring weakness, and everyone was on board. Martinez didn't feel that Game 1 was the right time to roll it out. But Game 2, with Strasburg on the mound, with him starting three days after throwing 34 pitches, seemed like the perfect time.

15

"What does comfortable mean?"

October 4, 2019

Some of the most important games in Nationals history unfolded, in anonymity, in the final weeks of September 2008. The first year at Nationals Park was rolling to a quiet halt. The Nationals were terrible, once again, and nearing their worst finish since arriving in DC. But every loss mattered in the final week of that season. At least they did for the Nationals, Padres, and Mariners.

On September 18, a regular Thursday, the Nationals were 58-95. So were the Padres. The Mariners were 57-95, having played one fewer game, and each team had three series left. It was a dead heat for the worst record in baseball. The winner of it—or, uh, the loser—would secure the first pick in next June's draft. The Nationals welcomed the Padres for three games, the Padres won them all, and that sunk their chances for thirtieth place. The field was narrowed to the Nationals and Mariners.

The Nationals went win, loss, loss, loss, loss, in their final five games, ending the year by getting swept by the Phillies. The Mariners, on the other hand, swept the Athletics in Seattle, playing hard until the season's last out. So when the dust settled on September 28, and a playoff field took shape, the bottom of the league standings looked like this:

San Diego Padres–63-99

Seattle Mariners–61-101

Washington Nationals–59-102

Washington locked up the No. 1 selection for the 2009 draft. There was a pitcher at San Diego State whom everyone was already talking about. Videos of him looked like a teenager playing Wiffle ball with kids. His fastball touched triple digits. His curveball could have been a physics lesson.

Stephen Strasburg was a phenomenon.

A year later, in the midst of another losing season, he was picked by Washington and treated as such. A group of reporters showed up in Viera, Florida, to watch and ask him about his first workout. *Sports Illustrated* had sent a reporter to profile him before the draft, then sent the reporter again to dig for more details. The *Washington Post* even assigned one of its top writers to follow him for a series titled "A Star Is Born."

When he joined the Harrisburg Senators, for a short stint in AA, each start drew a massive crowd. Adults hounded him for autographs. The strength coach's office was turned into Strasburg's mail room, and he was in there most afternoons, sitting alone, signing balls and photos before he had to pitch. All the excitement blunted his own, even though he was 21 years old, still a kid, supposed to be enamored of people being enamored of him. Instead, jaded by premature stardom, he was skeptical of any stranger who got too close.

His 2010 debut nudged Washington into the national spotlight, with his 14 strikeouts aired live on ESPN. Ask anyone in the organization, past or present, and they'll say that night signaled the Nationals' arrival. They had their ace. He was no longer a concept, an idea, just a name whizzing through the headlines and minor leagues. But Strasburg felt the price of providing hope.

He was on the cover of *Sports Illustrated* just two starts into his rookie year. The headline read, "National Treasure: Two Games . . . Two Wins . . . 22 Strikeouts . . . Stephen Strasburg (and his 100-mph fastball)." Mid-Atlantic Sports Network, the Nationals' TV rights holders, reported that ratings for Strasburg's debut were three times higher than their previous top-rated broadcast. Four DC restaurants began selling Strasburgers. The first lines of *SI*'s cover story were about fans lining up four or five deep to watch one of Strasburg's pregame bullpen sessions. Not in Washington. In Cleveland.

Strasburg was always shy and reserved. But friends and teammates believe that period of his career, and the speed dating with reporters, put up even more walls. He regularly turned down interviews. He walked through the clubhouse without making eye contact with those he wasn't familiar with. He wasn't approachable, and maybe he liked it that way, because it left him to focus on a craft that few understood. And he preferred that, too.

In 2012, after Strasburg made his first All-Star game, the Nationals shut him down. He'd pitched 159⅓ innings by early September, and his camp didn't want him going past 160. That the Nationals were in a pennant race, their first since returning to Washington, made it a massive deal with the local and national media. That they lost in the NLDS that October, falling to the Cardinals in five games, made it even bigger.

One local columnist wrote that the shutdown cost the Nationals a title shot. He insinuated, not so subtly, that the decision may haunt them forever. When manager Davey Johnson was on his way out the next fall, he told local radio hosts that the Nationals "probably" would have won the 2012 World Series if Strasburg was healthy and pitching down the stretch. Donald Trump, then just a prominent real estate mogul, chimed in on Twitter, writing, "When Strasburg leaves in a couple of years under free agency Washington will say 'what were we doing.' "

The Shutdown followed Strasburg. His shell got harder.

"I don't know if I'm ever going to accept it, to be honest," Strasburg told reporters after his last outing of that season. "You don't grow up dreaming of playing in the big leagues to get shut down when the games start to matter."

Everything, it seemed, was about why he wasn't pitching. *How* he pitched became a secondary story. Strasburg had a hand in that, since he was averse to discussing his process, his workout routine, or pitch grips. But each success—three All-Star appearances, a league-leading 242 strikeouts in 2014, a 15-4 record in back-to-back years—was balanced by a setback.

Injuries kept him below 25 starts in both 2015 and 2016. Early in his career, Strasburg dealt with shoulder inflammation and a torn ulnar collateral ligament that required Tommy John surgery. The issues in 2015 were upper-back and oblique strains. In 2016 it was another upper-back strain and elbow soreness. Then his body failed again in 2018, limiting him to 130 innings across 22 outings. Shoulder inflammation and a cervical impingement in his neck led to his fewest starts in seven seasons. And when he came off the injured list in late August, throwing four frames against the Phillies, there was an obvious concern: His velocity had dropped to the lower 90s.

The Nationals promised it would return, saying he was easing back to full strength. Strasburg stuck to that company line. Yet as he pitched, and that company line was repeated, the truth emerged. Strasburg could top out at 94 mph, maybe 95, but the 97s, 98s, and 99s were gone. Martinez stressed that Strasburg would take this development and become a better pitcher. His location would sharpen. His curveball and changeup, both devastating pitches, would be used more. He just had to adapt.

"There comes a point in everybody's career where you don't have the fastball that you can just blow by guys all the time," Strasburg would later say. "You have to learn how to pitch a little bit more."

September 26, 2018, brought the final home game of a trying season. There was a lightness in the clubhouse, as if a weight had been lifted, once a playoff-less year was accepted reality. Players chatted while stuffing clothes into cardboard boxes. Bryce Harper got there early, put on his full uniform for batting practice, and answered questions about possibly playing in Washington with the Nationals for the last time. He cracked jokes about an approaching storm. It was good for a few cheap laughs.

Yet Strasburg didn't join any conversations. An auction was upcoming, and the promotions team needed him to sign a few things. They handed him a glove, a few baseballs, then a small stack of old *Sports Illustrated* issues with him on the cover. There was the one from 2010, his motion frozen before he lets go of the ball, the teaser using his fastball velocity—100!—to pull readers in. The next was from April 1, 2013, the magazine's MLB preview, with Strasburg's blue eyes staring into a cracked pane of glass. The idea was that he'd shattered it, and could shatter something more, his right arm capable of shifting the Nationals' luck. The headline was "MR. OCTOBER: Stephen Strasburg . . . The Nationals Will Break Through and Win the World Series."

But they didn't. It was another hollow promise. Strasburg took a blue Sharpie and scribbled his name onto one copy, then a second, then a third that balanced on his knee. He formed a neat stack and set it on the floor. Then he looked at it, at what he was supposed to be, before leaving those reminders to be picked up.

Then he buried those reminders in the Nationals Park weight room that next winter. He melted them with sweat that dripped onto the rubber mats. Martinez would be in his office, figuring the clubhouse was empty, until Strasburg passed by and, without a word, gave a slight wave. Strasburg had a reshaped regimen with the Nationals' strength staff. It put him in peak shape once February 2019 rolled around.

Strasburg is always looser in the spring, when the stakes can be measured by teaspoons. But the flashes of a different guy were immediate. After his second-to-last exhibition start, a night game on March 17, Strasburg spoke with a handful of reporters by his locker in West Palm Beach. He appeared relaxed. He smiled while saying he was the "longest-tenured pitcher in the NL East." He made some more jokes about being old, the ripe age of thirty, and offered minor details about his fastball and slider.

"Stephen!" said Thomas Boswell, a longtime *Washington Post* columnist, once the interview wound down. "Was that that hard?" The group lingered, waiting to see if Strasburg would ignore Boswell or bristle at the backhanded praise. But Strasburg's cheeks turned pink and he laughed. He picked humility over irritation, and his manager and teammates noticed.

Yet it wasn't until July 18 that the shell slipped off. Strasburg ripped a 3-run homer at SunTrust Park in Atlanta, a laser out to left, and had a sinking thought while rounding the bases: he was going to have to dance. It was cardinal law by then anyone who homered had to break it down in the Nationals' dugout. Strasburg hadn't danced since his wedding, and he couldn't think of any moves. So he bounced from one foot to another, as if his legs were made of pogo sticks, and wagged his arms like a timid middle schooler.

"To be honest, it was pretty nerve-racking," Strasburg said, red-faced and smiling, after dancing in Atlanta. He was the first pitcher in franchise history to slap two hits in one inning. He was also the first pitcher since 2014 to record 5 RBI in the same game. "I didn't really have anything. I'm not a big dancer to begin with."

Next came the smallest of "Baby Shark" claps, just a touch of two fingers, following a late-summer single. After that came a surprising ending to his starts. Strasburg had once made a habit of disappearing when pulled from outings. A short talk with Martinez was standard. He'd pass out high fives and fist bumps, keeping his eyes in the distance, then duck into the trainer's room for a cool-down routine.

But Gerardo Parra and Aníbal Sánchez had a fresh idea. If Strasburg pitched well, and he often had, the two Venezuelans greeted him with a group hug. They rested their heads on Strasburg's shoulders, nestling in, and he stood as if stuck in a straitjacket. Scherzer joined in on one to smother Strasburg in public affection. Strasburg admitted he wasn't much of a hugger. Yet he wasn't much of a dancer, either, and decided to lean in.

In the afternoon before Game 1 of the NLDS, before the Nationals lost, 6–1, and their bullpen was exposed, Strasburg had a press conference at Dodger Stadium. This was required of the next day's starter, otherwise Strasburg would not have been there, a microphone in his face, a whole room hanging on whatever scraps of himself he may share.

"Going back to kind of the long view . . . ," a reporter started, and this was when Strasburg became his most guarded, grisly self. He glanced in the reporter's direction before dropping his eyes into his lap. "When you were drafted, kind of impossible expectations were placed upon you. How would you say you have dealt with those expectations over your career and managed them, if you will?"

A beat of silence passed. Strasburg's mouth turned into a strained grimace, and he dipped one toe into the past: "Yeah, you realize that the expectations are always going to be there, and I think it's pretty obvious that the expectations that people had for me from early on were a little insane. And I think you just become more comfortable with yourself, more comfortable with the results, and you set yourself to your own standards, and those are always going to be more important than what others think you should be doing."

Another reporter sensed something there, maybe a chance to peel back a layer and see what Strasburg might reveal.

"For you, what does comfortable mean? What does that incorporate?"

"What does comfortable mean?" Strasburg asked, and it was unclear if he was buying time or wondering aloud. In the last decade, ever since the Nationals had picked him first overall, comfortable felt like some distant dream. But now his definition of it had changed.

Once Game 2 began on October 4, and the offense gave Strasburg a first-inning lead, this is what domination looked like: Strasburg striking out two in the first, one in the second, two in the third, one in the fourth, and three more in the fifth. He leaned on his curveball, throwing it 34 times, and balanced that with 22 sinkers, 18 changeups, and 11 four-seam fastballs. The Dodgers were handcuffed by the off-speed-heavy approach. Strasburg carried a perfect game into the fifth, retiring the first 14 batters he faced, until catcher Will Smith poked a two-out single. Strasburg then struck out the next hitter with a changeup in the zone.

The Dodgers would swing and miss at 20 of Strasburg's 85 pitches. They looked at 15 more strikes. So with Strasburg cruising, and the Nationals ahead, 3–0, Martinez went and activated his all-in approach.

Sean Doolittle heard the voice before he could see whom it belonged to. He was stretching inside the tunnel at Dodger Stadium, as he normally does in the fifth inning, and listened to reactions from the home crowd. The noise was minimal. He expected to enter with the score close. But he was then interrupted by a question that cut through the darkness and grabbed his ears. He whipped around to answer, letting an exercise band dangle by his hip, and watched Max Scherzer emerge through a dark hallway running beneath the seats.

"Hey!" Scherzer barked at Doolittle. "How do I get to the bullpen?"

Doolittle's mouth opened but nothing came out of it. He just pointed, guiding Scherzer into a packed Dodger Stadium, and that's how the next phase began. After he returned to the club in September, Martinez called in Scherzer, Strasburg, and Corbin for individual meetings. The Nationals had a way to turn their awful bullpen into a nonissue. It was a little wacky, and a definite risk, but Martinez had gathered intel from pitching coach Paul Menhart, the analytics staff, then discussed the final touches with Rizzo.

They would avoid their own bullpen by hardly using it. That was the master plan.

To execute it, they needed Scherzer, Strasburg, and Corbin to take on even heavier workloads. Starters typically have a bullpen day between outings. The idea was that, in the playoffs, they would skip them in favor of high-leverage relief appearances. Doolittle and Daniel Hudson were viable options. But it was unthinkable to put in anyone else, shown throughout the regular season, then in Game 1 of this series. The pitchers sat with Martinez in mid-September to hear the specifics. Corbin shrugged and told Martinez he was up for whatever. Scherzer's face lit up at the thought of pitching more.

Strasburg was the one Martinez worried about. It wasn't that Martinez expected him to turn down the ball. He just knew that Strasburg was rigid in his routines. Strasburg preferred pitching every fifth day. He followed a schedule, and his schedule had a schedule, and there was something off-putting, maybe even scary, about adjusting on the fly.

Yet that was the old Strasburg. The new Strasburg threw three innings out of the bullpen in the wild-card game. The new Strasburg turned around three days later to start Game 1 in LA. That let Scherzer find Martinez before Game 2 and plead for an inning of relief. One person who witnessed the conversation says that "Max basically begged." And now he was in the bullpen, collapsed into a white folding chair, chatting with the other relievers while Strasburg entered the sixth.

Strasburg found a bit of trouble in the inning, once Matt Beaty singled, Joc Pederson doubled, and Justin Turner scored Beaty with a sacrifice fly. But that was all they managed off Strasburg. He got A.J. Pollock to smack a liner straight into his glove, the final out of a six-inning gem, and Martinez had the exact matchups he wanted.

Martinez first plugged in Doolittle to face Bellinger, Muncy, Smith, and Seager in the seventh. Since Bellinger, Muncy, and Seager are lefties, Doolittle had the matchup edge. He struck out Bellinger with a 96 mph fastball. He allowed a towering homer to Muncy, denting the Nationals' advantage to one run, then recovered to set down Smith and Seager with seven pitches. Doolittle shook his head after Seager popped out. Muncy's blast was rattling through it. But Doolittle had still delivered a lead to the next reliever, who had little experiences in spots like this.

Once the Nationals restored a 2-run cushion, Scherzer threw his last warm-up pitch and tapped gloves with bullpen catcher Octavio Martinez. Reliever Aaron Barrett later described Scherzer as a "mad dog in a cage" while waiting to enter. Javy Guerra avoided Scherzer's piercing stare. Doolittle wasn't sure if the Nationals would use Scherzer at all, since Strasburg had gone six and Doolittle got the first call out of the bullpen. But he peaked out to right during the seventh, after he'd recorded the second out of the frame, and caught a glimpse of Scherzer.

"I had a small window where I could see who was warming," Doolittle recalled. "It was him. I thought, 'Oh, let's fucking go.' "

Scherzer was humming right away. He started behind the rubber, arms hanging at his sides, and fixed that glare on catcher Kurt Suzuki. Scherzer's lips lifted at the corner of his mouth, as if he were about to unlock his jaws and growl. His first pitch, a waist-high fastball, registered at 98.1 mph. Its average velocity was 94.9. He struck out Gavin Lux on seven pitches, and Lux finished the at bat on one knee. A back-foot cutter left him collapsed into the dirt.

Next came a four-pitch strikeout of Chris Taylor, ending with a slider that corkscrewed out of the zone. Then Scherzer showcased his arsenal against Joc Pederson. He painted the outside edge of the plate with a curveball. He got Pederson to swing through a fastball that touched 99 mph. Finally, he went with a low cutter that Pederson thought he could hit. But his bat didn't even flirt with it. The result was three pitches, three strikes, and three outs that ticked by like a metronome set to warp speed.

Scherzer didn't celebrate while Pederson dropped his gear to the field. He didn't scream, or even pump a fist. He just stalked to the dugout, slapped a handshake from Dave Martinez, and paced around to blow off steam. He was back in his cage, finished after 14 sizzling pitches, but had done a critical job. Washington's inning-by-inning staff ERA told a clear story during the regular season. It worsened later in games, when the bullpen was called upon, and the eighth was the most dangerous frame.

First inning–**4.17**

Second inning–**2.44**

Third inning–**3.61**

Fourth inning–**4.56**

Fifth inning–**3.11**

Sixth inning–**3.72**

Seventh inning–**4.67**

Eighth inning–**6.39**

Ninth inning–**5.70**

But this eighth inning was easy, if not a bit dramatic, since Scherzer can't do much without flair. It kept a 2-run lead intact and gave Hudson a chance for the save.

Since joining the Nationals in early August, Hudson had lobbied to do anything but close. He'd wanted Doolittle back in the role once Doolittle came off the injured list. Hudson told reporters he wasn't built for the ninth. He didn't think he threw hard enough, or could get groundballs to strand runners, or should pitch with the game on the line. That he'd had success in jams—stranding 21 of 22 inherited runners with the Blue Jays, then 9 of 14 with the Nationals—was a statistical fluke. At least that's how Hudson spun it.

Yet here he was again, jogging out for the ninth at Dodger Stadium, jousting with a rush of pressure and nerves. Hudson's eyes looked a bit wider in high-leverage situations, as if he were bracing for the worst. That didn't change when Turner led off the inning with a ground rule double to right. He recovered to get the next two batters, A. J. Pollock and Bellinger, but that's when Martinez went rogue.

Once Bellinger popped out to shallow left and Rendon made a diving catch along the line, Hudson squared his focus on Muncy. Muncy had crushed 35 home runs during the regular season. He already had a homer and 4 RBI in this series, and Hudson knew he had to be careful. But even with first base open, he couldn't totally pitch around Muncy and put the tying run on. That's when Martinez made the radical decision to do just that. He signaled for an intentional walk, wiggling four fingers in the air, before Hudson had even gotten back on the mound.

Hudson later revealed that he "got so thrown off" by the intentional walk. He added that "the book says don't intentionally walk anyone in the ninth unless it's Barry Bonds." That wasn't a dig at Martinez, Hudson explained, but more that no pitcher wants the tying run to get a free pass. A pitcher who loathes the ninth, such as Hudson, will only get more rattled. Martinez's logic was that Muncy was a tough matchup for Hudson, and Hudson had a better chance to retire the right-handed Will Smith, and, runners aside, Hudson just had to worry about that.

But it seemed damn near suicidal. Hudson yanked three sliders to Smith that were not close to strikes. His next pitch was a high fastball that Smith watched for ball four. The bases were now loaded. Muncy, put on by Martinez, moved ninety feet and into scoring position. Hudson took a step back off the rubber and took a deep breath. Then he took another. He couldn't let the intentional walk keep eating at him. There wasn't time for that.

Suzuki put down the sign for a four-seam fastball and moved his glove to the outer half of the plate. Hudson fired a heater that Seager passed on for strike one. Seager's long swing made it hard for him to catch up to high-90s fastballs, and Suzuki had that weakness in mind while calling the at bat:

Fastball. Foul ball. 0-2 count.

Fastball. Foul ball. 0-2 count.

Fastball. Foul ball. 0-2 count.

Fastball. Ball. 1-2 count.

Fastball. Ball. 2-2 count.

Fastball. Foul ball. 2-2 count.

That's when Suzuki sprang out of his squat and went to visit Hudson. He had done so before the at bat to make sure Turner wasn't stealing signs from second. Now he asked Hudson what he wanted to throw for his out pitch. Suzuki was leery of the slider because of the three that Hudson had tried against Smith. He lobbied for another fastball, thinking Hudson could blow it by Seager with the right location, but Hudson wanted the slider. He wanted to put it right on the plate. The ideal pitch would start around Seager's knees, appearing as a strike, before it darted toward the ground. Suzuki nodded in agreement and patted Hudson's chest.

Slider. Swing and a miss. Nationals win.

The pitch was exactly how Hudson wanted it. In a half hour, he'd stand by his locker in the tight visitors' clubhouse, reporters swirling around him, and say he'd never called his shot like that. He just felt that because Seager was sitting fastball, and maybe expecting it again, the slider would be a surprise. That put a punctuation mark on the gutsiest plan of Martinez's managerial career: 15 outs from Strasburg, 3 from Doolittle, 3 from Scherzer, 3 from Hudson. Then fly to Washington, the series level, 1-1, to keep stretching fate.

"You can be thrown right into the mix whenever," Scherzer said after the victory. "There is no routine in the postseason. There is no routine right now. It's come to the park ready to compete."

"Each year that you get into your career, you realize how special an opportunity it is to play in the postseason. You maybe feel that window closing a little bit, or you start to really appreciate these opportunities," Doolittle said of Scherzer and Strasburg. "We realize we have something special going on here. Guys are willing to do whatever it takes to give us the best chance."

"I would say it was more a little bit of a wall from the relief outing," Strasburg said when asked why he came out after five innings, revealing one drawback of this approach. Arms could get tired. And fast. "I think they had that number in mind and luckily I was able to go as long as I could, but I just kind of started to feel a little fatigued there. But again, that's I think more so from pitching in the wild-card game."

The Nationals then faced a short list of pressing questions: Could this work? Could they really ride a six-pitch staff? And who was their Game 3 starter now that Scherzer had come out of the bullpen? Scherzer was already telling the press that he could go in two days. That would have meant 77 pitches on Tuesday, 14 more on

Friday, then a Sunday start when Aníbal Sánchez was well rested and available. Martinez had a lot to weigh.

But first the Nationals squeezed every drop of optimism out of this night. They felt —no, they knew—that the pressure had shifted to the Dodgers. LA was heavily favored. They were supposed to advance. Yet Game 2 showed a clear way for the Nationals to compete: It started with Strasburg, like much of this had, and finished with doing anything to win.

16

"You can't replicate it."

October 7, 2019

But even the best-laid plans can fold with a single swing, or a slider that never bites. That's baseball. The Nationals learned that, and quickly, once Game 3 rolled along, they found a chance to win, and Martinez's aggression backfired.

The Nationals had bumped Max Scherzer to Game 4 and started Aníbal Sánchez in his place. He was opposed by lefty Hyun-Jin Ryu. In theory, the thirty-five-year-old Sánchez was a tough matchup for the Dodgers, who could struggle against soft throwers. Sánchez's repertoire was headlined by low-90s heat and two changeups, one that faded into right-handed hitters, and a second, called the "butterfly," that floated through the zone like a blimp. Martinez often said Sánchez had an "invisiball," since it was impossible to tell which of his seven options left his hand. The result, on his good days, was flailing hitters and blank frames. The problems arose without pinpoint fastball command.

That wasn't an issue in his first start against the Dodgers, on July 27, when Sánchez retired 20 consecutive batters in a dominant win. Now he picked up where he left off, escaping a bases-loaded jam in the first, then cruising through the second, third, and fourth. The Nationals grabbed a 2–0 lead in the first, once Juan Soto clocked a high fastball over the center-field fence. Sánchez then slipped in the fifth, allowing the Dodgers to score, yet soon exited, after 87 pitches, with a slim advantage intact.

Martinez needed the bullpen to account for 12 more outs. He remained hell-bent on avoiding his middle relievers. He turned to Patrick Corbin, knowing the lefty wouldn't make another start in the series, and everything went wrong.

What Corbin did, across two-thirds of an inning, was allow 6 earned runs on 4 hits and 2 walks. But what he'd done, in the bigger picture, was put the Nationals' season on life support. It was not what they'd envisioned upon signing Corbin to that six-year, $140 million contract the previous December. This was not how he thought his first shot at the playoffs would go. He was Martinez's latest chess piece, the closest the manager had to a sure thing out of the bullpen, yet was bullied in every which way.

The two-thirds of an inning is what the box recorded. But Corbin faced eight batters in all and appeared close to breezing through the sixth. He yielded a leadoff single to Cody Bellinger, the star's first hit of the series, before getting back-to-back strikeouts. Yet now it was Dave Roberts's turn to make a few moves. The Dodgers' manager possessed the most versatile offense in baseball. He had the ability to start one lineup, let it take a round of hacks or two, then make wholesale changes to shift the matchups in his favor.

So after A. J. Pollock had struck out, and Corbin seemed well in control, Roberts began his hockey subs. He pinch-hit the right-handed David Freese for the left-handed Gavin Lux. Freese laid off a low slider, the pitch Corbin needed batters to chase, and poked a 2-0 fastball to right for a single. Next Russell Martin ripped a 2-run double that flipped the scoreboard in the Dodgers' favor.

They led, 3–2, and Corbin was on an island. Roberts pinch-hit the right-handed Chris Taylor in the pitcher's spot. Corbin walked him with four pitches that were nowhere close to the zone. Roberts pinch-hit the right-handed Enrique Hernandez for the left-handed Joc Pederson. Hernandez ripped a hanging, down-the-middle slider for a double that scored two more runs. Corbin intentionally walked Max Muncy. Then Martinez came to peel the ball from Corbin's fingers.

Corbin walked off the field, Nationals Park hushed around him, and kept his eyes on the ground. His first relief appearance since 2017 was a disaster. Each of his 35 pitches seemed flatter than the last. They looked as if he had thrown 107 pitches three days before—since he had—and he left a mess for Wander Suero, with two runners on, before Suero misplaced a cutter to Justin Turner. Turner cracked it out to the left, and that tacked the fifth and sixth run onto Corbin's final line.

The Dodgers scored each of their seven runs with two outs and two strikes in the inning. It showed how slim a margin separated winners from losers in October. It also showed that, despite their best efforts, the Nationals could only hide their deficiencies for so long.

The immediate aftermath brought a search for solutions. A 10–4 loss is always bound to. Yan Gomes, who'd caught every one of Corbin's pitches this season, explained why the lefty struggled. Corbin's two-pitch approach requires time to set up his slider. But coming in as a reliever, and in the middle of a tight game, didn't afford Corbin any wiggle room. He had to go straight at the Dodgers, they knew he would, and that was a dangerous mix.

But Corbin's lapse, however frustrating, was a secondary concern. The Nationals were one loss away from elimination. The Dodgers had wrecked them in Game 3, like a replay of Game 1, and Roberts had outmanaged Martinez at every turn. Washington now needed two wins to advance—one at home, the other in Los Angeles—and the *good* news was that Scherzer and Strasburg were lined up to start.

That's what the players pointed to while October 6 wound down. A smug confidence centered on the two pitchers. There wasn't a cloud above the clubhouse, and it didn't feel like the beginning of an end. There was just a broken record player, spinning the same clichés, saying what the Nationals had all along. They were focused on *going 1-0* tomorrow, Martinez's go-to phrase, and were sure they could. They'd been up against the wall since May 24, they explained, the day—if you'd forgotten by now—that started a historic stretch. What was one more dance with death?

The local media had handed out its three annual awards at the end of the regular season. Strasburg was named Washington pitcher of the year. The honors for best player went to Rendon. Sean Doolittle received the Media Good Guy award for the second straight season, for his willingness to always speak with reporters. But he wanted to express a concern, even with the series, and season, slipping away.

"I don't know if I like the name Media Good Guy. It sounds too nice, like I don't have an edge, you know?" Doolittle lobbied by his locker, holding the plaque like a newborn baby. Daniel Hudson, not one to joke in tense moments, smiled from a few stalls over. Erick Fedde pulled on a pair of sneakers and shook his head. Doolittle smirked, his beard bending at its ridges, and kept on going. "Maybe we could change it to like Greatest Pitcher Ever award. Or maybe Local Humanitarian Who Saved the World . . . award. I'm just throwing some ideas out there."

This was the Nationals, too calm to panic, or too old and experienced to let it show. They had Scherzer on the mound for Game 4 on Monday. He set the Nationals back in the first, allowing a solo homer to Turner, and the ballpark hummed with angst. But Scherzer found a rhythm, and the offense was quick to back him. Rendon knotted the score with a sacrifice fly in the third. He inched the Nationals ahead with an RBI single in the fifth. Then Zimmerman saw a high fastball and left no doubt.

It came later in the fifth, when reliever Pedro Báez entered to face Zimmerman with one out. Rendon and Howie Kendrick were on base. Zimmerman had a chance to break the game wide open. He took Báez's first pitch, a low slider for a strike, but then Báez challenged him above the zone. Zimmerman's bat met the bottom of the fastball, shooting it straight into the air, and his eyes flicked toward an ink-black sky.

He searched above the tangle of hotels and parking garages beyond Nationals Park, trying to find the speck of white, hoping, maybe even praying, that it had the distance. When it did, sticking a soft landing in the grassy batter's eye, Zimmerman balled his fists, then stung first-base coach Tim Bogar's hand with a high five. He would later say he felt lucky for this opportunity, to play so many years in Washington, to be at the plate with his club in need.

But in that moment, in the thick of delirium, it was tough to tell who the lucky ones were. Was it the old first baseman, his feet worn down, his home-run trot not looking so different from his best sprint? Or was it the 36,847 around him, their voices going hoarse, all lifted by the player they'd watched for fourteen years? Maybe the feeling was mutual.

"That's why sports are special. You can't replicate it," Zimmerman said during a postgame press conference. The Nationals went on to beat the Dodgers, 6–1, to force a decisive Game 5 in Los Angeles. Scherzer sat to Zimmerman's left in the interview room, having allowed a lone run in seven innings. Doolittle and Hudson handled the final six outs. But Zimmerman soon signed the game ball before Martinez put it on the shelf.

The Nationals were guaranteed one more game. That was it. But there was assurance in giving Strasburg the ball. His career postseason ERA was shaved to 0.41 in 22 innings. His wild-card performance, with three scoreless innings out of the pen, further established him as one of the best playoff pitchers of all time. Those were the numbers that appeared on TV, and aired on the radio, and filled conversations that were somehow full of hope.

But Strasburg wouldn't be what separated Washington from the Dodgers. Not in the most practical sense. He would do his part, gut out six innings, allow one run to give the Nationals a fighting chance. He'd then wind up as one of the many reasons this fall didn't finish like the others. Yet his effort only gave way to a hero no one saw coming. Howie Kendrick was used to that.

17

"Do you believe it?"

October 9, 2019

It was on a gravel driveway in Callahan, Florida, a skinny stick in hand, that Howie Kendrick first swung and made contact. The stick was his bat. The ball was any pebble he could find. He tossed them to himself, a five-year-old spinning in circles, until wood found rock and he heard the pebble click along the sunbaked pavement. His grandmother sat inside, sometimes watching from the window, wondering what might come of this boy she was raising.

Ruth Woods didn't want her grandson staying in Callahan, a two-stoplight town between Jacksonville and the Georgia border. So few got out and made something of their lives. So she sent Howard to the local Little League fields, the stick replaced by a worn-down bat, and he fell in love for the first time. He couldn't take his child eyes off baseball.

The other kids called him Sloppy, because he was smothered by baby fat and his clothes never fit. He lived with Woods because his mother was in the army and deployed overseas. Once Woods sent him to the park, figuring the driveway was too small, Kendrick had little interest in other sports. Richard Pearce, the varsity baseball coach at West Nassau High School, thought Kendrick, if he wanted to, could have starred in football, basketball, maybe even soccer.

Kendrick was quick despite a stout frame. He had the best hand-eye coordination Pearce had ever seen. One day after baseball practice, when Kendrick was a junior, he challenged the school's top tennis player to a match. He held his own, sprinting around the court, taking big hacks that looked like home-run swings. His teammates didn't call him Sloppy for much longer. He went by Howard, and they all wanted to be like him.

"He always looked sloppy when he was on the Little League field," recalled Pearce, his voice low and gravelly, a familiar sound on the Panhandle. "Not in high school. Howard got to high school and he wasn't Sloppy no more."

But colleges didn't rush to recruit him. Few even gave Kendrick a glance. Callahan was offset from Florida's traditional baseball towns, and Kendrick didn't have the build of a Division I player. He was five feet seven and had slimmed down to 110 pounds. Pearce drove him to tryouts and showcases, pitched coaches over the phone, begged for someone, anyone, to come watch Kendrick in person. Pearce promised it would be worth it.

He finally convinced Lake City, a nearby community college, to come out. Kendrick made an error at shortstop in the early innings and the coaches left. He later hit the game-winning home run with few people in the stands. Other colleges agreed to watch video but never called back. Then Pearce and Kendrick drove an hour south to St. Johns River Community College in Palatka, Florida. Then they took him, trusting Pearce, and Kendrick began an all-American season. Then Tom Kotchman got a call he will never forget.

Kotchman, a Florida-area scout for the Angels, was always looking for tips. It was 2002, before social media could make a star out of nothing, and information traveled the old-fashioned way. It didn't matter that Kendrick was hitting, and playing a sound shortstop, and hitting some more. He'd look into the crowd during games and see not a single scout. But he impressed Ernie Rosseau, the head coach at Brevard Community College, and Rosseau was friendly with Kotchman.

Rosseau reached Kotchman with a simple message: there was a player he had to check on. Rosseau even called Kendrick "must-see." Kotchman preferred tips from opposing coaches, knowing the bias was cut out. He went out to St. Johns, his expectations still tempered, and noticed he was the only scout there. The visiting team was from Illinois and short on prospects. Kotchman would typically slow-play a trip, leave his camera in his bag for the first couple innings, be careful not to show other teams whom he was keying on.

But since he was alone, Kotchman took out his camcorder and began filming. He loved Kendrick's swing. He was impressed with how hard the ball flew off his bat. The fielding was fine, his running was average, but Kotchman was ready to sell Kendrick on hitting alone. When Kotchman met with Donny Rowland, then the Angels' scouting director, Rowland pressed him on those same concerns. It was the standard line of questioning, and Kotchman was ready to knock it aside.

Can Kendrick field? He can hit.

Can Kendrick run? He can hit.

Can Kendrick hit? He can hit.

Rowland's job was to be skeptical, to poke holes in a scouting report until it looked like a standardized test sheet. But he was drawn to the grainy tape of Kendrick's swing. Kotchman's major league comparison was Ray Durham, a second baseman who'd hit 20 homers for the White Sox in 2001. Each report comes with a "comp," as the scouts call it, to give a director such as Rowland some idea of how a player projects. Kotchman projected a mix of power and contact. They both projected power from the way Kendrick used his wrists and legs.

They picked him in the tenth round of the draft in the spring of 2002, behind 293 other players. The other clubs didn't think much of it. Most had never seen Kendrick play.

Torii Hunter looked up at his locker, filled with new shirts and gear, before scanning the stalls to his left and right. It was the spring of 2008, Hunter had joined the Angels after nine seasons in Minnesota, and he didn't know anyone too well. But he was right next to Howie Kendrick, a young outfielder who didn't talk much, and wondered where Kendrick was from, whom he looked up to, how he, an African American man, wound up playing baseball for a living. Kendrick was slow to share. Yet once Hunter cracked him, after hours spent in two folding chairs, the stories poured out.

Grew up with his grandmother before bouncing between homes. Nearly joined the Navy SEALs instead of going to college. Recruited by a single program out of high school. Only attended St. Johns because a books-and-tuition scholarship made it possible. Scouted by a single major league team and only here, at the Angels' spring training facility in Tempe, Arizona, because Rosseau called Kotchman, and Kotchman made the drive, and Kendrick hit well enough to create belief from scratch.

There was beating the odds. And then there was Howie Kendrick.

"The more I learned about him, he starts telling me about how no schools wanted him, how it was really hard to stay confident," Hunter recalled a decade later, "I just kept thinking, 'This guy could have really fallen through the cracks.' "

Hunter often stood behind the cage while Kendrick pounded baseballs into the outfield. Most batters got front or back spin with their swings. Kendrick's didn't produce either. He hit the ball so hard, and in the perfect spot, that it knuckled through the air. It looked as if the red seams were stuck between rotations, and the ball was speeding up and slowing down at the same time. Hunter had seen just three players do this. The other two were Mark Kotsay and Hall of Famer Tony Gwynn.

Kendrick hit .292 and averaged 28 doubles a year across 9 seasons in Anaheim. Washington traded for him in 2017 and signed him to a two-year deal the next winter. They were drawn to his hard contact and defensive versatility. He could play first base, second and third, the corner outfield spots, and was Dave Martinez's favorite right-handed pinch hitter. But that all changed on May 19, 2018, once Kendrick chased a ball into the left-field corner, fell onto the Nationals Park warning track, and couldn't get up. The diagnosis was quick and painful. A ruptured right Achilles tendon. Out for the rest of the season.

The recovery process was daunting for any player. For a thirty-four-year-old, it was like staring up a mountain.

"I always try to look at everything on the bright side," Kendrick told reporters. "I'm always positive, and even though this sucks, I got to find something to do. There's no point in being mopey about it. It won't heal as fast. The happier I am, the faster I'll heal."

But Kendrick privately considered retiring. He would have to regain range of motion in his right foot, spend months on an anti-gravity treadmill, and labor in the weight room to make sure his upper body didn't fall behind. He wasn't sure he had it in him. If he didn't have a year left on his contract, he told his agent, he would have walked away. Yet he taught his sons, Owen and Tyson, about commitment, and this was a chance to set an example. And by spring of 2019, Kendrick could say he was healthy, ready, and in the best shape of his life.

A minor hamstring strain kept him off the Opening Day roster, but he soon made sure the Nationals' awful start wasn't worse. When Anthony Rendon, Juan Soto, Trea Turner, and Ryan Zimmerman were all on the injured list, Kendrick carried the offense. He hit .314 with 4 homers in March and April. His stats improved in May, up to .333 with 5 home runs, and that's when he stepped in front of the team.

It was the first time Martinez called a meeting to clear the air. The Nationals were in the midst of being swept in Milwaukee, between May 6 and 8, and everyone had the chance to speak up. Paul Menhart remembered the room staying still while Kendrick spoke. Kendrick told the team that they would be fine. He had been on good teams that played poorly, he explained, but none were as talented as this one. He urged them all to believe, to hang on, and they listened.

He didn't have the name recognition of Rendon or Soto, Scherzer or Strasburg, or even Turner, Robles, or Zimmerman. But he was the undercurrent of the Nationals' charge through summer, always coming up with a timely knock, and often making solid-to-searing contact. MLB Statcast, a league-run analytics site, defines a "hard hit" as traveling 95 mph or faster off the bat. Kendrick was among the leaders in hard hits during the season, with 48.3 percent of his batted balls qualifying as such. That's how he put together the best season of his career, fourteen years in, and got penned into the playoff plan.

He would play every day after splitting time in the regular season. The Nationals wanted him at the plate.

How he got there on October 9, to the batter's box with a chance to win it, would sit with two cities forever. For Washington, there would be Rendon's swing, and Soto's swing, and then Kendrick's swing that changed everything. And Los Angeles would have to live under a pile of Dave Roberts's mistakes.

The night started with Strasburg getting rocked in the first two frames. But Strasburg held a 3-run deficit in place, Juan Soto dented it with an RBI single in the sixth, and Strasburg stranded a runner on second in the bottom half. That's when Roberts began his questionable decision-making.

Roberts had already pushed Buehler to a career-high 117 pitches despite having a fresh bullpen. His 110th, one below his season high, led to Soto's hit in the sixth. But Roberts's next move, or lack thereof, is what drew sharp and immediate criticism.

First he hooked Buehler and plugged in Clayton Kershaw to face Adam Eaton with two outs in the seventh. Kershaw looked like his old, dominant self, striking out Eaton on three pitches. But it was not a good barometer for how Kershaw was feeling. Eaton's worst matchup is a lefty who throws a lot of low-breaking balls. Kershaw was always bound to handle him. But Roberts rode him into the eighth anyway, brushing analytics aside, and the Dodgers paid.

Roberts had Kenta Maeda, his most reliable reliever, rested and raring to pitch. Even other options seemed better than the least effective version of Kershaw. But it felt like the idea of Kershaw, once the best pitcher of his generation, decked with milestones and mystique, led Roberts to put him back out there. Practicality would have formed a much smarter plan.

Kershaw's second pitch of the seventh was lofted by Rendon for a home run. Now Roberts had a chance to right a wrong before it was too late. Lefty Adam Kolarek had been Roberts's answer for Soto throughout the series. Soto was 0 for 3 against the sidewinding Kolarek and hadn't come particularly close. Left-handed hitters had a .178 average against Kolarek during the regular season. Plus, the benefit of using Kershaw against Eaton was lining up Kolarek for Soto.

Kolarek never even warmed up that inning. Instead, in the sort of move Martinez was expected to make, Roberts kept Kershaw in. His first pitch to Soto was a hanging slider that landed far up the stands in right-center. Tie game. Soto slapped his chest as he rounded second. Kershaw crouched to the mound, stared into the dirt, then peeked over his shoulder as the homer disappeared into a sea of Dodgers fans. Soto burst into the dugout and did a spirited dance with his Dominican teammates. Kershaw walked the other way, his ears filling with boos, until he slumped onto the wooden bench, then hung his head in shame.

Maeda came in and struck out the side while Kershaw stewed. Martinez turned to Tanner Rainey in the seventh, got two outs from the twenty-six-year-old, then went to Corbin to finish the frame. Corbin was only three days from combusting in relief at Nationals Park. But he retired all four batters he faced to keep the score knotted. When he exited after the eighth, and Hudson warmed behind him, Corbin ran through some simple logic: If Hudson held off the Dodgers in the ninth, the Nationals had the meat of their order coming up in the tenth. They would score, Corbin figured, he just didn't yet know how much Roberts would help.

Roberts brought in Joe Kelly for the ninth and survived. But Kelly was more often erratic than good, and too prone to blowing up altogether. That Roberts got a one-two-three inning from him was a steal. That he got greedy, and used Kelly for another inning, is what finally did the Dodgers in.

Kelly started the tenth with only 10 pitches. But his command was off from the beginning of the frame. Kenley Jansen, the Dodgers' closer, sat in the bullpen and waited for the phone to ring. Kelly walked leadoff batter Adam Eaton on six pitches. He yielded a ground rule double to Rendon, the third baseman's third hit of the game. Then Roberts decided to walk Soto intentionally, loading the bases with no outs, and Kendrick strode toward the plate.

Kendrick had had a nightmare series to that point. His two errors helped sink the Nationals in Game 1. In Game 3, after Corbin was shelled, he made a baserunning mistake that short-circuited a rally. Those "little things" Martinez preached about in spring—sound defense, being smart on the basepaths, situational hitting—had not plagued the club in months. But now Kendrick had his shot at redemption.

Kelly, still in beyond far bounds of logic and reason, was visited by pitching coach Rick Honeycutt before the at bat. If the advice was to attack Kendrick inside, it wasn't particularly good. Kelly's second pitch ran right into Kendrick's bat, the kind you dream about in the backyard growing up, or maybe in your grandmother's driveway beneath a beating Florida sun. So Kendrick used that fastball to make Washington baseball history. He smacked a grand slam, shattering the tenth-inning tie, and put the Nationals within three outs of their first trip past the division series.

Dave Jageler watched the flight of the ball from the radio booth behind home plate. The broadcaster, part of the Nationals' radio team since 2006, sat up in his chair to gauge how far it would travel. But instead of waiting, with no time to spare, Jageler let the reactions spill out of his mouth, his voice crescendoing: "Swing and a fly ball center field . . . Deep! . . . Bellinger's back! To the warning track! To the wall! . . . It's a graaaaand slam! Howie Kendrick has done it!"

A short pause on the airwaves revealed a stunned crowd inside Dodger Stadium. Trea Turner later described it as a "pin-drop silence" he'd never forget. Jageler looked to the Nationals' dugout and saw players spilling off the railing and onto the dirt.

Jageler grew up in Windsor, Connecticut, two hours from Boston, and his favorite sports memories were from 2004. That's when the Red Sox rallied from a 3-0 series deficit to beat the Yankees in the ALCS, then won their first World Series in eighty-six years. Jageler, a lifelong Red Sox fan, was gripped to every second of that fall, from Dave Roberts's steal in Game 4 of the ALCS, to David Ortiz's walk-off hits in Games 4 and 5. Jageler was thirty-three, a sports-radio host in Boston, and believed, once the Red Sox broke their curse, that even the worst luck could change.

Now there were kids all over Washington, Maryland, and Virginia feeling that for the first time. Soto's single off Hader was only a beginning. Kendrick's grand slam was real proof. The scouts tried to ignore him. An Achilles tear tried to end his career. But Kendrick was here, delivering the perfect swing, lifting a team that capsized back in May. Those Nationals were 3-0 in elimination games this postseason. They were headed to St. Louis, to play in the NLCS, to an uncharted phase of October.

This was redemption. *This* was getting over the hump. *This* was a goddamn exorcism on a baseball field.

"They're going crazy in the Nationals dugout!" Jageler continued, calculating the history and heartbreak. He had seen that hit go against the Nationals, so many times, and it was finally enough. ". . . Howie Kendrick with a grand slam! Here in the tenth inning of Game Five! . . . The Nationals, seven! The Dodgers, three! . . . Do you believe it?!"

It was a reasonable question. But once Sean Doolittle worked through the bottom half, and Michael A. Taylor ended the game with a diving catch, another celebration was the answer. The Nationals came prepared with now-familiar props: Doolittle had his glowing blue lightsaber. Turner had the NC State football helmet and skinny bottle of Clase Azul tequila. The additions to this party, crammed into the tiny visitors' clubhouse, were Fernando Rodney gnawing on ears of corn, and Yan Gomes mowing through a fourth-meal cheeseburger.

Max Scherzer walked out of the clubhouse, rubbing his eyes. They were red and stung by alcohol, and he was back minutes later wearing a pair of ski goggles. Roenis Elías, still sidelined with a hamstring strain, hid behind the plastic sheets and popped out to scare Wander Suero. Suero jumped before pouring a full Budweiser down Elías's neck. Kendrick was in the middle of it, his teammates rubbing his bald head, and his voice losing out to the thump of a crackling base.

"I can't ever describe that. It's just one of the greatest moments of my career. Being able to come through in that situation, it's what we dream of," Kendrick said before he was cut off by Mike Rizzo.

The general manager took his thumb off the top of a champagne bottle, raised it above Kendrick, then tilted the liquid onto the veteran's face. Rizzo yelled—drawing out a long "Hoooooowwieee! Are you kidding me?!"—until the Campo Viejo was nearly gone.

They danced until the plastic tore off the walls, then fell to the floor, then became something for the players to wipe their sandals on while packing up. "Closing Time" by Semisonic played over the speakers. Word spread that the buses were leaving, with or without the players, and guys hustled to pull on jeans and track pants that smelled like booze.

The buses rumbled down California Route 110, cutting through a breezy night, until parking at the Langham Hotel in Pasadena. They refilled in the morning, after a short night's sleep, with the Nationals now heading to St. Louis to face the Cardinals. Those rides are usually quiet, especially when players are nursing hangovers. But now there was no interest in that. A forty-minute trip was filled with off-key singing of the same song. They had Randy Newman's "I Love L.A." on repeat.

18

The Eye Test

October 10, 2019

Hours before the Nationals beat the Dodgers in Los Angeles on October 9, Jim Cuthbert settled into a seat behind home plate at SunTrust Park in Atlanta. He scanned the field behind a pair of wraparound shades. He cradled an iPad Pro, its screen reflecting the sun, and got ready to punch mounds of information into it.

The Nationals' most valuable arms belonged to Max Scherzer and Stephen Strasburg. Their most valuable bat belonged to Anthony Rendon, or maybe Juan Soto. Their most valuable glove was owned by Victor Robles, who often turned sure doubles into stinging outs, and Trea Turner had their most valuable legs. But Cuthbert possessed the club's most valuable iPad. He used it to plug data and analysis into advanced scouting reports, from Opening Day to right now, the most critical games of the season.

Cuthbert joined Washington before the year in a restructuring of its advanced-scouting department. Many teams around the league had cut advanced scouts in favor of analytics and new video technology. *Baseball America* reported that sixty traditional scouts lost their jobs in 2018, while *The Athletic* reported that the Astros, Yankees, Rays, and Braves, all on the cutting edge of modern trends, each employed at least fifteen data analysts. Trust in the eye test was phasing out.

But the Nationals still depended on balance. Rizzo had evolved over the years, and took the wave of numbers and fresh evaluation tools, yet stayed committed to the base of his career. Traditional scouting mattered to Rizzo, even in 2019, and that's why he brought in Cuthbert to seek out the smallest advantages.

Advanced scouts have a pretty simple job: travel one step ahead of the team, always watching the next club they'll play, and file detailed reports on tendencies, tics, and stats that support a given theory. Cuthbert was the Nationals' lone advanced scout during the regular season and racked up millions of travel points from his home in Allentown, Pennsylvania. But the operation ballooned once the playoffs rolled around. Rizzo wanted eyes on every team, in both the National and the American League, so Washington would be prepared for any series.

Cuthbert was used to scouting by himself, kept company by work and the game broadcast. He liked listening to the announcers for additional insight. He used the delayed video for plays he wanted to see again. If he missed home, and he often did, he reached into his Rawlings briefcase and looked at a drawing by one of his two sons. Anthony was eight years old, Nicholas was seven, and Cuthbert kept their artwork with him at all times. It helped clear his head before sinking into a game. It also eased the strain of being alone on the road.

But in Atlanta, ahead of Game 5 of the NLDS, he was joined by Kasey McKeon, Steve Arnieri, Dan Jennings, and Bob Schaefer. McKeon and Arnieri were in charge of watching the Braves. Jennings and Schaefer had the Cardinals. Cuthbert observed both, chatted with the others, then synthesized all their findings into digestible advice for the Nationals.

The entire advanced scouting crew for the postseason included Cuthbert, McKeon, Arnieri, Jennings, Schaefer, De Jon Watson, Bob Boone, Jay Robertson, Ron Rizzi, Jack McKeon, Terry Wetzel, and Mike Cubbage, all members of the front office or scouting department. This provided perspectives from longtime amateur scouts, former players and managers, guys who had just joined the organization, and others who had been around for years. That mix was important to Rizzo.

Wetzel and Cubbage scouted the Brewers in person ahead of the wild-card game. Robertson and Watson tracked the Dodgers before the Nationals faced them in the NLDS. Cuthbert couldn't be everywhere, but did keep up with everyone else, gathering their notes at all hours, and clarifying key points in texts and phone calls. By October, the Nationals' advanced scouting team had gone from one pair of eyes to twelve. It was overseen by Jon Tosches in the Nationals' video room, and Cuthbert was the quarterback on the ground.

The Cardinals-Braves game began and Cuthbert charted each pitch. It was a bright afternoon, and a shadow cut through the outfield. The stadium's brick facings was bathed in an off-yellow hue. It didn't take long for the Cardinals to stomp the Braves out of contention. St. Louis scored 10 first-running runs while the home crowd sagged into despair. Braves starter Mike Foltynewicz was hooked after recording one out and allowing 7 runs. The Cardinals were already celebrating as if they'd moved on.

While watching the rally, and ten Cardinals cross home plate, Cuthbert quickly noticed something the Braves had missed. The Braves' way of attacking a Cardinals' weakness turned it into a serious strength. Cuthbert was about to take that intel and give the Nationals a critical advantage in the NLCS. He picked up his right index finger and began tapping the iPad screen.

Cuthbert often tiptoed through the Progressive Field hallways during the 2013 season. He had joined the Indians a half decade before as an amateur scout in the Carolinas and Georgia. He was promoted in 2010, into his first pro scouting job, then had another role change when Terry Francona took over as manager. Francona led two World Series winners in Boston. He was that manager with a cheek full of chewing tobacco, perched on the top dugout step, peering at the game through a pair of glasses. And Cuthbert was intimidated by him.

Francona had had two advanced scouts with the Red Sox and wanted at least one in Cleveland. The Indians didn't employ an advanced scout before he got there, but they bumped Cuthbert into the role. Cuthbert just hadn't been around a big-league clubhouse, or in a big-league manager's office, or known much aside from warm bleachers and empty highways.

He wasn't sure which meetings he was invited to. He was hesitant to speak with Francona unless the manager approached him. He stayed out of the way, floating on the margins, until one day Francona welcomed him in.

"The quality of your work is the ticket to my office," Francona told Cuthbert, and the scout's confidence soared. It was the same lesson he'd heard years ago, when he first started as an associate amateur scout for the Colorado Rockies. Cuthbert grew up in a blue-collar family in Brooklyn, the son of an architect and a teacher's aide. He became a catcher at St. John's University because of his smarts behind the plate. He was slow-footed and had no future as a player. But he wanted to make the majors and knew there was a way.

The other hopefuls took sports management classes, setting themselves up for a life in ticket sales or team marketing. Cuthbert felt that was too far from the sport. His St. John's coach connected him with Mike Garlatti, a Northeast-area scout for the Rockies, and Cuthbert became his understudy. He sat on Garlatti's back porch in Edison, New Jersey, and the veteran scout walked Cuthbert through his player reports. Cuthbert was unpaid and kept steady jobs to support himself. He spent a year selling bulk uniforms around the city for a company called Team Wearhouse. He then worked for the Roberto Clemente All-Stars, a travel baseball organization, and helped youth teams book trips to Puerto Rico.

He'd finish working in the early afternoon, go straight to the subway, and be the first at the field once high schools let out. He was living half his dream, but wanted to have a business card with a major league club's name on it. He wanted to walk up to strangers and say, "Hi, I'm Jim Cuthbert from the . . ." He wanted to find the next Frank Thomas, Barry Bonds, or Mark McGwire. Garlatti's targets were infielders from Monmouth or Stony Brook Universities, and long-shot high schoolers from New York.

Cuthbert was soon sent out on his own, to scour Brooklyn and Staten Island, the Bronx and Queens, all the parks and programs he grew up around. But familiarity could be a trap. Garlatti's No. 1 rule was to never be wrong. As a scout in a low-talent area, one tended to squint too hard for talent. The danger was chasing, juicing a recommendation, having the team use a draft pick on your player, then that player not working out. That was one way to ruin a career. A scout only had his word and whatever followed.

Jason Bryan was the first player who piqued Cuthbert's interest. Cuthbert was working for the Texas Rangers, making $3,000 a year, saving for a wedding and trying to find that star. It was 1999. Bryan was an outfielder for New Utrecht High School in Brooklyn. Cuthbert was drawn to his six-foot-three, 195-pound frame, how muscular he was for a teenager, and the fluidity of Bryan's swing. He was already polished in center. But then Cuthbert considered Garlatti's advice. He couldn't just bring the Rangers glowing notes about Bryan's skill set. He had to dig.

So after Cuthbert got close to Bryan's coaches at Utrecht, he found the sandlot Bryan grew up playing in. Cuthbert spoke to the adults there, the other kids, pried as if he were writing Bryan's biography, not scouting him for the MLB draft. He did an in-home visit with Bryan and grew even more impressed. Bryan took three buses to school and practice. Cuthbert waited for him at the field one day, just to see if that was true, and Bryan hopped off the bus with his gear. Then Bryan took an empty field and set up a tee on the right-field line. The only sound was balls pinging off the fence, one after another, and Bryan tuning his swing without knowing anyone watched.

That bundle of information led Cuthbert to suggest Bryan for the upcoming draft. Cuthbert was twenty-three, not much older than the player, and the Rangers sent a cross-checker to review the outfielder. That was common in scouting, for a veteran to swoop in predraft to confirm or deny. Cuthbert and the cross-checker went to watch Bryan together, and Cuthbert was nervous. But after one of Bryan's at bats, the cross-checker assessed, "Jimmy, if this kid is in Florida, he goes in the top two rounds."

The Rangers selected Bryan in the tenth round, 316th overall, and the process showed Cuthbert a way forward: root his work in tireless research, and get it right. That led him up the ladder, from the Rockies, to the Rangers, to the Indians, and then into Francona's office. Francona told him to approach advanced scouting like he did everything else. The results would speak for themselves. Cuthbert did that job for three years, left to become the director of amateur scouting for the Marlins, then was cut loose when Derek Jeter took over the organization.

He was jobless until Rizzo called in November of 2018. The Nationals were rethinking their advanced scouting and wanted Cuthbert on board. They'd slipped into a cycle that was not working. The focus was too heavy on the opposition's weaknesses, and too light on how the Nationals' own strengths could exploit them. Cuthbert's reputation and résumé made him a logical fit for a new approach. He was not only qualified to break down other teams, but to analyze the Nationals and tailor his reports to their plans and personnel.

Cuthbert spent all six weeks of spring training with the club in West Palm Beach. He hung in the batting cages and listened to hitting coach Kevin Long talk. Cuthbert went to pitching meetings. Dave Martinez wanted him involved in everything, and the manager reminded Cuthbert of Francona. No door was closed. No spot of the field was off-limits.

"When I met him last December, it was 'Hey, you're a part of my staff, I want you with us from day one in spring training. I want to lean on you, I want to talk to you, we're going to work very closely together,'" Cuthbert recalled of his first conversation with Martinez. "He was closely inclusive with me so much more than the average manager would be with a scout."

That spring let Cuthbert and Tosches devise a blueprint for the season. Tosches was in charge of breaking down opposing batters for pitching coach Paul Menhart, the catchers, and pitching staff. Tosches also scouted opposing outfields to see arm strengths and trends in defensive positioning. Greg Ferguson, an advanced-scouting coordinator, worked with Long. Together they zeroed in on opposing pitchers and compiled notes for the Nationals' hitters and base stealers. The last team member was video intern Kenny Diaz, who, among his many duties, helped translate information to the club's Spanish-speaking players.

They all stuck together in the weeks leading into the season. Cuthbert was used to quickly turning reports around, and was expected to upload each before the Nationals boarded their flights to the next city. Now he had to learn their system, how they laid out their data, and, most important, what they wanted him to key on.

A standard report included a ten-to-twelve-page summary of the team Washington was about to face. Cuthbert designed his own template to chart at bats and weigh that data against human tendencies. Maybe a base runner shifts his weight a certain way before attempting a steal. Maybe his secondary lead puts him off-balance, and a catcher could get him with a back-pick throw. Maybe a batter's numbers say one thing, such as he can't hit low-breaking balls, but he has since adjusted to reach that pitch.

Those observations filled columns on the side of Cuthbert's spreadsheets. He later jotted them into the written summary for coaches to review and discuss. The next element was a report on each opposing player. They were one page, double-sided, and Cuthbert's notes were condensed into a paragraph or two at the top. The rest was done by Tosches, his team, and the analytics department, who provided video analysis, relevant sabermetrics, and colorful heat maps.

Batter reports had one side of data for him against right-handed pitchers, with the other for him against lefties. Pitcher reports were flipped, covering right- and left-handed hitters. But they had grown more detailed in the last few years. Tosches had infused more visual elements, including the blue and red heat maps, and catered to specific requests from players.

This process didn't just prepare Washington for any situation. It illustrated a conscious blend of old- and new-school tactics. The Nationals are often painted as being behind the times. Rizzo is one of the last remaining GMs with a traditional scouting background. The Nationals didn't rush to Edgertronic or Rapsodo cameras, popular technology that splits mechanics into a thousand tiny frames. The Astros, known as a very modern franchise, did not use a single advance scout during the regular season or playoffs. And they, not the Nationals, were much closer to the norm.

But the Nationals had gradually increased their commitment to staying current. Martinez wanted as much information as possible. Rizzo came around to that, too. The players were split—some liked all the data, others were weary of being turned into machines—yet it was always available to them. Tosches simplified the numbers when asked. The new-school side required his delicate touch, unending effort from Ferguson and Diaz, and an analytics staff that weighed internal data against stats from public sites. The old-school side required Cuthbert, McKeon, Arnieri, Jennings, and Schaefer all sitting at SunTrust Park.

Both of Cuthbert's reports were almost finished by the morning of Game 5 in Atlanta. He had one for the Cardinals, one for the Braves, and still had no clue which he'd be sending, or if the Nationals would need it at all. A loss in Los Angeles would have sent him straight back to Allentown for the winter. A win would kick-start another scramble to get everything in on time.

Cuthbert always left himself room for final touches. He, McKeon, Arnieri, Jennings, and Schaefer watched that Game 5, and the lopsided first inning, as if they were starting from scratch. And that's when Cuthbert saw what the Braves hadn't. Surface-level stats suggested pitching the Cardinals outside. It had been their team-wide cold zone all season. But knowing that weakness, the Cardinals inched up on the plate for Game 5 and focused on covering the outer half.

Foltynewicz, the Braves' starter, seemed to have clear instructions to pound the Cardinals low and outside. But since they didn't set up those pitches, and went straight to that spot without creative sequencing, the Cardinals feasted.

The Braves changed pitchers, swapping Foltynewicz out for Max Fried, but the damage was done. The Cardinals were on their way to a blowout. Cuthbert shifted all his attention to the Cardinals report. He gathered insights from the group, tapped out twelve pages on the team, polished notes for each player on the roster, then sent it by sundown. He was still unsure if the Nationals would ever use it. But once they won and were headed to St. Louis, Cuthbert booked his flight from Atlanta to meet them there.

During the regular season, he did his best to begin each series with the club. That way he could conduct an advanced meeting with coaches and answer any questions. But he never sat in on player meetings until the afternoon of Game 1 at Busch Stadium. Aníbal Sánchez was starting after Martinez had exhausted Scherzer, Strasburg, and Corbin to beat the Dodgers. Sánchez was heading to sit down with Menhart and catcher Yan Gomes, and spotted Cuthbert in the hallway.

"Hey! Jim!" Cuthbert remembered Sánchez saying. "Why don't you come to the pregame meeting today?"

It was different, and maybe a bit weird, but Cuthbert was more than willing. He was Washington's leading expert on the Cardinals. Sánchez saw him throughout the year, always saying hello, but had never tapped into the resource like this. The veteran was known for his tireless preparation, studying for days before he faced a lineup, jotting thoughts in a notebook that was always tucked in his locker or backpack.

And now, before the biggest night of his season, he picked Cuthbert's brain in a small room off the visitors' clubhouse. Cuthbert went through his observations. They led to the first inning of Game 5, to when Foltynewicz was hammered, and Cuthbert explained what he saw then: The Cardinals expected to get pitched outside, and the Nationals could use that against them. Their effort to cover the outer half of the plate left them susceptible to inside pitches. That's where sequencing was key.

If Sánchez started the Cardinals outside and teased that he'd approach them the way the Braves did, he could pound them inside and get bad swings. His sinker could get inside on right-handed hitters. His cutter could get inside on lefties. Sánchez's seven-pitch arsenal helped turn Cuthbert's advice into a practical plan. Menhart and Gomes made their suggestions, Sánchez refined it to his liking, and there was added urgency once they broke for warmups.

The Nationals needed Sánchez at his very, very best. The reason became public in the early afternoon. They were still only using six pitchers in close games, and one of them was missing.

19

"Worth the world"

October 11, 2019

Daniel Hudson stayed on the edges of the clubhouse celebration in Los Angeles, letting his teammates empty the tubs of alcohol. He had a Budweiser in his left hand, his iPhone in his right, and he stared into the bright screen. He was both texting his wife, Sara, and checking his flight information. He and Sara's third daughter was due the next day. So instead of flying with the Nationals to St. Louis, he would head to Phoenix, where his family lives year-round, to be with his wife.

"I need to sleep at some point. Plane leaves at seven a.m.," Hudson told himself through a half smile. He got somewhere between two and three hours, and caught a 5:00 a.m. UberX from Pasadena to Ontario International Airport. Sara and their two daughters were waiting for him when he landed later that morning. Sara, a delivery nurse, immediately asked how his right knee felt following the trip.

Hudson had dealt with a strained medial collateral ligament, or MCL, for the past three months. He made sure to book an exit-row seat, with no row in front of it, so he could stretch out in the air. But it didn't matter how he felt. That was just Sara's way. He quickly turned the focus to her, and they discussed how the birth would play out.

Detailed family planning is common in baseball. It is best for babies to come in the off-season, when players are home and can support their wives. Hudson, though, didn't have a job when they learned Sara was pregnant. They figured mid-October was safe either way, since only four teams went past that point. But he joined the Nationals at the trade deadline, and the Nationals were one of those four teams, and now the couple had a shrinking window before Hudson was expected in St. Louis.

Sara's experience with deliveries was a big help. The initial plan was for her to be induced Thursday morning, have the baby ten to twelve hours later, and Hudson would make it to Game 1 on Friday. But even the best-laid plans can fold when the hospital is short on beds. Women having natural births got priority. Her doctor told her to return around 8:00 p.m. and get induced by midnight.

First pitch for Game 1 was at 7:08 p.m. There was no way Hudson could be there for a Friday-morning birth and make it to Busch Stadium in time. Sara told him he could go, that she'd be okay, that she knew how important he was to the Nationals. Hudson never considered it.

"I was there for both of my first two. I just felt like I had to be home for this. How would I explain to my third girl why I wasn't there?" Hudson recalled later. "There was never a thought of me potentially missing the birth to be at a game. It was more 'This is the way it's going to be, but we'll deal with it.' "

Hudson spoke with Rizzo and Martinez, texted a bunch of teammates, and none of them pushed back. Martinez often told his players that family was more important than any game. The manager had kids toward the end of his sixteen-year career and visited whenever he could. He hated missing birthdays and holidays, and wanted his guys to make every effort to be there, too.

In the spring and fall, Sánchez flew to Miami on just about every off day to be with his wife and two kids. That's when Anabella, his seven-year-old daughter, was in school and not able to live with him in Washington. Sánchez and his wife, Ana, wanted her to stay in one school while growing up and settled in Miami during the 2018 season. So if the Nationals were off, and Sánchez wasn't pitching right after the off day, he flew down to drive his daughter to school, play with his one-year-old son, Aníbal, and help Anabella with her homework in the evenings. Then he'd fly north to rejoin the club.

His outlook on parenthood was rooted in tragedy. His first son, Alan, was born in September of 2006. A year later, during the 2007 season, Sánchez and his first wife brought Alan to their hometown in Venezuela. The one-year-old baby then contracted dengue fever from a mosquito bite and died that December. Sánchez had Alan's face, dimpled and smiling, tattooed to his right shoulder. He'd learned, in the hardest way possible, that every second with a child is "worth the world."

"If I can help it, if I can make the late-night flight or the long drive, I never want to miss a thing with my kids," Sánchez said. "There is really nothing more important to me."

That became a team motto of sorts. Martinez was fine with Sánchez's Miami trips, so long as he was always ready to pitch. Martinez was then proud of Hudson for sticking in Phoenix, and Sánchez felt the same. Hudson had done so much for the Nationals since coming over from Toronto in August. He filled in for Sean Doolittle when the lefty needed to rest. He finished both ends of a doubleheader on September 24, the day Washington clinched a playoff spot. He was their closer, whether he wanted that role or not, and never turned the ball down.

Now he needed his teammates to pick him up. He and Sara's third child was born at 7:02 a.m. on October 11, 2019. They'd known the gender of their first two daughters before they came into the world.

This time, they chose to wait. Baylor and Parker were giddy about having a new brother or sister. And it was a sister, weighing eight pounds one ounce, and fitting perfectly in Hudson's arms.

Her parents were undecided on a name and took suggestions from their daughters. Hudson and Sara had settled in the postpartum room by afternoon, laughing with Baylor, Parker, Baby Girl, and Jeff Passan, an ESPN reporter there to chronicle the family's day. It was not yet known outside the hospital and Nationals' clubhouse that Hudson would miss Game 1. But that changed when Washington posted its official roster for the NLCS.

There were the usual sections for catchers, infielders, outfielders, and pitchers. The odd one, tacked onto the bottom, was "Paternity List." Hudson's name was written beneath it. He was the first player to use the league's paternity list during the postseason. The Nationals had to designate one player to come off the roster once Hudson returned, and they picked reliever Wander Suero. Then they blasted the news out to the press, and social media detonated.

Hudson had sworn off Twitter three years ago. He only had an Instagram to follow Sara, look at pictures of Baylor and Parker, and never posted himself. Negativity spiked during the tough stretches of his career, and he preferred to stay in the dark. But Sara lay in bed and scrolled through tweets about Hudson skipping a baseball game. She read some of her favorites out loud.

The most viral came from David Samson, a former executive for the Marlins, who tweeted a pointed take: "Unreal that Daniel Hudson is on paternity list and missing game 1 of #NLCS. Only excuse would be a problem with the birth or health of baby or mother. If all is well, he needs to get to St. Louis. Inexcusable. Will it matter? #waittosee." Sean Doolittle later responded to Samson, telling reporters, "If your reaction to someone having a baby is anything other than 'Congratulations, I hope everybody's healthy!' you're an asshole."

All Hudson wanted was to be a good dad and husband. That he triggered a national conversation about parenting and priorities—and was at the center of it—was never his intention. The broadcast began and the announcers kept talking about him. He and Sara opened a bottle of wine and kicked back. They still had to pick a name for Baby Girl.

They both liked Millie, and how it was a homophone for Sara's maiden name. But aside from that conversation, and cradling his new daughter, Hudson was nervous while Sánchez took the mound. He knew that he, Sánchez, Doolittle, Scherzer, Strasburg, and Corbin were the arms Martinez favored. Hudson knew the fragile approach depended, in large part, on him.

"I don't feel like I should be there," Hudson remembered thinking as the game began. "I just really, really hope they don't need me tonight. And something happens, and I'm not there, and we lose because of it."

But his anxiety waned once Sánchez got going. Then it disappeared. Sánchez baffled the Cardinals with a healthy mix of pitches and velocity. He also had success working inside, with Cuthbert's report shining in the first inning. Sánchez started Kolten Wong outside, flashing what the Cardinals expected, before inducing a groundout with an inside fastball. The next hitter, All-Star first baseman Paul Goldschmidt, flew out on an inside cutter.

The Nationals nudged ahead in the second when Gomes scored Howie Kendrick with a double. There was slight drama in the fifth, when Cardinals starter Miles Mikolas took mocking exception to the Soto shuffle. Mikolas retired Juan Soto, chomped on his gum, and grabbed his crotch while walking to the dugout. Soto had done so during the at bat, as part of his elaborate routine, and Mikolas threw it back at him. But Mikolas was laughing, Soto was laughing, too, and the Nationals doubled their lead when Kendrick singled in Adam Eaton in the seventh.

Yet Sánchez was the show, and one run was all he needed. The thirty-five-year-old had a perfect game until he walked Wong in the fourth. Sánchez kept sneaking inside, running his sinker into the righties, and the Cardinals couldn't solve him. If anything could knock Hudson out of the national conversation, it was Sánchez's ability to change speeds.

His butterfly changeup sparked a rush of interest. His velocities went from 66 mph, a butterfly changeup that hit Yadier Molina in the back, to 93 mph, a sinker to Goldschmidt. Sánchez tossed 20 different velocities throughout 103 pitches. Seven pitches took one turn on the radar gun—66, 69, 70, 72, 75, 80, 93—and eight pitches in the 70s kept the Cardinals guessing, and guessing wrong.

When the eighth arrived, Sánchez had only walked Wong and plucked two more batters. He was six outs away from joining Don Larsen and Roy Halladay as the only pitchers to throw playoff no-hitters. Sánchez was at 89 pitches going into the inning. He had topped 100 in just 6 of his 30 starts during the regular season. But the ball was Sánchez's until he allowed a hit.

Tommy Edman lined a down-the-middle sinker toward first. It seemed bound for outfield grass, and maybe the right-field corner, until Ryan Zimmerman sprang to make a diving grab. Sánchez pounded a fist into his mitt. It was the sort of play that happened in every no-hitter, that signaled everything was on the pitcher's side. He followed by inching inside against Paul DeJong. A fly ball settled in Michal A. Taylor's glove, and Sánchez was one out from ending the eighth, and four from history. But José Martínez spoiled the fun. The tall righty knocked a seventh-pitch changeup into center. The St. Louis crowd gave Sánchez a standing ovation. His manager hooked him right then, thanking him for the effort, and Sánchez clapped toward José Martínez before ducking into a line of hugs and handshakes.

Martinez called on Doolittle to finish off the gem. It could have been a situation for Hudson, depending on the matchups, but

Hudson was confident in Doolittle. The lefty recorded the final four outs without any stress, ending the game by striking out Ozuna, and Hudson took a deep breath in Phoenix. It was the first time Doolittle had pitched more than an inning since returning from the injured list in September. Hudson hugged Sara and kissed his baby on the forehead. The Nationals had won, and his absence hadn't hurt them, and one of the best days of his life was capped by relief.

They had not yet settled on naming their third child Millie. Martinez couldn't have known that from St. Louis, but still took his chance to throw an option into the mix. Sitting in his small office, not 10 minutes after the game, Martinez took out his phone, laughed, and sent Hudson a text.

"You need to name your daughter Anibala, Sean."

20

A Beautiful Place

October 15, 2019

Mark Lerner had a whole two rows to pace through, up and back, while the Nationals tried to secure a spot in the World Series. Had it not been so cold on October 15, or spitting rain, or if a midfall wind wasn't whipping through the park, those seats would have been filled with Lerner's friends and family. But now they were empty aside from him, the team's managing principal owner, who used the space to vent his nerves and stretch out.

He pumped his fists while Patrick Corbin struck out the side in the first inning of Game 4. The Nationals had a 3-0 series lead, were on the cusp of moving on, and Lerner could feel it. He squeezed the grip of his wooden cane. He limped along the concrete, turned to high-five fans, and was out of breath by the end of the first. Washington scored 7 first-inning runs to take full command. Lerner had screamed so much, and so loudly, that he felt his heart beating against his chest. He walked to the end of his row and slumped into a rain-slicked seat, careful not to get the chip in his prosthetic leg wet. He just needed a minute to reset.

It was already a month of firsts for Lerner, who had his life split in two in 2017. There was before cancer and after it, and before and after that cancer forced doctors to amputate his left leg. Before,

Lerner was always at Nationals Park, sitting in that same seat behind the club's on-deck circle, cheering with a red Nationals cap pulled tightly onto his head. He traveled with the team, making it to about twenty road games a season, and loved chatting with players in the clubhouse, by the batting cage, wherever there was a chance to shake hands and swap stories. That was before.

After, Lerner could only watch a few innings before heading home. He grew too tired too quickly, his stamina all the way gone. He stopped traveling altogether. His body felt weak at night, planes were a no go, and his prosthetic made it hard to move around. He missed being at the stadium. He missed greeting fans on the way to his luxury seats. Yet no matter how much he missed it, and how disconnected it made him feel, Lerner didn't have the energy to push back. That was after.

But when this team was angling toward the playoffs, and the surgery was two years in the rearview, Lerner told his wife, Judy, that he was ready for nine innings. They picked the night of September 24, the end of that doubleheader against the Phillies, and hoped the Nationals would clinch. And when they did, Lerner was in the celebration, face creased by a smile, telling himself it wasn't close to midnight, but rather early in the afternoon. Mind tricks went a long way. So did grabbing ahold of a magical run.

Lerner's view made it hard to track Juan Soto's hit off Josh Hader in the wild-card game, and he yelled because everyone else did. Then, like a kid reading beneath the sheets, Lerner stayed up replaying the single on his iPad. He couldn't sleep. It was good practice for when the Nationals played in Los Angeles. When they beat the Dodgers, on the heels of Howie Kendrick's grand slam, it was 12:23 a.m. in Washington. Lerner was awake and teary-eyed in his living room. The team his family had bought in 2006, the one that sunk below miserable before shooting up, had kicked its October curse.

Then Lerner flew to St. Louis.

The trip was a reminder of what spindle-cell sarcoma took. Lerner went with his sons, Jacob and Jonathan, and stared at the big Nationals logo on the team charter plane. He checked into the team hotel, saying hellos in the lobby, and pushed into a back seat for the short drive to Busch Stadium. Lerner was always anxious on game day. His father had taught him that. But while Ted, the club's founding owner, was a calm observer, his son's emotions showed.

Ted handed control to Mark in June of 2018. The group of principal owners included Mark and Judy; Mark's two sisters, Debra Lerner Cohen and Marla Lerner Tanenbaum; and his two brothers-in-law, Robert Tanenbaum and Ed Cohen. They all weighed in on decisions big and small. Ted, ninety-three years old when the NLCS began, remained tangentially involved. But he'd entrusted his baseball team to his kids and put Mark in charge.

That's why Mark Lerner felt this pull back to the field, to see the fans, to watch the club he once urged his father to purchase. He grew up on stories about the Washington Senators, about how Ted, the son of two immigrants, would sell the Saturday evening *Washington Post* to save up for a ticket. Other times he got into Griffith Stadium by working as an usher. Ted would do anything to watch a baseball game, lose himself in the subtle rhythms, and park in the old bleachers until he had to leave. And that's why Mark was in St. Louis, fighting fatigue, to see the Nationals' first dance into the NLCS.

Lerner loved everything about this team. He loved the stars, the glow of Max Scherzer and Stephen Strasburg, of Juan Soto and Anthony Rendon, of Ryan Zimmerman and Trea Turner, and if you didn't stop him, Lerner would keep on listing. But he loved the oddities, too.

He loved Gerardo Parra and watching the "Baby Shark" clap. He loved how the Nationals were fixed on wearing their navy-blue alternate uniforms. They hadn't lost in them in six games. Lerner loved that. He loved each superstition, however weird, however silly it was for the relievers to have assigned seats in the bullpen, and was now nagged by one of his own: He was in Washington for the Nationals' two road wins during the NLDS. What if going to St. Louis brought bad luck?

But it didn't. First came Sánchez's near no-hitter in Game 1. Next came Scherzer, taking his turn with the Cardinals, and he wove through their order with a mix of fastballs, changes, sliders, and curves. The sun over St. Louis was an additional aid. The shadows inside Busch Stadium helped. Because it was an afternoon game, starting at 3:10 p.m., Busch Stadium was covered in shadows that favored Scherzer and Adam Wainwright.

A straight line of shade cut through the infield when Scherzer warmed up for the first. The hitters were in the dark, the pitchers in the light, and that made it hard for hitters to read the spin of each pitch, turning many at-bats into a guessing game. Scherzer sandwiched a first-inning walk with three strikeouts. He carried a no-hitter into the second, then the third, fourth, fifth, sixth, and seventh, leaving his hometown quiet, and the Cardinals fooled.

Washington had a one-run lead off Taylor's solo homer in the third. Wainwright otherwise matched Scherzer, using the shadows himself, except his club still couldn't hit. It was the second time in playoff history that teammates held an opponent hitless through five innings of consecutive games. The first was in 2013, when a pair of Tigers pitchers dominated the Red Sox in the ALCS.

Their names? Aníbal Sánchez and Max Scherzer.

Now here they were again, six years older, carving with even sharper knives. Sánchez shut out the Cardinals for 7⅔ innings. Scherzer kept them scoreless for 7. His no-hitter ended in that frame, once Goldschmidt poked a leadoff single to left. His final line—1 hit, 3 base runners, 11 strikeouts—made up the best postseason start of his career. The lead stretched in the eighth, when Adam Eaton ripped a 2-run double, and Martinez lined up Doolittle, Corbin, and Hudson for the finish.

The Cardinals scored in the eighth after Taylor overran a line drive he should have caught. But Doolittle worked around the mistake, handed the ball to Corbin, Corbin retired Wong, the only batter he faced, and Hudson, a day after Millie's birth, running on little sleep, notched the last two outs. Like clockwork.

Lerner avoided the clubhouse after Game 1, not wanting to change the perfect formula. Yet he couldn't resist once the Nationals locked down a 2–0 lead. He leaned on a leather sofa while players cycled by for quick conversations. Patrick Corbin gave him a one-armed hug. Scherzer offered a subtle fist bump. Lerner's cheeks were red with excitement, and his hat was tilted to the side, and it appeared, for a few short moments, as if he'd been there all along.

The owner had a short chat with Martinez before the manager walked to his postgame press conference. The topics were standard until the microphone found Thomas Boswell, a longtime columnist for the *Washington Post*, and a lifelong baseball junkie who'd waited decades to chronicle this. Boswell grew up in Capitol Hill and rooting for the Washington Senators. His mother worked at the Library of Congress, and he'd spend days working through the hulking section of baseball books. His father showed him those endless shelves and had one piece of advice: make sure you don't go blind.

Boswell joined the newspaper in November of 1969, fifty autumns before this one, and was an Orioles beat writer, then a national baseball columnist, then finally had a local team to cover come 2005. He spent the first two weeks of October saying he'd seen little like this Nationals team. His columns were rewriting a tortured history, and dripped with perspective only he could share. Now Boswell wanted Martinez to offer his.

"Are you getting a sense of kind of how unusual it is to have a pitcher take a no-hitter into the eighth, a no-hitter into the seventh, a guy back from paternity leave to save the game, the manager leaves to go have a heart procedure a few weeks ago?" Boswell laid out. "It's getting to be a really long list of unusual things."

"It sounds like a book." Martinez laughed, as if it were a crazy thought, but Lerner only smiled when he read that quote in Boswell's next piece. Lerner couldn't have agreed more.

The Nationals had turned into a bulldozer without breaks. They bludgeoned the Cardinals in Game 3, winning 8–1, behind another lights-out pitching performance. Strasburg struck out 12 batters, gave up 1 unearned run in 7 innings, and shaved his career postseason ERA to 1.10 in 41 innings. His case for being the sport's best playoff pitcher—not in 2019, but ever—took a significant leap. And St. Louis was left hanging by a thread.

They'd scored 1 earned run in the first 27 innings of the series. Washington's starters had allowed zero earned runs across 21⅔ frames. The Nationals scored three in the third inning of Game 3 alone. Another route was on. To that point of the postseason, they had recorded 165 outs across six wins. All but two of those outs were handled by Scherzer, Strasburg, Corbin, Sánchez, Doolittle, and Hudson. Tanner Rainey was responsible for the rest. But with a widened gap in Game 3, and the Cardinals looking like a limp punching bag, Martinez reached deeper into his bullpen.

The manager hooked Strasburg after 117 pitches and plugged in Fernando Rodney. Martinez gave Rainey the ninth, resting his high-leverage arms, and both pitchers set the Cardinals down in order. News vans dotted the pavement around Nationals Park. They had reporters pick off fans, mad-dashing to the metro, and ask what the night was like. They were some of the first 43,675 people to see the Nationals play in the NLCS. One win separated their team from the World Series.

But that wasn't entertained in a calm clubhouse. The players, to no surprise, stuck to Martinez's *one day at a time, let's go 1-0* approach.

"We still have work to do. We've accomplished nothing yet," Zimmerman said when pressed about winning the National League pennant. "We'll come in tomorrow like we have the last three, four months and try to win the game that day. That's all we're going to worry about."

"Nothing is won yet," Scherzer repeated, not five minutes later, while standing in the middle of the room. "We have to bring the same kind of effort we've brought the whole time."

They didn't want to give off a sniff of complacency. Take Soto, the Nationals' twenty-year-old left fielder, who was watching video while his teammates met the media. He was disgusted by his NLCS results. Since he'd tagged Hader for that game-winning single, Soto had felt entirely off at the plate. He was 7 for 34 overall in the playoffs, good for a .206 average, and 1 for 12 in this series with 7 strikeouts. He struck out twice in Game 3 and slammed his bat after the second. His confidence looked shot.

He caught the last out of the victory at 11:05 p.m. Around midnight, while everyone else filtered home, he found hitting coach Kevin Long and asked for a session in the cage. They stepped into the tunnel of nets and beneath a row of harsh lights. Soto told Long he thought he was pulling his front hip. Long agreed, saying that's why Soto was out in front of each pitch. That made him antsy and prone to chasing pitches. And *that* made him feel as if he were in quicksand.

Soto had slumped a bit in September, hitting .206 across the whole month, and was seeing more sliders than usual. His numbers saw a considerable dip against that pitch, he struggled most when his brain began to expect it. Then the tiny breakdowns piled up.

Long had a drill in mind. He placed seven balls on the ground and in a diagonal line toward Soto and the plate. The seventh was farthest away, at the edge of where Soto's bat could reach, while the closest was deep in the zone. Long wanted Soto to be more aware of where he made contact. That was one way for timing to improve. He had Soto swing, connect, and immediately call out a number—from one to seven—to guess where his bat met the ball.

"Three!" Soto yelled after hitting a fastball.

"No, that was a one," Long recalled telling him. Soto was flustered. He wasn't used to being wrong, especially in the batter's box, but had a realization. Pitches were getting deep on him because he anticipated breaking balls. To combat that, Long suggested Soto load earlier than usual. Long added that Soto should try making contact between three and four, and Long recalled Soto making that tweak within pitches. He started smacking line drives up the middle, one after another, and smiled at his coach.

"Oh my God," Soto said to himself. "There it is."

About a half hour went by before Soto recalibrated his swing. About nineteen hours passed until they were all back inside Nationals Park, with Lerner hanging on each pitch. Corbin typically throws his fastball in the low 90s. Now he came out and got back-to-back-to-back strikeouts on 95 mph heat. That set up the offense to explode in the bottom of the first, and seven runs scored before the Cardinals could blink. Soto accounted for the second with an RBI double to left. RBI singles by Victor Robles, Yan Gomes, and Turner capped the flood.

Next came the Nationals' longest countdown to 27 outs. Everyone knew they were advancing. The city was already uncorked. They just had to get another round of champagne and beers into the clubhouse. Corbin had his own shutout until Yadier Molina homered in the fourth. He allowed three more runs in the fifth, and the Cardinals had a runner on second with one out.

Pitching coach Paul Menhart visited for a short talk. Lerner kept pacing, using every inch of his empty row, and shook his head a few times. The Cardinals had yet to create any tension in Washington. Here, with the Nationals' lead cut to three runs, were a few hints of it. But Corbin ended that by striking out the next two batters.

The stadium boomed with cheers. Lerner raised his arms above his head. Corbin walked off, his night finished at 94 pitches and 12 strikeouts, and the bullpen kept cruising. Rainey worked a scoreless seventh. Doolittle took care of the next five outs, but left a bases-loaded jam for Hudson in the eighth. Once Hudson escaped it, getting a groundout to second, Anthony Rendon approached Martinez and put his hand on the manager's chest. Rendon was checking Martinez's heartbeat. Martinez laughed, told Rendon he was okay, and bear-hugged the third baseman from behind.

Hudson went back for the ninth. Then he was on the mound, eyes titled skyward, watching that 27th out soar toward Robles. This was a regular sight by now. Robles settled under the fly ball, the noise growing as he did, and Hudson had a planned celebration. He liked how Doolittle chucked his glove once the Nationals won the NLDS. So when Robles made the catch, and DC would host its first World Series in eighty-six years, Hudson wound up and threw his mitt at the backstop.

The Nationals mobbed him while mobbing one another. The coaching staff had its mob by the dugout steps. There were mobs throughout the stands, of hugs that didn't want to end, and red fireworks shot out of the video board. The ballpark staff had practiced every small step of the ceremony. Players and coaches received gray T-shirts for winning the pennant. A stage was erected on second base. Everyone was ushered there, once the immediate joy wore off, and speeches were then broadcast on national TV.

Martinez hated public speaking of any scale. Press conferences felt like a chore. Television appearances made him anxious. This, with the stadium still full, and millions watching from their living rooms, was the opposite of a good time.

It's not that he didn't want to be there, standing atop the platform, officially the manager who'd brought the World Series back to Washington. Of course he did. But he kept glancing at a microphone that inched his way. Ted Lerner put his hands on the NLCS trophy. It was his 94th birthday, and Mark later cried while describing his dad's face, his smile, when their usual postgame handshake turned into a long embrace. The crowd went crazy when Ted lifted his fingers off the trophy and gave them a thumbs-up. Mark Lerner and Mike Rizzo talked, praising the club, and that triggered more screams. Now Martinez had to think—and think fast—of what to say.

He stalled by telling them he didn't have words. His voice cracked with emotion, a familiar sound, and that's when it came to him. That's when his mother's voice popped into his head.

"I'll say this," Martinez started. "Often bumpy roads lead to beautiful places. And this is a beautiful place."

The place went ballistic. The players smacked his shoulders in approval. He added that they cured his heart, a line he'd repeated across the last five weeks, and then the moment passed. *Bumpy roads lead to beautiful places*. Lillian Martinez often told her son that while he was growing up. But it wasn't always easy to believe. Those hitting slumps filled Martinez with doubt. So did his first season as a manager, and the beginning of his second, and how he'd felt while strapped into the back of that ambulance in mid-September.

Yet now that he'd arrived at a beautiful place, and the end of a long and bumpy road, he knew Lillian was right. He was glad to share her wisdom with a massive audience. The rest of the night unfolded in a blur. Howie Kendrick was named NLCS MVP for hitting .333 with 4 doubles and 4 RBI in the series. He was thirty-six years old, the Nationals' starters were all over thirty, and the key veterans had adopted a saying: *Let the* viejos *play*.

MLB was marketing its young stars with the "Let the Kids Play" campaign. It doubled as an effort to remold a rigid culture for a younger generation of fans. The league wanted bat flips, and it wanted flair, and it wanted its budding stars, many of them Latin American, to showcase their culture without restraint. The Nationals had two of those players in Soto and Robles. But the Nationals' twist on the slogan fit baseball's oldest roster. The Spanglish translated to "Let the old guys play."

Kendrick, a thirty-six-year-old *viejo*, was the deserving MVP. Scherzer, a thirty-five-year-old *viejo*, leaned against a metal guardrail while reporters swarmed. When asked to explain why this team was special, and how it dismembered the Cardinals across four games, Scherzer laughed while saying, "We're just a bunch of *viejos*, man. That's it." The sport was weeding them out across the country. But Washington had turned age into a market inefficiency. They made it both effective and cool.

Ryan Zimmerman, a thirty-five-year-old *viejo*, was often blunt when discussing the importance of veterans. But having made his first World Series, and having spent all fourteen years of his career in DC, Zimmerman let that go for now. He posed with his wife, Heather, in front of the words NATIONAL LEAGUE CHAMPIONS. He couldn't believe they referred to him, finally, and disappeared into the clubhouse, then a cloud of champagne spray, then into Scherzer's arms once the Latin music thumped.

The ace had gone from relaxed to reflective. He stumbled away from Zimmerman, into a quiet corner of the room, and stole a few seconds for himself. He hopped up and down. He couldn't stop grinning. Then he approached a row of plastic-lined lockers, stared straight into them, and cried. It was a good cry, scrunching his face, suppressed by years of missed opportunity, but it didn't last long. He wiped his red cheeks, drops of alcohol flying off them, and jogged back into the mix. He had a few dozen teammates to party with. And once this faded, they had one more party to chase.

"It took the entire roster," Scherzer yelled over a fuzzy blend of bass and words. "Everyone on the roster had a hand in it."

Doolittle, a thirty-three-year-old *viejo*, had his blue lightsaber. Brian Dozier, a thirty-two-year-old *viejo*, lost his shirt again. Yan Gomes, another thirty-two-year-old *viejo*, was shirtless, too, and helping guys use the NLCS trophy as a beer funnel. Martinez tried it, despite his doctor's orders, and joked that cameramen had to kill the footage. Strasburg, a thirty-one-year-old *viejo*, basically a kid, let Bud Light slide down his throat before he was nudged away for an interview.

Strasburg had lived every step of the march to right now. He'd seen great teams make it and lose, one year after another, as if they were dominoes and bound to fall. He felt the blows of 2012, of 2014, of 2016 and 2017, every false hope and stunning defeat. It all made him the perfect person to ask a puzzling question: What was it about these Nationals?

Why were they 82-40, a .672 winning percentage, since flatlining on May 24? Why were they 16-2 since starting that five-game series with the Phillies in late September? Why had they eliminated the Phillies, Indians, Brewers, Dodgers, and Cardinals in three weeks? Why were they one of two clubs that would play for the World Series? The Nationals. How could that make any sense?

"It's kind of tough to say what's going to happen in the playoffs," Strasburg said, Budweiser dripping off his beard, a grin stretched across his face. "You have a great year, and you can run into a buzz saw. Maybe this year we're the buzz saw."

Gerardo Parra, a thirty-two-year-old *viejo*, called for Strasburg while blowing a whistle. It gave Strasburg an excuse to peel off and rejoin the fray. Parra extended his right hand, Strasburg clasped it, and they swayed back and forth in a drunken dance. Strasburg put his arm around Parra's waist. Cameras clicked and flashed. Maybe Strasburg would resent those videos in the morning, when he sobered up and checked the damage. Or maybe this really was different.

21

Clash

October 21, 2019

Six full days.

When the NLCS was over and the hangovers cleared, the Nationals had six full days before Game 1 of the World Series. The calendar rarely afforded such a break. They had been going since early February, playing games since late March, and, outside of a four-day breath for the All-Star Game in July, had had few chances, if any, to stop and rest.

If you bent the numbers a certain way, resting before the World Series was a bad idea. Baseball players are conditioned to work every day. Anecdotal evidence suggests that prolonged rest is the enemy of rhythm. Since 2012, when the playoff field expanded from eight to ten clubs, teams with six or more days of rest were 0-4 in the World Series. They were 6-7 overall since 1994. Before October of 2018, when the Red Sox rested for five days, then beat the Dodgers for the title, teams with more rest had lost nine consecutive times.

But the Nationals needed a rest in many ways. It was a rare opportunity to organize their hectic lives. Most of their apartment leases had ended when the regular season did. A deep playoff run is never planned. Juan Soto was living at National Harbor, a waterside resort and casino in Maryland. Sean Doolittle and his wife were in a hotel by the ballpark, and their laundry was piling up. The day after they swept the Cardinals, Doolittle slept in, woke up in the early afternoon, then went right back to bed. Then he emerged the next morning, threw in mounds of laundry, bought bagels, and sneaked off to a bookstore. He felt born-again.

All of the players' bodies needed to recover. The starters had taxed their arms to beat the Brewers, Dodgers, and St. Louis. Doolittle and Hudson were handling the heaviest workloads of their careers. Howie Kendrick hadn't played every day in a long time. His thirty-six-year-old limbs could feel the strain. The same went for Suzuki, who turned thirty-six on October 4, and Zimmerman, who turned thirty-five on September 28. And the same went for the younger guys, for Soto, Robles, Turner, and Rendon, who'd taken just a handful of days off since spring.

The challenge was to not let these off days shake the Nationals' groove. Dave Martinez told his players to stay home Wednesday and Thursday. Most listened, aside from those who needed medical treatment, and they reconvened Friday for a light workout. The World Series was set to start Tuesday in either Houston or New York. The Astros led in the AL Championship Series, 3-1, when the Nationals stepped into a bright afternoon in Washington.

It was as if the Nationals were back to the basics, to what they did in spring training, to shake any rust off. They lined up and jogged the bases. They spread out in the field, filling every spot but the pitcher's mound, caught pop flies and grounders, and threw balls to each base.

This was just the beginning of a multistep plan to stay fresh. Martinez's biggest worry was his players' legs. His second-biggest worry was falling out of "game shape." They were connected, in a way, but the latter was trickier. He had to keep his club ready to play without . . . actually playing. Max Scherzer and Aníbal Sánchez cruised to the World Series with the Tigers in 2012. The Tigers swept the Championship Series and, like the Nationals, had six days to rest. Then they were swept by the Giants, who rested for two days before the World Series, forcing Scherzer to wonder, for years, what the hell went wrong.

There wasn't one explanation. But Scherzer could point to one potential issue. All World Series games are played in prime time. The bulk of the Tigers' pre-series workouts were during the day. That left a preparation gap that was never filled. Once the Series began, and the sun went down each night, it had been a week since the Tigers had faced live pitching under the lights. They were shut out in Games 2 and 3. They scored 3 three runs in both Games 1 and 4.

Martinez did not need Scherzer's input to correct that mistake. In 2016, when Martinez was a bench coach for Joe Maddon and the Cubs, the Cubs had just three days of rest between the NLCS and the World Series. But Maddon made sure the Cubs worked out at night, and Martinez now did the same with his team. After the Friday workout, the plan was to meet each evening for simulated games. Hitters and pitchers could partake in live at bats. It doubled as a way to keep the competitive juices spiked.

The clubhouse was open to the media after the workout, and just about every player was asked about the conundrum of rest. Most brushed it aside, saying the six days were welcomed, even necessary, and the narrative was overcooked. But another one, that the Nationals were the anti-modern baseball team, was about to really swell.

It was sealed on October 19 in Houston, that Saturday night, once José Altuve lifted a walk-off, 2-run homer out of Minute Maid Park: the World Series would be a clash of ideologies.

The Nationals had long been carrying the torch for tradition. The Astros were known for bashing it with a sledgehammer. They had built through the draft, much like the Nationals, and won a title in 2017 after adding star pitcher Justin Verlander at the trade deadline. But their methods and approach were otherwise very different from Washington's.

That started with Jeff Luhnow, their clean-cut GM, who had never worked for a professional club, or even played high school baseball, before the St. Louis Cardinals hired him in 2003. That was the same year *Moneyball* brought a tectonic shift in how teams viewed numbers and roster-building. William DeWitt, the Cardinals' owner, wanted a front office that operated like the Athletics did in Michael Lewis's book. So he hired Luhnow, who was working at McKinsey & Company, a global consulting firm, to be his vice president of baseball operations.

Under Luhnow, the Cardinals tethered their player-evaluation process to new-age analytics. The Astros would do the same once Houston hired Luhnow in 2012. They lost a franchise-record 111 games in 2013. They lost 82 more a year later. But they made it count once the draft rolled around each June. That's where they got a core of Altuve at second, shortstop Carlos Correa, third baseman Alex Bregman, outfielder George Springer, and lefty starter Dallas Keuchel. That is the group that rose to relevance in 2015, raising the Astros' year-to-year win total by 16, then lost in the first round of the playoffs. Then they won it all two seasons later.

The Astros had cut down their number of traditional scouts. They used video and data analysis for the draft and continued those practices in player development. Their pitchers were taught the importance of spin rate and spin axis. They made a habit out of restoring discarded arms, such as with the once-struggling Collin McHugh, or reliever Ryan Pressly in 2018. They were the team everyone wanted to duplicate.

Yet even with copycats around the league, the Astros were often derided as robots. Their GM was a suit-wearing management consultant. His right-hand man, Sig Mejdal, was a former NASA engineer. The Astros had the culture of a Fortune 500 company, fired around a dozen scouts in 2017, and Luhnow told reporters it wasn't a cutback. He instead referred to it as a "reconfiguration."

So if the Nationals were painted as anti-innovation, the Astros were the anti-Nationals. They were the perfect foil for each other, even if, in both cases, the strokes were far too broad. Monday, October 21, was World Series media day at Minute Maid Park in Houston, and Dave Sheinin, a national baseball reporter for the *Washington Post*, was out to define these differences. Luhnow was from the corporate world. Rizzo was certainly not. The Nationals relied on advance scouts throughout the year. The Astros hadn't used one in the regular season or playoffs. Those were the facts.

Yet Luhnow and Rizzo pushed against too stark a contrast. Neither wanted to be too radical in one direction. Luhnow had baseball people to please. Rizzo liked the old-school label, and let it be stretched for narrative's sake, but was wary of appearing out of touch. Their comments to Sheinin reflected those insecurities.

"We're sneaky analytical," Rizzo told Sheinin on the eve of Game 1. The headline of Sheinin's story read, "At World Series, old school meets new in how Nationals, Astros approach analytics."

"And they're sneaky scouting," Rizzo continued. "We have an eight-person analytics department that we don't talk about very much. And they know what they're doing with scouting. I know because we've tried to make trades with them, and they know our personnel up and down."

"They're sort of sneaky in what they do," Luhnow told Sheinin. "They don't talk about it a whole lot, but they have good capabilities. We watch their moves. They're a smart organization, and they've got a lot of good people over there. And so do we. We're sneaky the other way. People label us an analytical organization, but we've got really good evaluators, and they use their eyes and their guts. We're more similar than people think."

Sheinin's write-up hit the internet at 8:14 p.m. local time and was drowned out eleven minutes later. That's when *Sports Illustrated* hit publish on a troubling story about Astros assistant general manager Brandon Taubman. The writer, Stephanie Apstein, was subject to Taubman's inappropriate behavior following Game 6 of the ALCS. Apstein reported that during the Astros' celebration, Taubman approached a group of three female reporters, herself among them, and repeatedly yelled, "Thank God we got Osuna! I'm so fucking glad we got Osuna!"

The Astros had traded for Roberto Osuna while he was serving a 75-game suspension for domestic violence in 2018. The move was widely questioned and underscored their reputation as soulless robots. The Astros publicly announced a "zero-tolerance policy" for domestic violence. They reportedly donated $214,000 to shelters and put hotline numbers in every women's bathroom at Minute Maid Park. But Luhnow bungled the save-face campaign when he stated the deal might "actually turn out to be a positive down the road" and "raise awareness."

Now Taubman, a thirty-three-year-old executive, targeted three women with his remarks. He was another nonbaseball person in the Astros' front office. He graduated with an economics degree from Cornell University, and worked for Ernst & Young, then Barclays, before the Astros took notice of his projection system for daily fantasy baseball. That later led him to the Astros as an "economist" in 2013. Apstein reported that one of the three female reporters wore a purple bracelet for domestic violence awareness. That reporter had ridiculed the Osuna addition in 2018, just months after he allegedly assaulted Alejandra Román Cota, the mother of his child. Apstein wrote, "The outburst was offensive and frightening enough that another Houston staffer apologized."

The Astros declined to comment for the story and did not make Taubman available for an interview. The *Washington Post* later reported that an Astros public relations staffer tried to dissuade Apstein from publishing, saying she could not know Taubman's intent. Their strategy was to deny, deny, deny. They tweeted a statement shortly after Apstein's story went live. It only threw a match into a growing fire.

"The story posted by *Sports Illustrated* is misleading and completely irresponsible," the statement read. "An Astros player was being questions about a difficult outing. Our executive was supporting the player during a difficult time. His comments had everything to do about the game situation that just occurred and nothing else—they were also not directed at any specific reporters. We are extremely disappointed in *Sports Illustrated*'s attempt to fabricate a story where one does not exist."

Sports Illustrated soon released a statement that defended Apstein's reporting and integrity. Male and female reporters confirmed her account of the incident. Hunter Atkins, a reporter for the *Houston Chronicle*, apologized for witnessing Taubman's outburst and not speaking up. A nationwide conversation ensued about clubhouse culture and a need for change. The Astros had tried, and very much failed, to hide from it. They were backpedaling toward a cliff, and the World Series was less than twenty-four hours away, and the focus was shifted away from their title bid.

The Astros had Gerrit Cole, the league's best pitcher, and Verlander, maybe the league's second-best pitcher, and then Zack Greinke, who was the best pitcher available at the trade deadline. Their lineup brimmed with talent, from Springer to Altuve, to Bregman, an MVP candidate, on down to Michael Brantley, Correa, and Yordan Álvarez, a rookie who slugged 27 homers in the regular season. Their bullpen, anchored by Osuna, featured Pressly, Will Harris, and the hard-throwing Josh James.

They finished with a league-high 107 wins for a reason. Oddsmakers made them the biggest World Series favorite since 2007. But few talked about that once Monday turned to Tuesday, and morning became afternoon, and the first pitch of Game 1 was no longer some distant concept, but ready to be thrown.

22

"It's just you and me."

October 22, 2019

Gerrit Cole pumped three fastballs at the top of the zone. Juan Soto couldn't touch them. They were all strikes, and all traveled 97 mph or faster, and Soto swung at each one—*whiff, whiff, whiff*—before yanking off his batting gloves.

Soto looked entirely overmatched. Cole looked ready to cruise through Game 1 the way he'd cruised through summer and fall. The twenty-nine-year-old had won 19 straight decisions. The Astros had not lost one of his starts since July 12. He had not allowed a run on a hit that was not a homer since August 28. Heading into the night, his first World Series start, he'd allowed just 1 earned run in 22⅔ innings throughout the postseason.

That's what the Nationals were up against. The afternoon began with A. J. Hinch, the Astros' smooth-talking manager, fielding questions about Taubman and a botched response. Hinch was often tasked with cleaning up the organization's mistakes. He was also adept at doing so.

"I'm very disappointed for a lot of reasons. It's unfortunate, it's uncalled for. For me as a leader in this organization down here in the clubhouse, on the field, I take everything that happens in the clubhouse to heart," Hinch said at the start of his pregame press conference. "No one, it doesn't matter if it's a player, a coach, a manager, any of you members of the media, should ever feel like when you come into our clubhouse that you're going to be uncomfortable or disrespected."

The Astros finally had an adult in the room. It was just too late, and too far buried by their attempt to smear Apstein. But the game went on, as it always does, and Cole struck out Rendon and Soto to work around a lead-off single. Scherzer walked Springer to start his outing, gave up a single to Altuve, got back-to-back strikeouts, then allowed a two-run double to Gurriel. The Nationals blinked and were in a hole.

But that didn't last too long. With two outs in the top of the second, and no runners on base, Cole missed his spot with a four-seam fastball. Zimmerman capitalized, lifting the pitch out to center, and the Nationals' first World Series run was scored by its first-ever draft pick. Martinez later admitted to shedding a few tears in the dugout. The Nationals had found a footing in unfamiliar territory. Then Soto and Cole engaged again.

No matter how versatile the Astros' staff was, they couldn't escape an obvious roster flaw: neither their rotation nor bullpen had a lefty. And while the Nationals had a handful of other left-handed hitters—Adam Eaton, Matt Adams, Gerardo Parra—that was most concerning with Soto. The Brewers had used Josh Hader against Soto, even if that didn't end well for them. The Dodgers used lefty specialist Adam Kolarek, even if they forgot to in the waning moments of Game 5. The Cardinals used Andrew Miller, even if Soto's adjustments had led to a sizzling hit off him in Game 4 of the NLCS. The Astros, though, had to hope a number of righties could handle the young star.

Cole did in their first matchup of the night. But when he went to the same spot with the same pitch, a high-and-away fastball, Soto crushed it 417 feet. Minute Maid Park has a makeshift train track above left field, and Soto's blast cleared the seats, climbing two stadium levels, and bounced onto the concrete beneath its metal rails.

That's where the ball rolled to a stop. When Soto made contact, he, catcher Martin Maldonado, and home-plate umpire Alan Porter all looked as if they were tracking a shooting star. They basically were. A reporter in the press box blurted out, "Where the fuck did that land?" The home crowd went quiet. Soto took a quick trip around the bases, Scherzer held the Astros down, and Soto then readied for a third meeting with Houston's ace.

It came after Eaton broke the tie with a single off Cole in the fifth. Soto stepped up with runners on the corners, a chance to widen the gap, and did so by lining an RBI double off the left-field wall. He drove a full-count, down-and-away slider that Cole tried to sneak past him. His bat made contact at the perfect point. He later singled in the eighth, capping a historic World Series debut, and provided just enough of a cushion.

Patrick Corbin got the Nationals through the sixth unscathed. The seventh brought trouble, once Tanner Rainey allowed a solo homer to Springer, and Springer inched the Astros even closer with an RBI double in the eighth. But Doolittle recorded the final four outs, retiring each batter he faced, and the Nationals had the series lead.

"I forget about everybody around. It's just you and me," Soto offered on his approach against Cole. The Nationals tagged Cole for 5 runs in 5 innings of a 5–4 win. He had allowed more than 5 runs in only 2 of his 33 starts during the regular season. That Washington got the best of him, and rode that effort to a Game 1 victory, sent them humming into the next night.

The cameras caught Alex Bregman in the act. He had just crushed a moon-shot homer off Stephen Strasburg, tying Game 2 in the first inning, and gathered his teammates for a quick meeting. The whole sequence played out on TV while speculation peaked: Bregman mimicked Strasburg in the dugout, holding an invisible glove to his chest, and seemed to indicate that Strasburg was tipping pitches. Bregman appeared ready for off-speed in a 2-strike count, sitting changeup, and crushed the pitch over the wall.

It was an odd start for another marquee pitching matchup. Strasburg had been untouchable all October. Verlander, a Cy Young front-runner, had a career 0-4 record in the World Series, and had been struggling at the start of games. Rendon, a Houston native, continued that trend with a 2-run double in the top of the first. But the lead evaporated with Bregman's shot, and now Strasburg had to wonder what the third baseman had seen.

For years, the Astros had a reputation as extensive sign-stealers. It was accepted around the league that players would glean signs from second base. That was part of the game. But the Astros were often quietly accused of cheating with technology, and using it to relay information to hitters at the plate.

(Following the World Series, an article on *The Athletic* detailed the Astros' sign-stealing practices during the 2017 season and their title run. Two players came forward and spoke on the record about a system that included videotaping, a hidden operation in the tunnel behind the dugout, and banging on trash cans to let batters know what pitches were coming. MLB then launched a full-scale investigation that began in November. On January 13, 2020, MLB released its findings, and issued one-year bans for Hinch and Luhnow. Astros owner Jim Crane fired both the same day. In a statement about the Astros' illegal practices, commissioner Rob Manfred made pointed remarks about Houston's organizational culture, writing: "While no one can dispute that Luhnow's baseball operations department is an industry leader in its analytics, it is very clear to me that the culture of the baseball operations department, manifesting itself in the way its employees are treated, its relations with other Clubs, and its relations with the media and external stakeholders, has been very problematic. At least in my view, the baseball operations department's insular culture–one that valued and rewarded results over other considerations, combined with a staff of individuals who often lacked direction or sufficient oversight—led, at least in part, to the Brandon Taubman incident, the Club's admittedly inappropriate and inaccurate response to that incident, and finally, to an environment that allowed the conduct described in this report to have occurred.")

Since Strasurg had ditched his full windup in 2017, he gave batters a cleaner look at his glove and throwing hand. That had led to a number of pitch-tipping concerns in the last few seasons. The Nationals quickly determined that there were no tells for Bregman to pick up. But they were aware of the Astros' ways, illegal or otherwise, heading into the Series.

To ease their paranoia, they set up an elaborate system to conceal their signs. Each pitcher had his own set. To keep the pitchers and catchers on the same page, the Nationals made laminated note cards. The catchers slid them into wristbands. The pitchers had them in their caps or back pockets. The note cards detailed five sets of signs for every pitcher, so they could switch whenever necessary.

But that wasn't it. Teams typically use multiple signs when a runner is on second base. The Nationals decided to for every at bat, just in case. They even set up tricky ways to relay signs from catcher to pitcher. One method was "outs plus one," meaning if there were no outs, the first sign was the pitch, and if there was one out, the second sign was the pitch, and so on. There was also "chase the two," meaning the sign came right after the catcher threw down two fingers.

"We did not want to take any chances that our signs could be stolen," pitching coach Paul Menhart explained later, and added that the Nationals had plans against the Brewers, Dodgers, and

Cardinals, too. "We thought we heard a whistle. That was the first thing. Whether we heard it or not, or our minds were placing tricks on us, that's a whole different conversation. But once it gets in your head that can be incredibly frustrating for a pitcher. We had to put a system in place that eliminated that worry and even the possibility that Houston, or whoever, could pick something up. We were ready for everything."

The goal, first and foremost, was to combat whatever the Astros could have been doing, whether that was illegal video sign-stealing or just dissecting Strasburg's tendencies. Strasburg and Kurt Suzuki shook up the pitcher's signs after Bregman's homer. But the real fix was that Strasburg made pitches when he had to. He allowed a hit in all but one of his six innings, a rare occurrence, yet steered away from danger each time. He struck out 7. He gave the Nationals a chance to pull ahead, exiting with a tie intact, and they did so in the top of the seventh.

Verlander was still in. Suzuki entered Game 1 with 15 hits in 42 career at-bats against him. But that didn't alter Suzuki's plan going into this game. The Nationals' hitters get detailed scouting reports for every pitcher they might face. He just looked for the first fastball he sees, the staffer explained, and tried to pull it as hard as he could.

That's what he did against Verlander, and drove a high fastball off the Lexus sign in left. The ball smacked the metal and dropped into the seats. A fan fished it off the ground and tossed it onto the outfield grass, triggering tired cheers. The Nationals were ahead, and their lead was about to stretch, and by the end of the seventh, an inning that started with Suzuki's homer, they had scored 6 runs to bury the Astros.

It was a warped frame from the beginning. Suzuki was 1 for 23 in the postseason before his blast. Then he got the best of a generational star. Eaton executed a sacrifice bunt, now an old-school artifact, to put Victor Robles and Trea Turner on second and third. Then the

Astros did something they hadn't in 173 games, counting both the regular season and the playoffs. They intentionally walked a hitter. It was Juan Soto. He took a free pass to first base, which was open after the bunt, and that's when Houston unraveled.

Verlander was pulled for Pressly. Kendrick tapped an infield single that Bregman couldn't handle at third. Then Asdrúbal Cabrera tapped a single to center. It left the bat at 75.7 mph and scored 2 runs. Then Ryan Zimmerman tapped an infield single to third that left the bat at 62.8 mph. Bregman fielded it and threw way past first. The error brought 2 more runs across. The Nationals sent 10 batters to the plate. In the era of boom or bust, with homers and strikeouts at record highs, none of those batters went down swinging.

And that was that.

They poured on 4 more runs to cap a 12–3 win. They were 18-2 since September 23, on a 7-game winning streak, and had every number in their favor. Fifty-five teams had taken a 2-0 advantage in the World Series. Forty-four won it all, including the past 11, and the Nationals had five contests to finish the job.

They were clicking in every possible way. Eaton and Michael A. Taylor had added late homers in Game 2. The wacky seventh showed that even luck was on their side. There wasn't one hero, a player lifting the rest onto his back, but Strasburg going 6 innings, and Rendon smacking the early double, Suzuki homering, Cabrera pitching in, and all the tiny contributions that, when glued together, form a buzz saw.

There was once reason to wonder if the World Series would ever make it back to Washington. Now, after just a few days in Houston, of all places, there was reason to believe these Nationals could win a title at home. They had to take two of three games, lined up for the weekend, to celebrate in their city, with their city, until the city drank itself to sleep. The thought crossed a few of their minds as they boarded a morning flight. Some whispered that it could be their last trip of the season, one full of bus issues, that train fire on the rails to New York, and that night in Philadelphia when they spent eight hours on the plane, waiting for an update, then scrambled into a fleet of Uber XLs.

Wouldn't it be nice to finish this at home and, just, stay there? What could go wrong?

23

Booooo

October 27, 2019

The answer was a blunt and painful truth.

Taubman's actions followed the Astros east. They were the reeling club, the one dealing with controversy, resting on a razor's edge between floating and finished. Taubman released a statement before Game 1 in Houston. Well, the Astros released it for him and probably wrote it for him, too, saying this, among other platitudes: "Those that know me know that I am a progressive member of the community, and a loving and committed husband and father. I hope that those who do know me understand that the *Sports Illustrated* article does not reflect who I am or my values. I am sorry if anyone was offended by my actions."

That came out Tuesday afternoon. By Wednesday afternoon, MLB was investigating the issue and interviewing those involved. By Thursday evening, Taubman was fired by the Astros. Being a committed husband and father wasn't enough to save his job. The Astros announced this during the travel day between Games 2 and 3, and Luhnow held a press conference at Nationals Park. He declined to reveal who wrote the initial statement that cut down Stephanie Apstein's report. He admitted to seeing it before publication, and that he thought it was wrong, and that the Astros should have waited.

Luhnow was grilled for twenty-four questions about Taubman, the Astros' response, and who was responsible for trying to damage Apstein's career. Joel Sherman, a dogged reporter for the *New York Post*, asked Luhnow why those who crafted the initial statement didn't lose their jobs, leading to this exchange:

"I don't know the answer to that, to be honest with you," Luhnow answered.

"You're one of the people who runs the organization," Sherman shot back.

"I run the baseball operations, as you know."

"Well, Jim Crane hasn't come today, Jeff," Sherman pointed out, referring to the Astros' owner.

"I understand that. And we're taking responsibility and accountability for that and apologizing for it. And at this point that's all I can tell you. I don't have anything else to give you. Sorry about that."

That last phrase, *sorry about that*, came up at the end of the interview. Luhnow was asked if he had apologized to any of the women involved in the incident. He explained that he'd been traveling and had not found the time, but he would as soon as possible. Stephanie Apstein was sitting in the room.

The Astros weren't alone in taking the focus off baseball. Teams are required to have some sort of media access during off days during the postseason. The Nationals were expected to open their clubhouse between Games 2 and 3, given how well they were playing, yet decided to keep it closed. The reason had popped into the news cycle that afternoon.

The White House announced that President Donald Trump would attend Game 5 at Nationals Park. The Nationals did not want players discussing politics before the most important games of their lives. They also did not invite Trump, a fact that soon leaked through anonymous reports. Major League Baseball and commissioner Rob Manfred did. The Nationals would rather he stayed away, especially with the ongoing impeachment proceedings down the road. But presidents and baseball had always been linked.

President Barack Obama threw out the first pitch for Opening Day at Nationals Park in 2010. There were rumors that Trump would in 2017, his first Opening Day in office, but they were met with widespread criticism. Fans wrote emails to the Nationals to object. Others promised on Twitter to boycott the game. It took only a few hours for the White House to announce that Trump would not do the honors, and many outlets reported it as breaking a "century-old" tradition.

That wasn't really the case. Only Warren G. Harding, Calvin Coolidge, Herbert Hoover, Harry Truman, and John F. Kennedy threw the first pitch in every year of their presidencies. Trump had thrown out two first pitches back when he was a celebrity real estate mogul, but was not expected to for Game 5. The Nationals had already lined up first pitches for each of the home games. Game 3 was Chad Cordero and Brian Schneider, a pitcher and a catcher from the inaugural team in 2005. Game 4 was Janyia Freeman, a standout student-athlete at the Washington Nationals Youth Baseball Academy. And Game 5 was José Andrés, the renowned chef and noted opponent of Trump.

Baseball clubhouses are not political places, and, in 2019, there was a reason for that. It was divisive to express pro-Trump opinions in Washington, as in any left-leaning city, and so the Nationals didn't. That does not mean Trump didn't have supporters on the roster. A handful of Nationals had voted for Trump or, at the least, were committed Republicans. That was fairly common for American players around the league.

Sean Doolittle, the Nationals' closer, was one of the rare bleeding-heart liberals in the sport. He wasn't shy about it, either, and was a go-to source for reporters on social and political issues. Doolittle did charity work within the LGBTQ community, among his many organizations. When a rash of hate-filled tweets were dug up in 2018, including a few from teammate Trea Turner, Doolittle tweeted, "It's been a tough couple of weeks for baseball on Twitter. It sucks to see racist and homophobic language coming from inside our league—a league I'm so proud to be a part of that I've worked really hard to make a more accepting and inclusive place for all our fans to enjoy."

Then Doolittle stood at his locker, straight across the room from Turner's, and told reporters he was not trying to "pile on" Turner. Turner's tweets, all from 2011, included the words "faggot" and "retard" and a racist joke about how once women "go black" they need a wheelchair. Doolittle and Turner had a few conversations about inclusivity and the power of hate speech, and Turner addressed the team with a tearful apology.

But those discussions only happen when controversies arise. Most players choose to live in their bubble, to "stick to sports," to avoid anything that reveals opinions and could make people upset. And that's why the Nationals avoided having their players talk about Trump.

"He's the president of this country," said Aníbal Sánchez, who was starting Game 3 and thus required to speak with reporters. "If he wants to come to the game, it's something that he wants to do. Of course everybody has to respect that situation."

Sánchez's next public appearance left him struggling through the Astros' order. They took an early lead Friday when Josh Reddick ripped an RBI single in the second. Sánchez had trouble missing bats. His fastball command was off, and that made it hard to mix his slow pitches effectively. He was tuned up for 10 hits and 4 earned runs in 5⅓ innings and exited with the Nationals trailing 4–1.

They hung around with Victor Robles's RBI triple in the fourth. He slid into third, popped straight up, then did a big shark clap that the dugout returned. But that was the lone run Washington scored.

They finished 0 for 10 with runners in scoring position. They made two fielding errors, tying their most of the postseason, and for the first time in a while, Martinez had a decision go wrong.

Tanner Rainey was warming up when Robles tripled in Ryan Zimmerman. Sánchez was due up after Robles. Once Robles tripled with one out, and the Nationals trailed by a run, it seemed like the right spot to sub out Sánchez for a pinch hitter, even if he was only at 65 pitches. Martinez knew he had to be a bit more conservative in the World Series, and mostly save Scherzer, Strasburg, and Corbin for their scheduled start days. So Martinez kept in Sánchez, he popped up a bunt for the second out, and Trea Turner ended the inning by rolling a dribbler in front of the plate. Sánchez recorded just 4 more outs while allowing 2 more runs. The Nationals never recovered.

"We've lost a game before. Everyone will be okay," said Zimmerman after a 4–1 defeat. He never thought too much of a win or loss, having spent fourteen years in a game built on failure. Then he had two runners on when the Nationals were down 2 in the fifth. He struck out swinging, missing an inside changeup from Josh James, and could only shrug it off. "Nobody thought this was going to be easy, and we have to play good baseball to win."

But by Saturday morning, with the Nationals grounded, one loss was a pretty small problem. They would soon realize that.

Brad Scherzer noticed his son struggling to pick up his daughter. That was the first sign. They were at Max's house in northern Virginia, passing the hours before Game 4, and Scherzer felt a shooting pain in his neck. Then the pain became consistent, stiffening each of his movements. He had dealt with this throughout his career, mini-bouts with his neck, and even went on the ten-day injured list in August of 2017. But the timing was never, ever this bad.

Scherzer went to the park early to meet the training staff. He was injected with a few different medications to alleviate neck spasms and pain in his upper-right trapezius. Scherzer would admit in the off-season that a misstep in treatment made the injury worse. But at the time, with panic rising, they were all looking for a quick fix. Patrick Corbin was scheduled to start Game 4 that night. Scherzer was supposed to have the ball for Game 5.

He did his usual pre-start throwing on Saturday and only further aggravated his neck. The new plan was to sleep on it and pray he felt better in the morning. Scherzer was tense in the dugout while the Astros raced ahead in Game 4. Corbin yielded 4 consecutive hits in the first, walked another batter, and escaped after throwing 26 pitches and allowing 2 runs.

The Astros, on the other hand, got a dominant outing from José Urquidy. They didn't carry a fourth starter on their World Series roster, pegged this as a "bullpen game," and wanted a couple innings from Urquidy before turning to a mash-up of relievers. But Urquidy tossed five scoreless innings while the Houston built a 4–0 lead.

Corbin appeared fatigued and too predictable. The Astros weren't fooled by his below-the-zone sliders, instead zeroing in on his sinker and changeup. Robinson Chirinos stalked a changeup for his second homer in as many games. The Astros finished with 13 hits, the Nationals finished with 4, and the score broke open when Alex Bregman smacked a grand slam off Fernando Rodney in the seventh. The Nationals lost, 8–1, and were now 1 for 19 with runners in scoring position since returning home.

When asked how to make more of constant traffic on the basepaths, Anthony Rendon smiled. He smugly told a reporter that the key was getting more hits. The reporter then asked how the Nationals could go about doing that, and Rendon put on a small show at his locker.

"So we have these bats . . . ," Rendon started, taking one from the top shelf of his locker, talking sarcastically about an issue that evened the Series. He pointed to the wood throughout his demonstration. It made it seem as if there were little else to say. "You try to square it up, and there's a baseball, and then you hit the outfield grass and usually they are hits."

"We've been doing this all season," Corbin said a bit earlier, keeping a far more serious tone. "We've had losses, big losses, and bounced back fine. Guys will be ready to go tomorrow."

Yet the looming question was if Scherzer could pitch. He got home a bit after midnight. He went right to bed, resting his neck on a pillow, and began to hope. The stiffness didn't go away. The spasms kept spasming. He woke up a few times, stirring in the darkness, and knew this wasn't good. Meanwhile, back at Nationals Park, Secret Service cleared the building by 2:00 a.m. They started an eight-hour sweep of the building, using multiple units and a pack of bomb-sniffing dogs, ending as Scherzer woke up.

He tried standing and fell to the floor. He needed help from his wife, Erica, to put on clothes. He needed Erica to drive him to the stadium, but he did not want to talk. Not at the house. Not in the car. Not while every bump on the George Washington Parkway sent sharper pains through his neck.

Erica wasn't having that. She told him it was going to be okay. She explained that everyone had their story, and his was unfolding in private, and he would be ready for Game 7, if one was played, because Strasburg was going to get them there. She believed every word, and just had to get her husband on board. Scherzer stayed quiet while taking it in. He wanted to post. He *needed* to post. Yet now he couldn't, and Joe Ross would start in his place, and so Scherzer delivered that news to Ross in a text message.

"Hey, get ready, you're going to be starting today. There's no way I'm going to be able to start."

Scherzer soon received a cortisone shot at Nationals Park. It was expected to alleviate the nerve irritation in forty-eight hours, and all he could do was wait. The media learned at the beginning of Dave Martinez's pregame press conference. The manager gave the particulars he could: Ross would take the mound. The injury was not related to what Scherzer dealt with in the summer. There was no incident, nothing that Scherzer did wrong, just his waking up Saturday with a stiff neck that would not cooperate.

"For Max to miss a game, especially a significant game like this, he's got to be really hurting," Martinez said when pressed on the severity. "So hopefully, within the next twenty-four hours, as he starts getting better, we start seeing signs of him getting better and then we'll go from there."

Next in the interview room was Scherzer. He walked in without the usual stomp in his step. He turned his full torso, instead of just his neck, to make eye contact with reporters. He remembered missing a start in San Diego for the same reason. He recalled another in Miami, when he tried to pitch through the spasms and his neck locked up during the game.

If he could have risked it again, he would have been preparing to pitch, not talking through gritted teeth about why he wasn't. But that was never an option.

"I mean, I'm as disappointed as I possibly can be not to be able to pitch tonight. It's Game Five of the World Series. I've pitched through so much crap in my career that that would be easy to pitch through at this point. This is literally impossible to do anything with." The frustration filled his eyes. But he fought it off and expressed full confidence in Ross.

Ross spent the season bouncing between the majors and AAA Fresno Grizzlies. He was once a staple of the Nationals' future and even pitched Game 4 of the NLDS in 2016. But he underwent Tommy John surgery the next season, missed about fourteen months afterward, and had not been the same since. The Nationals tried him in the bullpen in the spring. It was a disaster. They sent him back to Fresno, with the goal of stretching him back out, and Ross returned in August to make a string of solid starts.

A line drive in Pittsburgh bruised his right knee at the end of that month. With this setback, Ross fell behind Austin Voth and Erick Fedde in an evolving pecking order. The Nationals left Ross off the roster for the wild-card game, NLDS, and NLCS. They carried Voth as their emergency long reliever. But Voth's shoulder tendinitis flared up in a bullpen session during the NLCS, and Washington had to shut him down for the year. They activated Ross, considering him a last-ditch option, and he pitched 2 scoreless innings in their Game 3 loss.

Then, out of nowhere, he was tapped to start Game 5 of the World Series.

Ross entered a sold-out stadium at 7:39 p.m., his eyes fixed straight ahead, his ears full of a long, loud ovation. The crowd chanted, "Let's go, Joe!" They screamed while he tossed his first warm-up throws in right field. They were behind Ross, giving him everything they could on October 27. Then came the boos.

Trump had arrived by motorcade before first pitch and was escorted to his suite above the visitors' dugout. Snipers and Secret Service agents had guarded the area all day. He was joined by the first lady, his daughter Ivanka Trump, and twelve members of Congress, all of whom were Republican.

The Nationals were already behind, 2–0, when Trump flashed onto the videoboard. It was after the third inning, once the typical salute to the military had ended. The camera panned to Trump, and the crowd erupted in boos. There were chants of "Lock him up!" mimicking how Trump supporters jeered Hillary Clinton during the 2016 election. That blended into chants of "Impeach Trump!" a topical choice, and the president did not flinch.

He smiled. He waved at fans. He turned to Kevin McCarthy, the House minority leader, for idle chat, and then sat down. Trump hardly ever appeared in Washington outside of the White House and his own properties. He stayed away from restaurants he did not own. This was his first Washington sporting event since he was elected, and here the fans showed why. He stayed until the eighth, and it was common for someone to remember his presence, turn toward his open-air box, and start screaming. It was one way to get the anger out.

The Nationals' bats were still dead. The Astros were still surging. They had Cole on the mound, and he was back to his dominant self, and Ross made two mistakes—a sinker to Yordan Álvarez, and a hanging slider to Carlos Correa—and that decided it. Álvarez went deep with a 2-run homer in the second. Correa did the same in the fourth. Juan Soto scored the Nationals' only run, homering off Cole for the second time in the series, but it wasn't nearly enough.

Washington had carried every ounce of momentum back from Houston. They looked like the better team, and the team of unbending fate, but that was all slipping away. Ross thought he had Correa struck out with a low-and-out slider, yet home-plate umpire Lance Barksdale did not move. Victor Robles thought he worked a walk, with one on and two outs in the seventh, but Barksdale rung him up on a questionable call. Cole's fastball looked high and outside the strike zone. Robles jumped off the dirt, squeezed his bat with two hands, then lobbed every piece of his gear in Barksdale's direction.

Would it have mattered? Would a walk, with the Nationals trailing by 3 runs, even make a dent in the final score? Who knows. What mattered was that image, of Robles boiling with frustration, of the Nationals appearing desperate and fraught. The Astros bullied them again, taking Game 5, 7–1, and a 3-2 lead in the Series.

He looked a little spent. The Nationals had scored 3 runs across three home games. The Astros had managed to plate 19. Washington finished with 17 hits across Games 3, 4, and 5, and were 1 for 21 with runners in scoring position. Scherzer's neck spasms only deepened the disappointment.

No team had ever won the World Series with four road victories. But the response was to *go 1-0*, to *stay in the fight*, to do what the Nationals had for months, whenever they were doubted, and just play Game 6 in Houston.

"What's new? That's kind of our feeling. What's new?" Adam Eaton repeated after the loss. "Backs against the wall. Winners come to play when their backs are against the wall."

"They didn't win a hundred and six games for nothing. They're really good," Martinez explained in his postgame press conference. Reporters dangled questions about Barksdale and the umpires, pointing to the call for Correa and against Robles. Martinez didn't bite. "They've got a well-balanced lineup. Their pitching is good. Their bullpen gets out. We knew this coming in. They're a game up with two games left. So let's just worry about Tuesday."

Worry was an interesting word choice. The Astros found confidence in starting Verlander for Game 6. The Nationals rested theirs on Strasburg. But past Tuesday, and the only game they were guaranteed, was nothing but uncertainty. They were really banking on a cortisone shot.

24

"Remember your heart!"

October 29, 2019

It took two pitches for Jonathan Tosches to notice.

Strasburg was blatantly tipping his pitches. This time, Tosches was sure. It wasn't a false alarm like when Bregman thought he saw something in Game 2. It was the exact same tipping Strasburg did in Phoenix on August 3, when he gave up 9 runs on 9 hits to the Diamondbacks. The Astros, like the Diamondbacks, knew what pitch was coming by watching Strasburg's glove. He squeezed it when gripping a fastball. He flared it when gripping a changeup or curve. By recognizing each tell—for the staple of his arsenal, and his best out pitches—the Diamondbacks had made him look like a wide-eyed rookie. Now the Astros were doing the same.

That left Tosches with a critical decision. He sat in the video room by the visitors' clubhouse, staring at the monitor fixed on Strasburg, and ran quick calculations. It was against his personal policy to bother pitchers during starts. He was the coordinator of advance scouting, respected at thirty-seven years old, but was not supposed to rattle their brains. Telling a pitcher he is tipping can completely throw him off. Telling Strasburg could both agitate and upset the veteran. He *had* changed this year and seemed more open to criticism, but he was still Stephen Strasburg. No one, let alone Tosches, dared talk to him while he pitched.

That's why Tosches didn't sound any alarms in Phoenix in August. Strasburg knew something was off when he exited that game. He approached the video staff, the way Tosches preferred it, and asked if they noticed anything. Tosches showed him the squeeze and the flair. Strasburg corrected it, and, across 14 starts before this one, Tosches had never seen it again. The timing of its return, in Game 6 of the World Series, with the Nationals a loss from elimination, could not have been worse.

Tosches grew restless as the first unfolded. George Springer stalked a first-pitch fastball for a double. José Altuve scored him one batter later with a sacrifice fly, and Altuve appeared ready for a 2-strike curveball. The Nationals had scored in the top half, when Anthony Rendon singled in Trea Turner, but their lead was already erased. Then Alex Bregman stepped in and ripped a fastball out to left. The stadium swelled with excitement, and Bregman trotted down the line, watching the ball carry, before dropping his bat around first base.

Enough was enough. All Tosches ever wanted was to help a team in the major leagues. His playing days flickered out at the University of Massachusetts Amherst, and he worked for Fidelity Investments after graduating. But he missed the game, went back to UMass for a sports management degree, and soon took an operations job with the Nassau Pride.

The Pride was an independent-league team with no budget. When it folded, Tosches worked his connections to land a gig at the Nationals' spring training facility in Viera, Florida. The job was a blend of player development, business, and facility management, and Tosches did it for half a decade. But he always asked to do more, to go on scouting trips, to see every nook of the organization. That's what led him to the Nationals' video room in 2016, and to become head of advance scouting two years later. Tosches, like Jim Cuthbert, like everyone who never made the show, backed each recommendation with loads of reason and research. That's how he gained trust from coaches and players. He also took a few risks along the way.

So Tosches ditched his post after the first inning and sprinted to the dugout in Houston. He was there a minute later, a bit out of breath, and called for Paul Menhart's attention. Menhart had watched Strasburg pitch since he was twenty-one years old and could spot the tiniest flaw in Strasburg's mechanics. He saw the tipping, too, and started predicting each pitch Strasburg was about to throw. Every guess was right. When he turned to see Tosches, an unusual sight midgame, Menhart knew what was coming.

"Paul," Tosches said once the first ended, "he's doing it again."

Tosches's job was finished. Next Menhart had to decide the best way to approach Strasburg. Menhart scanned the tunnel, where Strasburg often went to avoid the frenetic energy of the dugout. There was no dancing, no banging on the rails, just him, his thoughts, and a small TV that told him when to retake the mound.

"Stephen," Menhart said once he found Strasburg, "you're doing it again."

"Show me," Strasburg shot back. "Show me exactly how. Right now."

Strasburg held out his black leather glove and Menhart took it. The coach slipped the mitt on and pantomimed the pitch tipping. He showed Strasburg how he squeezed it for fastballs. Then he flared it for off-speed pitches. Strasburg recognized these as the same issues he'd fought in Phoenix. But while they fixed those between starts, and by watching video on loop, Strasburg had just minutes before he'd keep facing the Astros.

This was the second time he and Menhart had met like this in the postseason. During Game 2 in Los Angeles, Strasburg thought he heard a whistle before releasing the ball. He grabbed Menhart and complained about the noise, thinking the Dodgers had picked something up and were relaying signs to the batter's box. Then, Menhart urged him to forget about the whistles and keep dominating. Now, he urged his pitcher to make a change. He wanted Strasburg to shake his glove before each pitch, so it looked the same no matter the grip. Strasburg immediately pushed back.

"I always thought that looked so stupid," Strasburg told Menhart.

"Well, guess what? We're in the sixth game. You can get your ass handed to you or you can make this adjustment."

"All right," Strasburg muttered, and they didn't talk about it again.

"It's an awful, lonely feeling on the mound when you're tipping pitches," Menhart later explained. "By giving him something to do, it took his mind off the fact they might know what was coming, and he absolutely dominated."

"We had to do it," Tosches recalled. "I would have regretted not speaking up for the rest of my life."

Shaking his glove was one key adjustment. Another was something Yan Gomes had picked up during Joe Ross's start in Game 5. Gomes caught Games 2, 3, 4, 5, and 6 while Kurt Suzuki nursed a lingering elbow injury. For the first three contests, the plan was to pitch the Astros outside. They had power up and down their lineup, and the way to limit it was to make them go the other way. But Ross's stuff did not fit that approach.

His power sinker is best used inside against righties. So Gomes called it there, and called it there some more, and the Astros had trouble. If Ross's outing looked like a wash—two costly homers, then a lopsided loss—it had value beneath the surface. Gomes gained new insight on the Astros' hitters. He brought it to Strasburg before Game 6, and Strasburg was intrigued. Strasburg's sinker was a bit different from Ross's. It moved side to side, while Ross's had some dip, but the principle was the same: Houston didn't like velocity on its hands.

Two of Strasburg's three outs in the second came on inside fastballs. The second was a sinker that ran in on the right-handed Correa. Strasburg pounded José Altuve inside before getting him to pop up and end the third. Strasburg retired nine straight between the first and fourth, shaking his glove all the while, and struck out Correa to finish that frame. Two inside heaters set up a third-strike curveball in the dirt.

The Nationals were down a run, but that was about to change. Strasburg and Gomes were not the only ones making subtle tweaks. Adam Eaton felt off heading into the World Series and had a .194 batting average across the wild-card game, NLDS, and NLCS. He still got on base, working six walks, and was an effective number two hitter behind Trea Turner. But Eaton's production was limited to a small handful of at bats, and he felt his timing was the worst it had been all season.

When he went to Kevin Long, the hitting coach already had a fix in mind. He thought Eaton should eliminate his stride altogether. That would give him a chance to load early, be ready for high velocity, and adjust if he read off-speed out of the pitcher's hand. It had been a long time since Eaton had cut down his stride. But he listened to Long and had 6 hits and a homer in the first 5 games of the series.

Now Eaton lifted his foot during Verlander's delivery, dropped it in the same spot, and saw the twisting seams of a slider. He waited a tick, loading his hands behind his left shoulder, and ripped his bat through the zone. Verlander's pitch caught too much of the plate. Eaton got all of it. The ball landed fifteen rows beyond the right-field fence. Eaton blew a bubble while rounding first.

A dance line waited in the dugout, and Kendrick waited to race some cars. They revved their engines, punched their invisible gears, and, once Rendon popped out to right, watched Juan Soto do a Juan Soto thing. The score was now tied, 2–2, when Soto kicked dirt around the batter's box. Verlander took exception to the Soto shuffle. Verlander missed with an inside fastball, Soto spread his legs, grabbed his junk, and, after Verlander argued the call, turned to home-plate umpire Sam Holbrook and said, "Ball. That's a ball."

"Not here!" Verlander barked from the mound, seeming to tell Soto to cool it. "Not here!"

Soto only grinned. Verlander then challenged him with a similar pitch, high-and-tight heat, and Soto murdered it. The ball came in at 95.9 mph. It exited at 111.4, bound for the park's closed roof, until it floated deep into the upper deck. Soto froze by the plate, gazing at his blast like a piece of art, and decided to mimic Bregman. Soto carried his bat up the line, held it out toward the Astros' dugout, and flipped it into the grass in front of first-base coach Tim Bogar.

Bogar chucked it back toward home. He was upset with the gesture, as was Dave Martinez, as were many of Soto's veteran teammates. It broke some unwritten code to copy a celebration that was already out of line. But Soto's defense was pure innocence. He later told reporters that he'd thought Bregman looked cool and wanted to try it himself. And believe him or not, the Nationals had the lead.

Strasburg kept the Astros in check from there. He stranded runners on second and third in the fifth. He left another on in the sixth, after a leadoff single, and punctuated that inning with his second strikeout of Correa. That brought the top of the seventh, and Gomes punched a lead-off single. Then Turner tapped a dribbler in front of the plate, busted toward first, and Brad Peacock, pitching for the Astros, flung a sidearm through to first. It whizzed past Yuli Gurriel and into foul territory. Turner's leg knocked off Gurriel's glove once the ball was past. So Turner raced to second, Gomes raced to third, and the Nationals had two runners in scoring position with no outs. Eaton, Rendon, and Soto were coming up. It was a prime opportunity for at least one insurance run.

But Holbrook was motioning at Turner. The umpire thought Turner had run too far inside the baseline and interfered with Peacock's throw. He called runner's interference, meaning Turner was out and Gomes went back to first. Turner stood on second and turned his palms to the ceiling. Martinez took one step onto the field and lost it.

"Bullshit! Bullshit! The hell are you doing?" Then Martinez stomped toward the umpire while pointing at the base line. He urged that Turner ran straight to the bag. He threw in a few more curse words. Turner may have started a bit inside the line, but corrected that before reaching first. It was the usual path for a right-handed hitter. Plus, Peacock's errant throw would have missed Gurriel either way.

The umpires convened and put on headsets. Everyone thought they were reviewing the call. But the discussion centered on whether the Nationals could play the rest of the game under protest. Crew chief Gary Cederstrom spoke with the league office in New York. Since Holbrook had made a judgment call, however questionable it was, the Nationals were not permitted to protest or request a review.

That's when cameras caught Mike Rizzo, the Nationals' general manager, screaming from his seat behind the dugout. Rizzo quickly straightened up, typed an angry text message, and hit send. He was later told by an MLB staffer that he could not talk to the commissioner like that.

Turner stood on the dugout steps and simmered. He is calm by nature and rarely shows emotion, but could not hold his anger in. First it was all over his face. Then it was picked up by nearby TV microphones. "Hey, he's right there! Just ask him! Why's he hiding?" Turner yelled while pointing at Joe Torre, MLB's chief baseball officer. Torre oversaw all umpires in that role. Turner wanted him pulled into the mix. "We can't replay this, it's like a protest of the game. Joe Torre is in charge of all the umpires and he's right there. And he's sitting with his head down trying not to look up!"

The shortstop stared straight at Torre. But there was nothing Turner or anyone else could do. Holbrook had made his decision, there was no reversing it, and it might affect the game. The Nationals went from rallying to square one. Eaton popped out to third base to give the Astros two outs. But Rendon made sure the call wouldn't sting Washington. He may have bailed out the league, too.

When his 2-run homer cleared the left-field wall, Rendon sank into a light jog. Turner was still too angry to react. He stood straight up, his eyes on fire, and watched the lead stretch to 3 runs. The rest of the dugout erupted. But Martinez, like Turner, would not let Holbrook off easy.

Martinez waited until the top of the seventh ended before making his next move. Once it did, and the players were off the field, he went right back to shouting at Holbrook and Cederstrom. It appeared that Cederstrom raised a finger at Martinez and told him to calm down. Martinez was restrained by bench coach Chip Hale, repeated it back—"You got to calm down! You got to calm down! . . . Fuck you!"—and could not be settled.

Martinez snapped at Holbrook again: "The fuck are you looking at?" So Holbrook looked right at Martinez and threw him out, triggering the manager even more. He tried spinning past Hale, who now looked like a small offensive lineman, and tugged down the front of Hale's jersey. Bogar stepped between Martinez and the umpires. Menhart rushed over to help. While they peeled Martinez away and ushered him off the field, the manager heard a shrill voice from behind their dugout.

"Davey! Your heart!" a woman yelled out of the first row. Martinez glanced up to see that she wore a Nationals shirt. Or maybe he was just seeing red. "Remember your heart!"

In some ways he did. A doctor soon visited the trainer's room to check Martinez out. The game resumed, Hale managed in his place, and Strasburg and Rendon made that an easy task. Strasburg pitched a one-two-three seventh, mixing in one of his 7 strikeouts, and used just 5 pitches to get through the eight. Rendon's next at bat came in the ninth, and he smacked a 2-run double over Springer's head in center. That gave Rendon 5 RBI and the Nationals a 5-run lead. Rendon had 6 at bats in the seventh inning or later of four elimination games, and his numbers were ridiculous: 2 homers, 3 doubles, a single, and a walk for good measure.

The Nationals' stars played like stars. This run was built on a lot of things—starting pitching, experience, fun—but it still depended on the best players shining in the biggest moments. That's what Strasburg and Rendon did in Game 6, the pitcher shaking his glove before each throw, the hitter using three swings to deflate his hometown. Strasburg got his final out with a fastball off the low-and-outside corner. He'd spent the last few innings going away, away, away. It was even more effective once he'd lived inside for the first half of the night.

In another odd twist, as if the game needed it, Scherzer had warmed during the bottom of the seventh. The Nationals confirmed that he was ready for Game 7. They had not, however, indicated that he could pitch in relief. But if Strasburg had allowed a base runner in that inning, the plan was for Scherzer to face the heart of the order. Since Strasburg didn't and looked well in control, Scherzer wasn't needed.

Hale hooked Strasburg at 104 pitches and 25 outs. Sean Doolittle entered to record the last 2. Strasburg was now the first pitcher to go 5-0 in the same postseason. His career playoff ERA was down to a microscopic 1.46. He and Scherzer had had their differences. In July of 2018, Strasburg had left a rough outing and brushed off Scherzer in the dugout. That led to a heated exchange that aired on television. The pair wound up in the tunnel, both huffing mad, to vent their frustrations. Their personalities are polar opposites. It would be a stretch to call them close friends.

But that was buried by October 29, when their fates collided in Houston, when Strasburg pushed the Series to one final game.

Scherzer felt good before Game 6, came to Minute Maid Park, tossed in left field, and stretched out the distance to see what his neck could take. His motion was fluid. The ball flew off his hand. Then he charged toward the clubhouse with his usual urgency, passed the press and, without stopping, barked, "I'm good!"

No one had asked. He was pitching Game 7 if Strasburg could get him there. And once Strasburg did, putting the ball in Scherzer's hands, the two of them shared a quick hug. Erica Scherzer was right. Here was Max's chance.

25

One More

October 30, 2019

There is no good view of the visitors' bullpen inside Minute Maid Park. It is tucked beneath the left-field seats, behind the left-field wall, then shaded by a dark screen, as if something top secret is going on. The dugouts rely on small monitors to check activity. Reporters use binoculars from the press box. Otherwise, in a given game—let's say Game 7 of the World Series—it is a bunch of faceless bodies, stirring into motion when the landline rings, stretching a leg over here, or loosening an arm over there.

But on October 30, with Game 7 rolling along, everyone knew one certainty: no one was warming for the Nationals. Not after Max Scherzer allowed a solo homer to Yuli Gurriel in the second. Not after the Astros followed it with back-to-back singles. Not after Scherzer put two on in the third, or two on in the fourth, or two more on in the bottom of the fifth.

There *was* stirring in the bullpen. Legs were stretched. Arms were loosened and spun above heads like a windmill. But no pitches were thrown. Not one. With everything on the line, and no tomorrow to plan for, Dave Martinez had all his arms available. Patrick Corbin and Aníbal Sánchez began the game in the bullpen. Martinez joked in his pregame press conference that Strasburg could face a batter, even after throwing 104 pitches the day before. Or maybe Martinez was serious.

That's the nature of Game 7s, of doing or dying, when you have to play and manage as if nothing's beyond the last out. In this case, nothing was. But Martinez was still gambling, one batter at a time, trusting Scherzer to hold on, and holding off on a backup plan. Scherzer did not have his best stuff. He didn't even have his sort-of-best stuff. Not warming anyone, for if or when Scherzer imploded, was managerial malpractice. A pitcher did step on the bullpen mound in the second inning. Order seemed restored. Yet that pitcher was Aaron Barrett, who was not on the World Series roster, and who, throughout the playoffs, had stood on the bullpen rubber, bouncing a ball in his hand, to give the offense luck.

It had sparked a few rallies across the last few weeks. But the Nationals stranded Juan Soto at first, stayed behind, 1–0, and Barrett sat down. Corbin leaned against the bullpen fence and swung his left leg. Sánchez broke into a light jog behind him. Martinez and Paul Menhart chatted, considering the next move, yet decided that Scherzer was their top option in a jam—even if he'd created it.

Two were on after Gurriel's homer in the second. Scherzer then got Robinson Chirinos to pop a bunt to Yan Gomes. The runners stayed on first and second with one out. They moved to third with the next out, a grounder to first base, and were ready to score once George Springer smacked a liner to left.

Soto took two steps to his left, froze while judging the ball, then fell forward with his glove angled upward. He caught it with inches to spare. The ballpark went from exploding to one loud sigh, knowing the Astros had been a hit away from breaking this wide open. But Scherzer survived, the Nationals' bats had a chance, and all they had to do was solve Zack Greinke.

Greinke faced the minimum three batters in the first, four in the second, three in the third and fourth, four in the fifth, and went one-two-three in the sixth. He looked untouchable, his pitches finding each crevice of the zone, his blank stare firm under pressure. The crowd grew louder with each batter he retired. Then it went ballistic in the fifth, once Carlos Correa ripped a single down the line.

Gurriel scored to give the Astros a 2–0 lead. There were two outs and still no one up in the Nationals' bullpen. Scherzer wiped sweat off his forehead and stared down Robinson Chirinos. Houston had two more insurance runs in scoring position. If Scherzer wilted again and those runs came in, and the Astros opened a yawning lead with him stuck on the mound, Martinez might never have escaped it. The decision to push Scherzer, further and further, against all logic and sense, was a mix of gutsy and insane. But Scherzer struck out Chirinos, planting a changeup in the dirt, and had kept the score close.

That's when Corbin ditched his red sweatshirt and started tossing. He'd done his full warm-up routine before the game and only needed a handful of pitches to get ready for the sixth. That was one reason Martinez waited until Scherzer was done, at 103 pitches, to get Corbin going. The other was Martinez's limitless faith in Scherzer.

Corbin emerged after Greinke worked through the sixth on eight pitches. It was possible to project this very scenario in September, while discussing the future at a team dinner in Miami. Word of the postseason pitching plan, of riding six arms to exhaustion, had spread throughout the clubhouse. That's when some basic math began. If Scherzer was the first in line, and Strasburg was next, that meant Corbin could wind up with the season in his hands.

Scherzer remembered everyone telling Corbin this—"You're going to be the man, Pat! You're the man!"—while the lefty brushed it aside. Corbin is shy and reserved. The players fed off that and kept goading him. The conversation did pass, more wine was poured, but Joe Dillon, the club's assistant hitting coach, couldn't let it go quite yet.

"It's going to be you, Pat," Scherzer recalled Dillon saying. "You're going to be the guy on the mound."

Now Martinez expected Corbin to pitch one frame before Sean Doolittle came in. But Corbin induced a double play to end the sixth, went straight for Martinez on the dugout steps, and told his manager two words: I'm good. It was enough to keep Corbin in for at least another inning. It would only matter, though, if the Nationals did anything against Greinke.

This run was built on miracles big and small. There was the revival from 19-31, and there would always be, but consider what happened in October alone. Consider that wayward bounce past Trent Grisham in the wild-card game. Consider Game 4 of the NLDS, when the Nationals held a 5-run lead, the Dodgers had the bases loaded, and what would have been a Joc Pederson double—and given the Dodgers a prayer—landed centimeters foul. Consider Game 5, when Dave Roberts left in Clayton Kershaw, then left in Joe Kelly, then left Howie Kendrick to hit an NLDS-winning grand slam. Then consider that it didn't stop there.

The cortisone shot worked. The glove shaking did, too. In the second inning of Game 7, when Scherzer was teetering toward disaster, the Nationals caught a break on that grounder to first. Josh Reddick's roller hit the bag and still went right to Ryan Zimmerman. It could have easily shot to the right, or the left, or in any diagonal direction to extend the Astros' rally. But it didn't. Another little miracle.

Now the Nationals needed one more.

Adam Eaton led off the seventh and chopped out to shortstop. Greinke had thrown only 73 pitches. But on came Anthony Rendon for his favorite type of situation: hitting in the seventh inning or later of an elimination game. He watched a fastball go by to get ahead in the count. He fiddled with his batting gloves, fiddled with his bat, and quickly settled back into his familiar stance.

His knees bent a bit. His hands hovered between his shoulders and waist. His eyes watched Greinke's motion, his wrists waited, then they snapped toward a misplaced pitch. Rendon rocked a floating slider out to left, leaving him 360 feet to jog. For about 358 of them, maybe more, his face rested like a driver's license photo. But right before touching home plate, and halving the deficit to one run, Rendon's mouth became a semicircle, his palms faced the heavens, and he shrugged. One last dance line waited for him in the dugout, with chants of "Hey! Hey! Hey!" and Rendon shook his hips until he was crouched to the floor.

Through months of practice, and a lot of comebacks, the Nationals had grown comfortable when trailing. They even seemed to welcome the challenge, the four elimination games before this one, the ability to apply pressure from behind and make their opponent sweat. Rendon's homer was a leap in the right direction. But it was the next at bat, with Soto up, that shifted the entire game.

Soto took an outside fastball, swung through an outside changeup, watched another outside changeup, watched another, and laid off a low changeup for ball four, a call Greinke disagreed with. And those five pitches made all the difference. Greinke's total count was up to 80. A. J. Hinch had Will Harris ready in the bullpen. He had also warmed up Gerrit Cole, who was available in relief but never entered. With Howie Kendrick coming up, and the momentum teetering, Hinch chose a fresh Harris because of Greinke's two mistakes.

Everyone with the Nationals had the same series of emotions. They were shocked, relieved, and, more than anything, ecstatic that Hinch pulled Greinke. Mike Rizzo felt it from his seat behind the dugout. Owner Mark Lerner felt it in the owner's box. Scherzer had ducked into the clubhouse after exiting, his stomach a knot of nerves, and spent twenty minutes analyzing his start. But he was back in the dugout for the seventh and, like the rest, could not believe Greinke was walking off the field.

Harris was Hinch's go-to option, a do-everything righty who had dominated all season. He finished the year with a 1.50 ERA. He inherited 27 runners and stranded 22 of them. He was Houston's fireman, the pitcher who navigated trouble, and now in charge of gluing Soto to first base. The task brought him matchups with Kendrick and Asdrúbal Cabrera.

He began with a curve for strike one. Then he threw a cutter that started middle before diving away from Kendrick. If that pitch in Los Angeles was perfect, the one Joe Kelly ran into Kendrick's bat, this one was much tougher to handle. Ball met wood, the contact rattling Kendrick's forearms, and he sprinted out of the batter's box. It was sliced, and bent toward the right-field corner, drifting through the awestruck air, bending more, and more, until . . .

Dongggg.

In the hurried moment between result and reaction, that sound—*dongggg*—echoed through thousands of ears. It echoed through a silent stadium, through the streets of Houston, and, in Washington, the pixelated big screen at Nationals Park. Some thirteen thousand fans stood in there, soaked beneath a driving rain, and learned right then, right at the edge of their patience, why they kept showing up.

The ball struck the yellow foul pole. Howie Kendrick had done it again. Harris gazed out to right, his stare beyond blank, while Kendrick yelled his way around the bases. The Nationals led, 3–2, and went from reeling, to damn near finished, to nine outs away from a title. Another miracle meant another, final countdown. And that meant another two innings for Corbin.

Corbin's seventh lasted four batters and ended like his sixth: *I'm good.* His eighth, after Soto singled in Eaton to make it 4–2, went three up, three down, and put the Nationals three outs from a win. They would belong to Hudson. It was as if Corbin had earned a six-year, $140 million contract, and that massive dinner bill from Fiola Mare, with three spotless innings, in a role he was not signed to fill. He threw 44 pitches that shut the Astros down, and in the ninth, just before Hudson entered, Eaton ripped a 2-run knock to right.

Eaton fist-bumped Tim Bogar and directed a "Baby Shark" clap to the dugout. They returned it, all the way to the end, pressing their thumbs to index fingers. Then the bullpen door swung open, cutting a hole in the dark screen, and Hudson skipped across the warning track. Doolittle thought back to one of Hudson's September interviews. When Doolittle had returned from the injured list and was still finding his form, Hudson told reporters that, in the end, this team would celebrate around Doolittle. He was the closer, Hudson urged, and the ninth inning was his.

Doolittle couldn't help but laugh to himself. Look at them now. Hudson, the reluctant closer, the one who'd believed himself unfit for this, took the ball from Corbin, in the last pass of 2019. It was two pitches into the inning, when Springer got under a middle-in fastball, that Rizzo looked up, his son to his right, his fiancée to his left, their eyes watching a pop fly meet gravity. That's when he turned to Michael, to Jodi, to himself, even, and let those words slip out.

"We're going to win the fucking World Series," Rizzo stated, once and for all, and Hudson nudged them one step closer by striking out José Altuve on three pitches. Michael Brantley was the final batter in the way. They fell into a 2-2 count on fastball, fastball, slider, fastball. Hudson thought back to Game 2 of the NLDS, when he battled Corey Seager in Los Angeles, using a burst of fastballs to set up his put-away pitch. Seager went down on a slider in the dirt. Hudson felt like he could beat Brantley with the same.

So after Brantley fouled off another fastball, and Gomes called for a slider low and in, Hudson came set, his glove at his belt, and drew a deep breath. He was joined by people around the world. They had waited a long time for this, and would do the last part together.

Marissa Mizroch was at Minute Maid Park, sobbing on the concourse past the third-base line, thinking about her dad. John Mizroch died of lung cancer on February 23, 2019, right as spring training began. He was seventy years old. Marissa loved the Nationals because he did, because he recorded each game to watch it twice, because of the time he asked her to make a Trea Turner meme, without knowing what a meme was.

She grew up in DC, and now, at twenty-five, was a morning-show producer in Austin. When the Nationals made the World Series, and the Astros became their opponent, Marissa was set on making a game. Houston was a two-and-a-half-hour drive from her apartment. John would have traveled much farther. So she spent rent money on a standing-room ticket for Game 7, even if she'd have to turn her car around at midnight, win or lose, to start a 2:00 a.m. shift. She put on her favorite red Nationals shirt, the one she bought at the last game she went to with her dad. Then she was there, exactly where she was supposed to be, sobbing and shaking through the ninth.

Natan Bash watched Game 6 on a bench inside a Tel Aviv military base. It was near 6:00 a.m. and freezing when the Nationals secured that victory, so his officer allowed him to go home, thirty minutes north, to watch Game 7 with his family. They filled their little living room around 2:45 a.m. and now huddled around a TV, wary of waking their neighbors, waiting in the dead of night for Hudson to throw that pitch.

Zoe Jackson was in Cambridge, United Kingdom, watching on her laptop while playing the Nationals radio broadcast. She skyped with her parents and had them point their camera at the TV. She was far from home, studying history in a graduate program, yet felt back in Silver Spring, Maryland, among family, for each playoff game.

Jack Gillies tuned in to a shaky stream from a quiet morning in Barcelona. Eric Martin toggled his Wi-Fi to get a clear DirecTV feed on a flight from Mexico to New York. Sandy Pugh and Jim Lastowka, longtime fans, were flying from New York to Spain and booked the trip without considering this dilemma. The game was not offered in Delta's entertainment package. They pulled up MLB Gamecast on their iPad, just in time for the last few innings, and asked a flight attendant for two glasses of champagne.

Luiz Otavio was in São Paulo, Brazil, hiding out in a bathroom stall, watching the ninth inning on his cell phone. He was in the middle of a shift at the bank he works for, but kept glancing at his hip as the comeback unfolded. That's how he knew when to slip away for the finish. He dialed the volume down, to just loud enough that he could hear, and prayed no one noticed he was missing.

Todd Dixon was anchored off the Georgia coast, researching a mid-1800s wooden sailing vessel. By day, he scoured the sunken ship, once bound for Georgia from New York, for more than a million dollars in gold, rusted cannons, and other personal effects. By night, he was fixed on the Nationals. His girlfriend, Carrie O'Reilly, was at Florida State University, and they texted after each out of Game 7. But since Todd was fifteen seconds behind, his service slow from the bowels of a boat, Carrie waited for his reactions before offering hers.

Matt Stevenson and his wife, Michela, were checking into a Maui hotel when they heard commotion from the lobby bar. A small group of Nationals fans were going crazy over Howie Kendrick's go-ahead homer. The newlyweds dropped their bags in the room and rushed downstairs to join them.

Dustin Chaffee was in Yellowknife, in Canada's Northwest Territories, pacing about the living room with a blanket over his head. His wife and daughter thought he was insane. But Dustin had been a fan for thirty years, following the Nationals when they were the Montreal Expos, a reminder that one city lost its team when baseball returned to Washington. And back in the Washington area, at Holy Cross Hospital in Silver Spring, Luke Waidman and his wife, Jackie, held Millie Rose for the first time. Millie was born at 4:40 p.m. on October 30. She would never remember all the early playoff exits. She would only know what happened on her birthday.

Superstitions were also in full swing. In Vancouver, Washington, Soren Roth put on his lucky T-shirt—a faded long-sleeve from the Nationals' inaugural season—and gripped the handle of his rowing machine. He began working out in the sixth, before Zack Greinke exited, and couldn't stop once the scoreboard flipped. The radio call blared through his black headphones. Sweat beaded his forehead and close-cropped hair. In Oxford, Mississippi, Scott Wyant did the same on the elliptical, pouring his nervous energy into a steady jog.

In Alexandria, Virginia, Bo Macreery was banished upstairs to pick his guitar and sing, a routine he and his wife did to start rallies from home. Scorpions' "Rock You Like a Hurricane" seemed to always rev the offense. The Police's "Message in a Bottle" was for defense and pitching. Bo and his wife bumped their radios to max volume, making it so Bo could hear a floor away, and he slipped into a rhythm. Then Kendrick homered, he skipped down the steps, and his wife told him, no, stay put and keep playing. So he did, and when Hudson threw a slider to Brantley, and Brantley missed it, and deep breaths became a wide wave of screams, Bo dropped his guitar and screamed, too.

Luiz screamed from the skinny stall in São Paulo. Natan screamed and cried at 5:50 a.m. in Tel Aviv. Zoe screamed from Cambridge, Jack from Barcelona, Matt and Michela from Maui, and Luke and Jackie from a recovery room at Holy Cross, their family one baby bigger, their hearts never feeling so full.

Eric screamed from seat 9D of his JetBlue flight. Sandy and Jim did from seats 10D and 10F on Delta, and touched their champagne cups before taking a long sip. Dustin screamed in Yellowknife and collapsed beneath that knitted throw blanket. Soren screamed after ninety-three minutes on the rowing machine. Scott screamed after more than ninety minutes on the elliptical. Todd screamed from his bed on the boat, banging his head against the top bunk before texting Carrie—"!!!!!!!!!!!!!!!!!!!!!!!!!"—on a fifteen-second delay. Conor McBride screamed from Columbia, South Carolina, sprinted toward the door, then stumbled into a coffee table and tore the ACL in his left knee.

And in Houston, in a heap of Astros fans, Marissa screamed through heavy tears. Her cheeks were slick and her makeup runny. Sons called moms, and grandsons called grandmothers, and daughters called their fathers, or the other way around. That was all Marissa wanted once Hudson chucked his glove toward the Nationals' dugout. She wondered what John would say, how his face would have looked, why he had to watch all those empty years, replaying each loss, only to miss the ultimate thrill.

She missed him. There was no way around it. But while she watched the celebration, and the Nationals rush the field, it was as if Marissa were hanging with her dad again. It was the first time in a long time that something felt right. Dean Schleicher could relate. So could Darren Goldwater, Ryan Raley, Phil Gracik, and Stephen Baughan.

They all had lost someone who'd waited for this, who'd wished for it, who'd hoped against hope that this title would come. October 30, 2019, was about the Nationals, and it was about family, but it was really about John Mizroch, Richard Goldwater, Leo Schleicher, John Raley, Lewis "Happy" Gracik, and Grace Grimes. It was about every fan who didn't live to see this, yet was right there all along.

Dave Martinez thought about his father, about Ernie, who wanted to be in Houston, close to his son, but could no longer travel. The players spilled out of the dugout at 10:50 p.m. But Martinez froze in his seat, a lifetime running through his head, and let the rest take those first steps into glory. The coaches came by for one-armed hugs. His players shouted—"Let's go! Come on, skip!—and Martinez was slow to budge. He wanted to reflect, if only for a moment, on who was there, who wasn't, and a question he might never answer: *How the hell did we get here?*

The diamond brimmed with improbability. There was Hudson, the pitcher who had back-to-back Tommy John surgeries, considered retirement, began this year auditioning on a high school field, his career in the balance, and landed here, with Washington, still saying he did not want to close.

There was Scherzer, his neck pain gone, his eyes—the blue one, the brown one—searching for someone to tackle. There was Stephen Strasburg, undrafted out of high school, unable to stay healthy all those years, darting to the mix by Scherzer's side. There was Patrick Corbin, who first tried out his junior year of high school, never lost a game for Cicero–North Syracuse, then never looked back. There was Howie Kendrick, whom no college wanted, who nearly joined the Navy SEALs, and now had the two biggest homers in Nationals history. There was Anthony Rendon, Houston's own, hacking his way into his city's worst nightmares, one big hit at a time.

There was Trea Turner, still playing with nine fingers. There was Fernando Rodney, still pitching at forty-two. There were the kids, Juan Soto and Victor Robles, sprinting in from the outfield. There were all the *viejos.* There was Gerardo Parra, Baby Shark, who joined in May, right off the scrap heap, and changed the clubhouse culture. There was Aníbal Sánchez, Parra's other half, the thirty-five-year-old who was discarded, given a final chance, then ran with it, butterflies and all.

There was Asdrúbal Cabrera, another odd addition, who went from released and jobless in August, to playing and hitting every day. There was Adam Eaton, a nineteenth-round pick, a five-foot-nine, 175-pound spark plug who never let scouts look away. There was Sean Doolittle, who almost chose grad school nine years earlier, but gave his body one more shot, and was forever glad he did. There was Ryan Zimmerman—because there was always Ryan Zimmerman—not knowing what the future held, and, for now, not caring.

Then there was Martinez, pushing himself off the padded bench, wondering what happens if Joe Maddon doesn't call, if Martinez never coaches first base, if he doesn't relent at that Starbucks in Tampa, and commit everything to this game. And there was Mike Rizzo, standing and swept by tears, staring at what looked to him like the perfect Jenga tower.

Take one block out and the whole thing falls down. But keep them together, weather a 19-31 start, let the weight wobble, just enough to steady itself, and you get . . . well, you get this. You get to be the GM who brought Washington its first World Series title since 1924. You get to watch a few dozen players, a bunch of champions, sink into the daze of a long-shot dream. You get to see them look at one another, grip one another, their smiles spread and eyes widen, wondering, even with a win so fresh, how any of this could be real.

Epilogue

The Top

December 10, 2019

"We're going to win the fucking World Series," Rizzo repeats in his hotel room in San Diego, the view still perfect, the boats still zipping through the bay, leaving white foam that fades back to blue. "Can you believe that shit?"

He's remembering that moment inside Minute Maid Park on October 30, when he knew—like really, really knew—that the title was theirs. Michael, his son, put his arm around Rizzo's shoulder. Jodi, then his fiancée, now his wife, was near tears. Everything after that is a haze, the details blurry at the edges, the celebration stretching, then stretching some more, until Rizzo could look at a Bud Light and feel his head pound.

That night in Houston, while a party raged in the Nationals' clubhouse, Rizzo slipped into the hallway to make a call. His father, Phil Rizzo, a senior advisor in the front office and once a long-time scout, had stayed awake in Chicago to watch the ending. They always talked after games, and Phil usually shared advice, a possible tweak, often lacing his observations with a string of curse words. But not now. Mike Rizzo starts recounting their conversation and a tear rolls down his cheek.

What is there to say when someone has been there, right by your side, for fifty-eight years? And how do you tell someone else about that?

"We were just like, 'We did it,'" Rizzo says quietly, his nose red and his hands shaking by his lap. "Yeah . . . that's what it was."

The next part came in flashes. The clubhouse was subdued, a bit quiet, even, because the year was finally finished. The Nationals played for as long as the calendar allowed. They didn't drink as they had after clinching the playoffs in September, or winning the wild-card game, or taking the NLDS or NLCS. They seemed tired, reflective, wanting to clink beers, kick back, and savor one of their last nights together. A number of players wound up eating cold-cut sandwiches in the clubhouse cafeteria. They took pictures with the trophy, waving their families in, and that's when Adam Eaton brought his out to the field.

Eaton; his wife, Katie; his three-year-old son, Brayden; and his parents, Robin and Glenn, walked through the dark tunnel and into Minute Maid Park. The lights were dimmed. The stands were being cleaned for the winter. Eaton showed Brayden and Glenn where he put his feet in the batter's box. They stepped into the exact same spots and mimicked Eaton's batting stance. He told Brayden to jog around the bases, just like his dad had twice in the World Series, and Eaton watched, a huge grin on his face, his arm around Katie's shoulder.

He had one more wish before they headed to the hotel. He led them out to right field and they all turned to face the empty infield. Eaton wanted them to see his view of the final out.

"It's for everyone who helped you get there, for your Little League coaches, your high school coaches, your parents. That's who it's for," Eaton would explain later. "You work your entire life to win a World Series. It's all you ever want, from your first game of tee-ball. It took 25 years for me, really, and then when it happens, man . . . I don't even know what to say. It's sort of like this: One day you're going to die, and you're going to be remembered, and people will always say that you won it in 2019, that you were a champion. I guess that means a lot to me. Nobody can ever take that away."

By the next morning, when dreams met reality, they all sleep-walked onto a plane bound for Washington. Hundreds of fans gathered at Dulles International Airport to welcome them home. The parade was scheduled for that Saturday, straight down Constitution Avenue, and their lives followed the drumbeat of a strict schedule: Photos here. Photos there. Clean out your lockers. Team meeting. Breathe. Eat. Sleep. Get on a bus. Get on another bus. Then wait on those buses in downtown Washington, the motors humming, while the city gathered as one.

Rizzo, Dave Martinez, and Ryan Zimmerman were on the last float, arriving for the parade around 1:00 p.m. on November 2. They each had their families aboard. They also had two trophies, for the World Series and the NLCS, and spent hours lifting metal above their heads. The afternoon was sunny and crisp, a perfect fall day, and Martinez heard shouting from all directions.

"Davey! You're the fucking man!"

"You did it, Davey! You did it!"

"Let's go one and oh today, Davey! Stay in the damn fight!"

"Hey, skipper," Rizzo said, and Martinez spun around to face his boss. Rizzo wore a backward WORLD SERIES CHAMPIONS hat and dark sunglasses. A cigar hung out of the side of his mouth. "Sounds like they love you now, huh?"

"Sure does. And I love them, too."

It was love that soon sent Martinez running into the streets. His security guard told him that wasn't such a good idea, but he couldn't listen. They came for the Nationals, and they came for him, and so Martinez was fixed on getting closer to the fans. He skipped down the bus steps, the guard and his family behind him, and waited for the driver to pump the brakes. Then the door swung open, he leaped into the thick of a thousand yelling people, and children cried as he grabbed their hands.

His players were offering the same experience. Brian Dozier lost his shirt again. Sean Doolittle rode the bullpen cart for a few blocks. Max Scherzer held a championship WWE belt and scaled the roof of his bus. Mark Lerner put on Baby Shark glasses during a speech. The rally ended with the whole team onstage, the city looking on, the Capitol in the backdrop, and the players dancing to "Calma," that Pedro Capó song, while Dozier mouthed each word.

It was their second-to-last day as a full group. Their finale was a Capitals game the next night. The Nationals felt the Capitals had paved the way, that their Stanley Cup title, in the spring of 2018, taught Washington how to win. It broke a championship drought, the Capitals went on an all-out bender through the area, and it inspired the Nationals to follow their lead. So they went to Capital One Arena to say thank-you. They also liked hockey, and wanted more excuses to drink.

Cameras caught Yan Gomes pouring a beer into the crowd. During the second intermission, six players were invited to ride the Zamboni around the ice. Scherzer, Gomes, Trea Turner, Sean Doolittle, Adam Eaton, and Patrick Corbin raised their hands. They sat in the tunnel, waiting to go out, and Scherzer told the group they were taking their shirts off. The driver turned around and said that wasn't allowed. Scherzer kept saying it anyway, and the driver conceded that once he made his final turn, and not a second before, they could do whatever they wanted.

The final turn came. Shirts were ripped off. The building went nuts, and the Nationals were invited into the dressing room after a Capitals win. The two teams joined in a snaking conga line. Gerardo Parra took a selfie video, puck in hand, and shouted, "That's a baseball for the hockey!"

The Nationals wound up on the ice, the arena near empty, like a bunch of kids playing pond hockey. Capitals star Alex Ovechkin let Rizzo use one of his sticks. Aníbal Sánchez bet $800 that no one could shoot a puck from center ice and hit a beer can resting in the net. Gomes did it, but Sánchez called him on a technicality. Then Dozier did it and Sánchez paid up. Dozier was still shirtless, wearing a helmet, shorts, and a pair of skates. The joke was that he could use Sánchez's money to buy some clothes.

That night finished at the casino at MGM National Harbor. The Nationals had a private room, ordered up a blackjack dealer, and huddled around a table, their shirts in puddles at their feet, and gambled past 3:00 a.m.

They were expected at the White House in the morning, for a customary post-title visit with the president. The decision was made the Friday before, two days after Game 7, and lit a fuse among liberal fans. The choice to attend White House ceremonies had become polarizing since Donald Trump was elected in 2016. Many teams had declined, including the Golden State Warriors and Philadelphia Eagles—though Trump contended that he'd rescinded the Eagles' invitation—and he drew additional criticism for not hosting women's teams.

In the hours after the Nationals announced their plan, Doolittle told the *Washington Post* he would not attend. He did not want to come off as the liberal player who would not meet a Republican president. It was much more nuanced than that. He detailed his issues with Trump's history on race relations. He mentioned his wife's lesbian parents, and her autistic brother, and how Trump's rhetoric had denigrated the LGBTQ community and those with disabilities. Doolittle just couldn't bring himself to go.

"People say you should go because it's about respecting the office of the president," Doolittle began. The *Washington Post* story went viral, shared by Congresswoman Alexandria Ocasio-Cortez and the

Hillary Clinton Foundation. Doolittle felt he could not decline the invitation without explaining his side. Then he wound up making a very public stance: "And I think over the course of his time in office he's done a lot of things that maybe don't respect the office.

"The rhetoric, time and time again, has enabled those kind of behaviors. That never really went away, but it feels like now people with those beliefs, they maybe feel a little bit more empowered," Doolittle continued, referring to racism and white supremacy. "They feel like they have a path, maybe. I don't want to hang out with somebody who talks like that."

Doolittle was not the only player who sat out the event. Many players and coaches went, including Martinez, Rizzo, and Mark Lerner, but Anthony Rendon, Victor Robles, Michael A. Taylor, Javy Guerra, Joe Ross, Wander Suero, Tres Barrera, Raudy Read, Roenis Elías, and Wilmer Difo were absent. The team declined to discuss why specific players did not attend. But it was hard not to notice the diversity of that group.

Rendon later revealed that he had already made travel plans but was otherwise excited to meet Trump, a president he supports. But multiple players asked Doolittle and his wife, Eireann Dolan, for advice on navigating the situation. Robles, Suero, Read, and Difo are from the Dominican Republic; Elías is from Cuba; Barrera and Guerra are Mexican American; and Ross and Taylor are African American.

The Nationals then dotted the ceremony with kind gestures toward Trump. Kurt Suzuki put on a red MAKE AMERICA GREAT AGAIN hat while Trump hugged him from behind. Zimmerman stepped to the lectern overlooking the South Lawn, called the visit an "incredible honor," and, turning to Trump, added that the Nationals would like to "thank you for keeping everyone safe in our country, and continuing to make America the greatest country to live in, in the world."

The reactions went as expected.

Political divisions were one reality of this championship. The other was that Rizzo had to now shift his attention to 2020. Stephen Strasburg opted out of his contract the night of the parade. He joined Rendon, Zimmerman, Gomes, Kendrick, Dozier, Daniel Hudson, Gerardo Parra, Asdrúbal Cabrera, and Matt Adams as free agents off the World Series roster. Keeping the whole band intact was not feasible. So Rizzo had to move on, make the tough decisions, and plan for the future without considering the past.

He married Jody in Jamaica in mid-November. Their cake was shaped like the World Series trophy, and then it was back to work. That's what brought him to the Grand Hyatt in San Diego in mid-December. It is the Tuesday of the winter meetings, and less than forty-eight hours since he signed Strasburg to a seven-year deal worth $245 million.

The World Series MVP, the only pitcher to go 5-0 in the same postseason, was staying home. Rizzo is relieved. But the catch is that ownership never wanted to pay both Strasburg and Rendon. The third baseman was gone a day later, signing with the Angels for Strasburg's exact contract, except without payment deferrals. Strasburg agreed to some, and will have about $80 million of his contract paid across the three years following its conclusion. He did this so the Nationals could keep building a contender around him, Scherzer and Corbin. It just wouldn't include Rendon, who wanted his money paid in full by the end of his deal, and got the Angels to meet those terms.

The first key player to land elsewhere was Gerardo Parra. It seems fitting that he landed with the Yomiuri Giants in Japan. By making "Baby Shark" his walk-up music, and overhauling the Nationals' entire vibe, Parra became a viral celebrity, then a wanted commodity overseas. Rizzo would bring back Gomes on a two-year deal, Kendrick on a one-year, and try to fill the Rendon void by committee. He did that by re-signing Asdrúbal Cabrera and getting veteran Starlin

Cartro in free agency. He also signed Will Harris—the same Will Harris who gave up the World Series–winning homer to Kendrick—to a three-year deal worth $24 million. Three days later Hudson returned on a two-year, $11 million deal. Harris was thirty-five years old. Hudson was thirty-two with a spotted injury history. They were all a bunch of *viejos*, and maybe that's crazy enough to work.

The possibilities would gnaw at Rizzo in the coming months. But any stress is eased a bit by what happened in October. Rizzo smiles when he hears laughter in the next room of their hotel suite. The winter meetings can be tense, while Rizzo, Martinez, and the front office plot the future. Only now they are a bit distracted when a highlight plays on TV, whether it's Hudson striking out Michael Brantley, a Rendon homer, or any sliver of their final celebration. They were all prone to stopping in the middle of a meeting, looking around, and, with a smirk, saying, "Hey, we won the World Series."

Reminders were always welcome. Their players were doing the exact same. Turner underwent surgery in mid-November to repair the bone spur in his knuckle and scarred tendon in his fractured right index finger. Once he woke up from the procedure and felt that he could move the finger again, he typed this caption beneath an Instagram post: "Only took 7 months to get this finger fixed, but now my ring will fit better!"

In late December, just before Christmas, Adam Eaton lugged a big package into his off-season home in Brighton, Michigan. He had a good feeling about what was inside. He ripped open the cardboard, sparing none of it, and saw the outline of his World Series trophy, covered in Bubble Wrap. He'd ordered a replica as soon as they were available. Then he stood in the foyer of his house, alone in a quiet winter, and raised it above his head.

Gerardo would begin the new year by covering his forearm in a World Series tattoo. It includes a yellow Baby Shark, smiling through the gaps of the trophy, wearing the same rose-tinted glasses that

Parra popularized. Scherzer couldn't stop thinking about the season, how every small thing went right, how Martinez made the perfect moves, and the players carried them out, and everyone, from him down to the bottom of the roster, chipped in.

"The coolest thing about our team is that it wasn't just one guy that won it for us. It wasn't just Howie's home run, Strasburg, Corbin, it wasn't me, it wasn't Trea. We needed every ounce of Huddy, every ounce of Doolittle, everybody had a moment where they contributed to our team throughout the whole postseason," he rattled off around the holidays, and at one point Scherzer had to stop and catch his breath. "If one guy faltered, we lose. Everyone can look each other in the face and say we're teammates for life. We won the World Series. Everybody caught an opportunity and had success. It was contagious. That's the ultimate sign of a team, no matter what happens, everyone rises to the occasion. The way everybody responded with everything on the line, that's teammates for life no matter what we do."

So, Rizzo is asked, one last time, how did this happen?

It's not that there has to be an answer. Maybe there isn't. But it's worth pushing Rizzo, the architect, the one who dreamed this up on some dark Iowa highway in the early nineties, on why this team got it done. Were they as "old-school" as everyone believed? Is the formula repeatable? Will they try it again next year? Or was this a one-off, an aberration, a lesson in timing and patience, and not much else?

"You might say we did it the old-school way. The old way. Well, it's been done that way for a long time because it's good. It works. You know?" Rizzo says in San Diego, and it's unclear whether he's convincing doubters or himself. He fumbles through an explanation, starting and stopping, sounding like an unprepared salesman, not making much sense. "We've added a lot of things to it. I think we don't get enough . . . I think we get too much credit for this old-school type of team that won it. And we don't get enough . . . I think that's overblown that way. And I think it's overblown that we're not analytically driven or that type of thing. Which, we utilize it. You know, it's . . . to me, I think we've found a really perfect blend of . . ."

Rizzo lets the thought hang there, not rushing to finish it. He will soon enough, talking about a three-pronged process, the importance of scouting, player development, *and* analytics, how the eye test is best used with loads of information, not in place of it. But he also does not care what you think. Only two teams won more games than the Nationals in the last decade. They finished it with a title. There's not much more to say.

When the conversation ends, and Rizzo stands up, he lingers by the glass and looks over his shoulder. It's as if he is stuck between something, between leaving or staying in this room, holding on to the past or stepping toward the future. He lingers for a moment, maybe two, taking the top in. Then he makes his choice, the door clicks behind him, and it is back to chasing titles, and reaching for all this again.

Acknowledgments

This book doesn't happen if I don't fall for a girl at our college newspaper, then she takes an editing job in New York, then, while visiting her, I meet Sean Manning, her then colleague, at Bar Nine in Hell's Kitchen. Sean and I hit it off talking about our favorite books. So when the Nationals won the World Series, Sean, now an editor at Simon & Schuster, asked if I wanted to write one. Thank you for sending that email, believing I could do this, and taking a genuine interest in the story, from the first word to the last. The final product is as much yours as it is mine. And thank you, Lara, for being you, following your dreams in the first place, and making it so I could stumble into one of mine.

Thank you to Jon Karp at Simon & Schuster for green-lighting *Buzz Saw*, and everyone else there—Jackie Seow, Tzipora Baitch, Sherry Wasserman, Jonathan Evans, Brianna Scharfenberg—for the guidance, copyediting, teaching me how to use Microsoft Word, and, Bri, for your great efforts to publicize this book. Thank you to Daniel Greenberg, my very supportive agent, who took on a first-time author and walked me through this crazy process. Glad you did. Can't wait for our next one.

Thank you to Matt Vita, the *Washington Post*'s sports editor, for hiring me in 2017, trusting me with the Nationals beat less than two years later, and championing my work at every step along the way. Just the thought of writing this book made me nauseous when I first came to you after the World Series. But your saying I was the best writer for it, and that you couldn't wait to read, meant a whole lot. Thank you to Glenn Yoder, the *Post*'s MLB editor, for being a friend and sounding board, even at odd hours of the night. Thank you to Marty Baron, the *Post*'s executive editor, for trusting that I could balance this book with the daily demands of my job. And thank you to Tracy Grant, a managing editor at the *Post*, for everything.

I did around thirty-five additional interviews in the seven weeks I worked on the book. The Nationals' PR staff of Jen Giglio, Kyle Brostowitz, and Melissa Strozza were very helpful following the World Series, as well as during the season, my first covering the team. I owe a major thank-you to the few dozen people who made additional time for me this winter, a list of players, coaches, front office members, team staff, and fans, who shared their Game 7 stories.

Anthony Dabbundo, Andrew Crane, and Michael McCleary transcribed most of those interviews, a thankless job that deserves a big thanks right here. All three of them are budding journalists at Syracuse University and the *Daily Orange*, the school's independent newspaper. There is no better incubator for sportswriters than the *D.O.*, though I may be a bit biased. Hiring editors should look out for these three names in the coming years.

Research for this book reminded me how thorough, innovative, and illuminative the *Post*'s coverage has been since the Nationals came to Washington in 2005. I leaned on each of the writers who proceeded me on the beat, a short list of Barry Svrluga, Chico Harlan, Adam Kilgore, James Wagner, Chelsea Janes, and Jorge Castillo. Dave Sheinin, you're my favorite writer, an inspiring mentor—even if you'd hate to be called that—and I often pinch myself when remembering we're on the same team. And one of the most fun parts of this process was reading years of Tom Boswell columns. You're the best, Boz, and I'll never forget our many conversations, especially when you told me, at the start of the World Series, to "dig in and write from the heart."

These resources proved particularly helpful while writing and preparing for interviews: Svrluga's two Nationals books, *National Pastime* and *The Grind*; Svrluga's reporting on the Nationals' early years Dominican Republic scandal, and negotiations with Bryce Harper; David Nakamura and Marc Fisher's work for the *Washington Post* on the development and gentrification around Nationals Park; Sheinin's *Washington Post* profiles of a young Stephen Strasburg; Kilgore's reporting on Rizzo's relationship with his father; Castillo's reporting on the discovery of Juan Soto; Janes's first profile on Dave Martinez when he was hired by the Nationals; Stephanie Apstein's important and incisive reporting on the Brandon Taubman incident, the Astros, and clubhouse culture for *Sports Illustrated*; and the work of other outlets throughout the 2019 season, from Mark Zuckerman, Todd Dybas, Jamal Collier, Brittany Ghiroli, and Byron Kerr.

That brings me to Sam Fortier, my beat partner at the *Post*, whose section in these acknowledgments will always be entirely too small. Sam's reporting on the Nationals' bottoming out in New York, Erick Fedde's wild-card-game premonition, and Juan Soto's late-night hitting session with Kevin Long really helped re-create some critical scenes. He also read every word of this book before I submitted it, and offered both sweeping critiques and sound line editing. One example: "This is a really dope sentence." Another: "You're trying too hard here." Sam, you were a great colleague during an insane year. But, somehow, you're an even better friend.

Timmy, Niko, Elliot, Roman, Jeff, Jamal, Rob, Conor, Billy, Clayton, Danny, Jon, Frank—I couldn't ask for a more supportive crew of friends. Sorry I went missing this winter. Ris, Gus, Kate, Anna, Lindsey, Brooke, Brendan, Blake, Kora, Mason, and all the

Fortunatos—I couldn't ask for a more supportive family. Sorry for writing during Thanksgiving and Christmas.

And, finally, Mom and Dad. Nothing makes me prouder than being your son, and nothing is more important to me, in the whole wide world, than making you proud. Thank you. Thank you, thank you, thank you, a million times over. This book starts and ends with the two of you, and that is no coincidence.

Photography Credits

1. Jonathan Newton / The *Washington Post* / Getty Images
2. Mark Goldman / Icon Sportswire / Getty Images
3. Jonathan Daniel / Getty Images Sport / Getty Images
4. Scott Taetsch / Getty Images Sport / Getty Images
5. John McDonnell / The *Washington Post* / Getty Images
6. Tony Quinn / Icon Sportswire / Getty Images
7. Mitchell Layton / Getty Images Sport / Getty Images
8. Jonathan Daniel / Getty Images Sport / Getty Images
9. John McDonnell / The *Washington Post* via Getty Images
10. Mitchell Layton / Getty Images Sport / Getty Images
11. Will Newton / Getty Images Sport / Getty Images
12. AP Photo / Andrew Harnik
13. Doug Benc / Getty Images Sport / Getty Images
14. John McDonnell / The *Washington Post* via Getty Images
15. Jonathan Newton / The *Washington Post* / Getty Images
16. John McDonnell / The *Washington Post* / Getty Images

17. Jamie Squire / Getty Images Sport / Getty Images
18. Mark Goldman / Icon Sportswire via Getty Images
19. Rob Carr / Getty Images Sport / Getty Images
20. Richard A. Lipski / The *Washington Post* / Getty Image
21. Simon Bruty / *Sports Illustrated* / Getty Images
22. Bob Levey / Getty Images Sport / Getty Images
23. Rob Carr / Getty Images Sport / Getty Images
24. John McDonnell / The *Washington Post* / Getty Images
25. Mike Ehrmann / Getty Images Sport / Getty Images
26. Mike Ehrmann / Getty Images Sport / Getty Images
27. Bob Levey / Getty Images / Getty Images Sport
28. John McDonnell / The *Washington Post* / Getty Images
29. Tim Warner / Getty Images Sport / Getty Images
30. Alex Trautwig / MLB Photos / Getty Images
31. Stefani Reynolds / Getty Images Sport / Getty Images
32. Alex Trautwig / MLB Photos / Getty Images